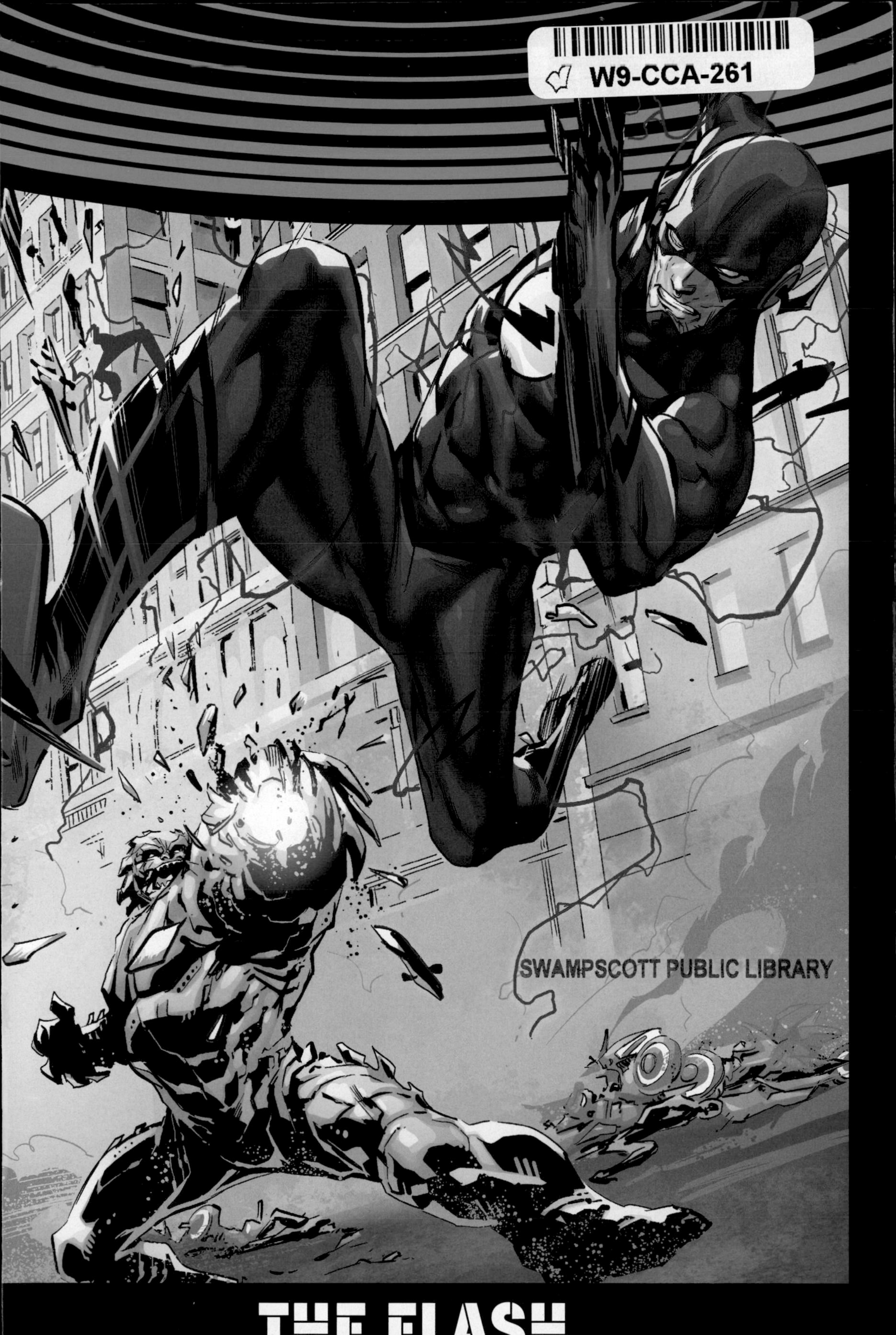

THE FLASH

VOL.5 NEGATIVE

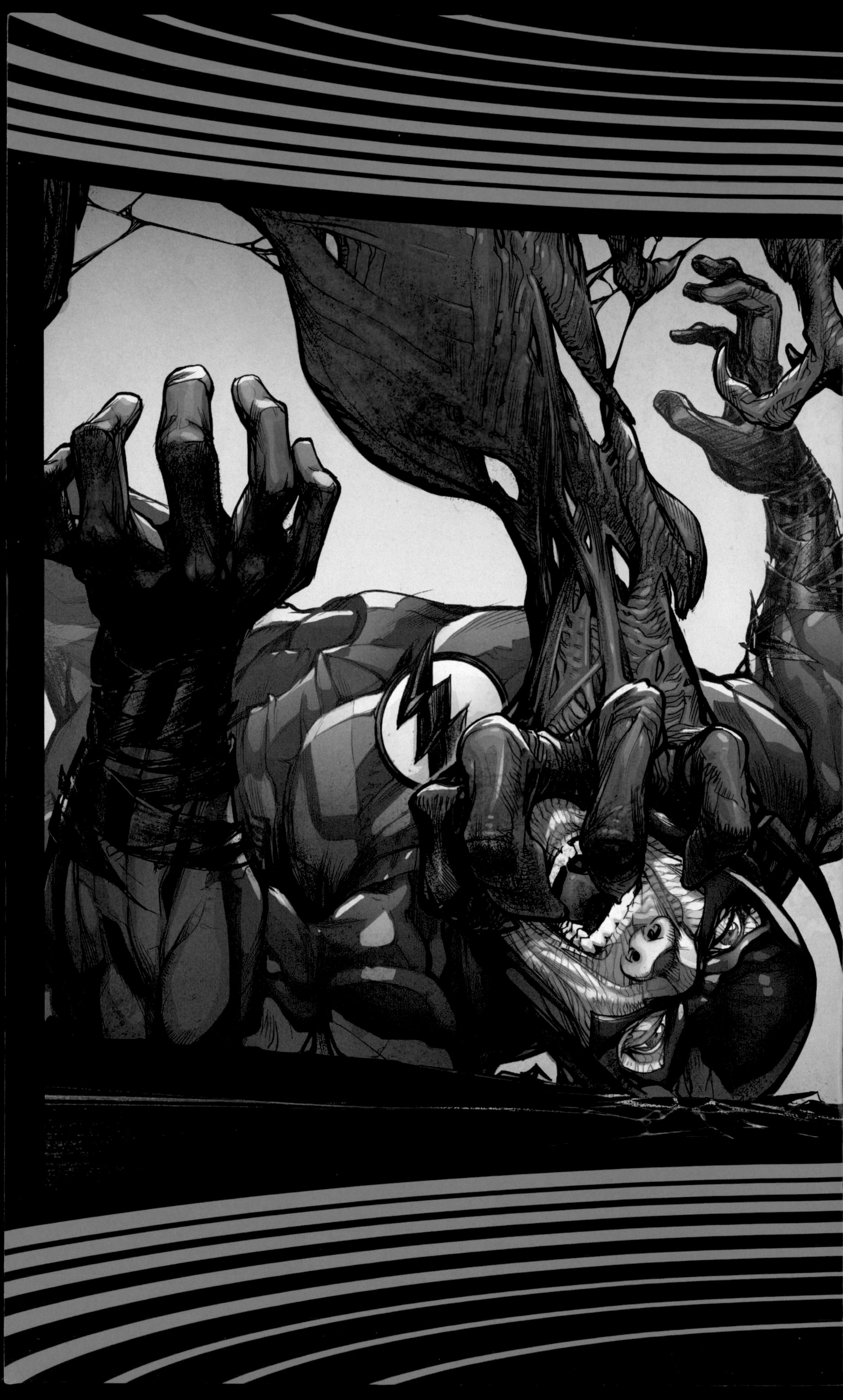

THE FLASH
VOL.5 NEGATIVE

JOSHUA WILLIAMSON
writer

NEIL GOOGE * **CHRISTIAN DUCE** * **CARMINE DI GIANDOMENICO**
POP MHAN * **GUS VAZQUEZ**
artists

IVAN PLASCENCIA * **HI-FI**
colorists

STEVE WANDS
TOM NAPOLITANO
letterers

NEIL GOOGE and IVAN PLASCENCIA
collection cover artists

SHRAPNEL created by **PAUL KUPPERBERG**
IRON HEIGHTS PENITENTIARY created by **GEOFF JOHNS** and **ETHAN VAN SCIVER**

BRIAN CUNNINGHAM Editor - Original Series ✻ **REBECCA TAYLOR AMEDEO TURTURRO** Associate Editors - Original Series
JEB WOODARD Group Editor - Collected Editions ✻ **ERIKA ROTHBERG** Editor - Collected Edition
STEVE COOK Design Director - Books ✻ **MONIQUE NARBONETA** Publication Design

BOB HARRAS Senior VP - Editor-in-Chief, DC Comics
PAT McCALLUM Executive Editor, DC Comics

DIANE NELSON President ✻ **DAN DiDIO** Publisher ✻ **JIM LEE** Publisher ✻ **GEOFF JOHNS** President & Chief Creative Officer
AMIT DESAI Executive VP - Business & Marketing Strategy, Direct to Consumer & Global Franchise Management
SAM ADES Senior VP & General Manager, Digital Services ✻ **BOBBIE CHASE** VP & Executive Editor, Young Reader & Talent Development
MARK CHIARELLO Senior VP - Art, Design & Collected Editions ✻ **JOHN CUNNINGHAM** Senior VP - Sales & Trade Marketing
ANNE DePIES Senior VP - Business Strategy, Finance & Administration ✻ **DON FALLETTI** VP - Manufacturing Operations
LAWRENCE GANEM VP - Editorial Administration & Talent Relations ✻ **ALISON GILL** Senior VP - Manufacturing & Operations
HANK KANALZ Senior VP - Editorial Strategy & Administration ✻ **JAY KOGAN** VP - Legal Affairs ✻ **JACK MAHAN** VP - Business Affairs
NICK J. NAPOLITANO VP - Manufacturing Administration ✻ **EDDIE SCANNELL** VP - Consumer Marketing
COURTNEY SIMMONS Senior VP - Publicity & Communications ✻ **JIM (SKI) SOKOLOWSKI** VP - Comic Book Specialty Sales & Trade Marketing
NANCY SPEARS VP - Mass, Book, Digital Sales & Trade Marketing ✻ **MICHELE R. WELLS** VP - Content Strategy

THE FLASH VOL. 5: NEGATIVE

Published by DC Comics. Compilation and all new material Copyright © 2018 DC Comics. All Rights Reserved.
Originally published in single magazine form in THE FLASH 28-32, DC HOLIDAY SPECIAL 2017 1. Copyright © 2017 DC Comics. All Rights Reserved.
All characters, their distinctive likenesses and related elements featured in this publication are trademarks of DC Comics.
The stories, characters and incidents featured in this publication are entirely fictional.
DC Comics does not read or accept unsolicited submissions of ideas, stories or artwork

DC Comics, 2900 West Alameda Ave., Burbank, CA 91505
Printed by LSC Communications, Kendallville, IN, USA. 2/16/18. First Printing.
ISBN: 978-1-4012-7727-7

Library of Congress Cataloging-in-Publication Data is available.

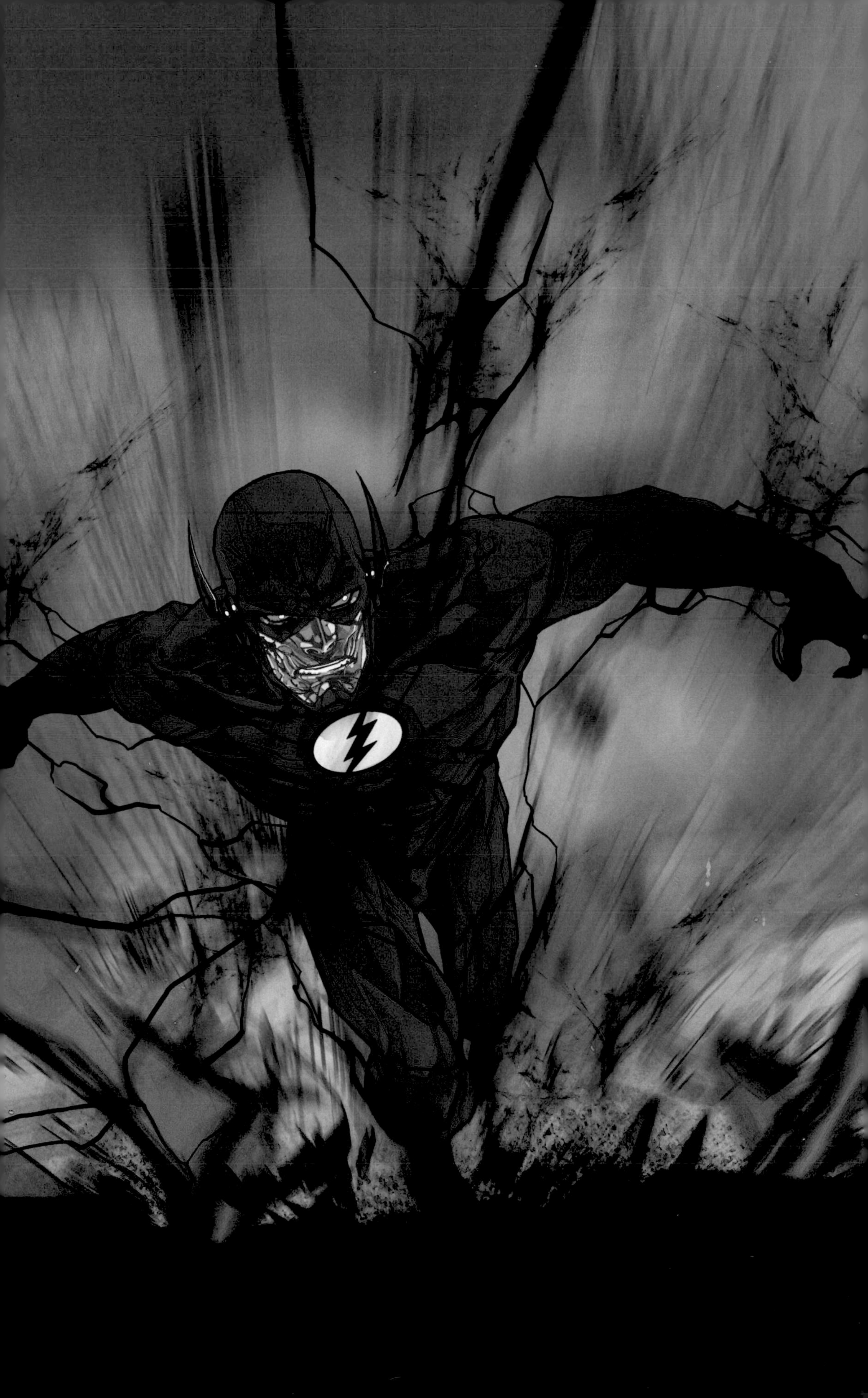

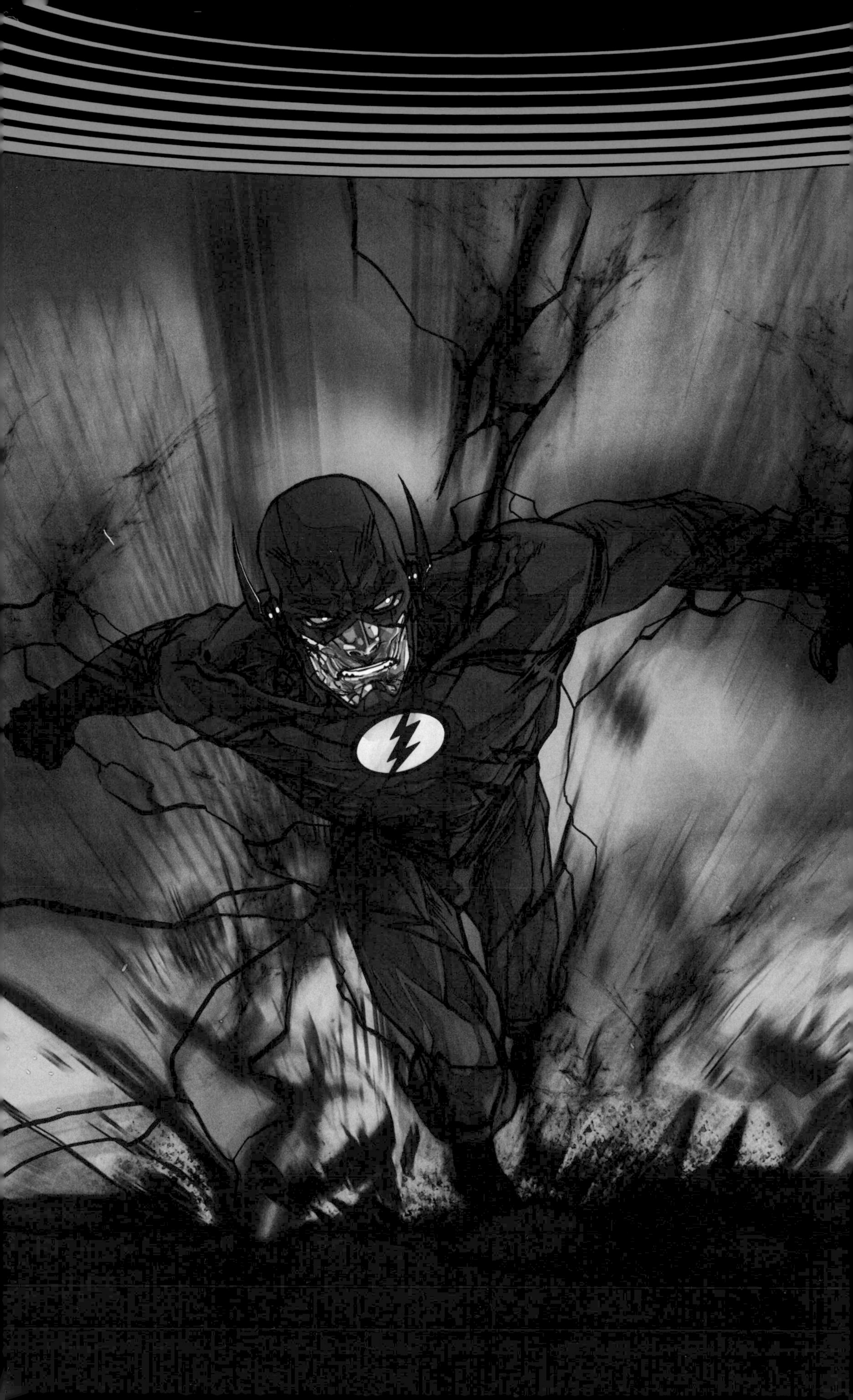

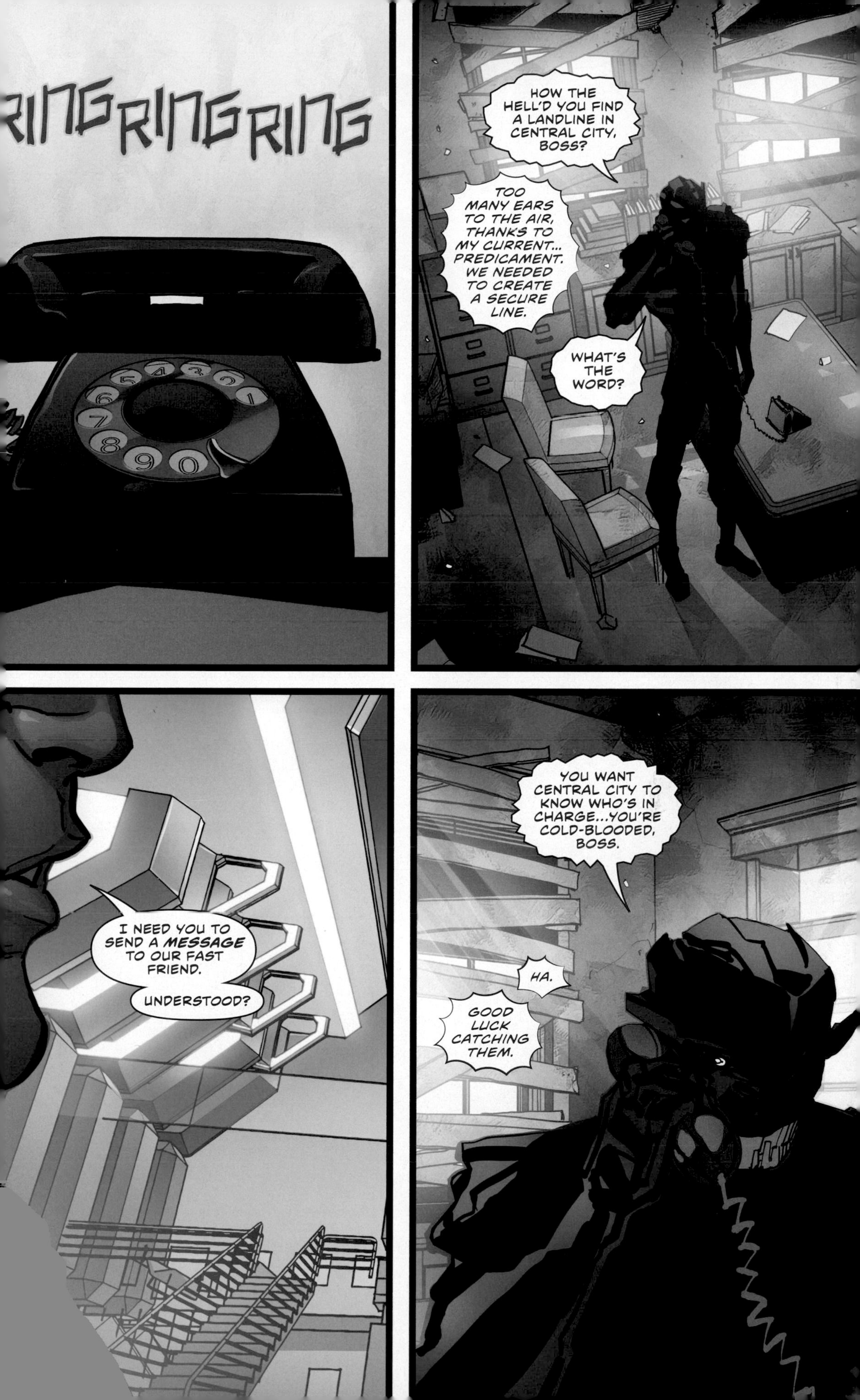
RING RING RING
HOW THE HELL'D YOU FIND A LANDLINE IN CENTRAL CITY, BOSS?
TOO MANY EARS TO THE AIR, THANKS TO MY CURRENT... PREDICAMENT. WE NEEDED TO CREATE A SECURE LINE.
WHAT'S THE WORD?
I NEED YOU TO SEND A MESSAGE TO OUR FAST FRIEND.
UNDERSTOOD?
YOU WANT CENTRAL CITY TO KNOW WHO'S IN CHARGE...YOU'RE COLD-BLOODED, BOSS.
HA.
GOOD LUCK CATCHING THEM.

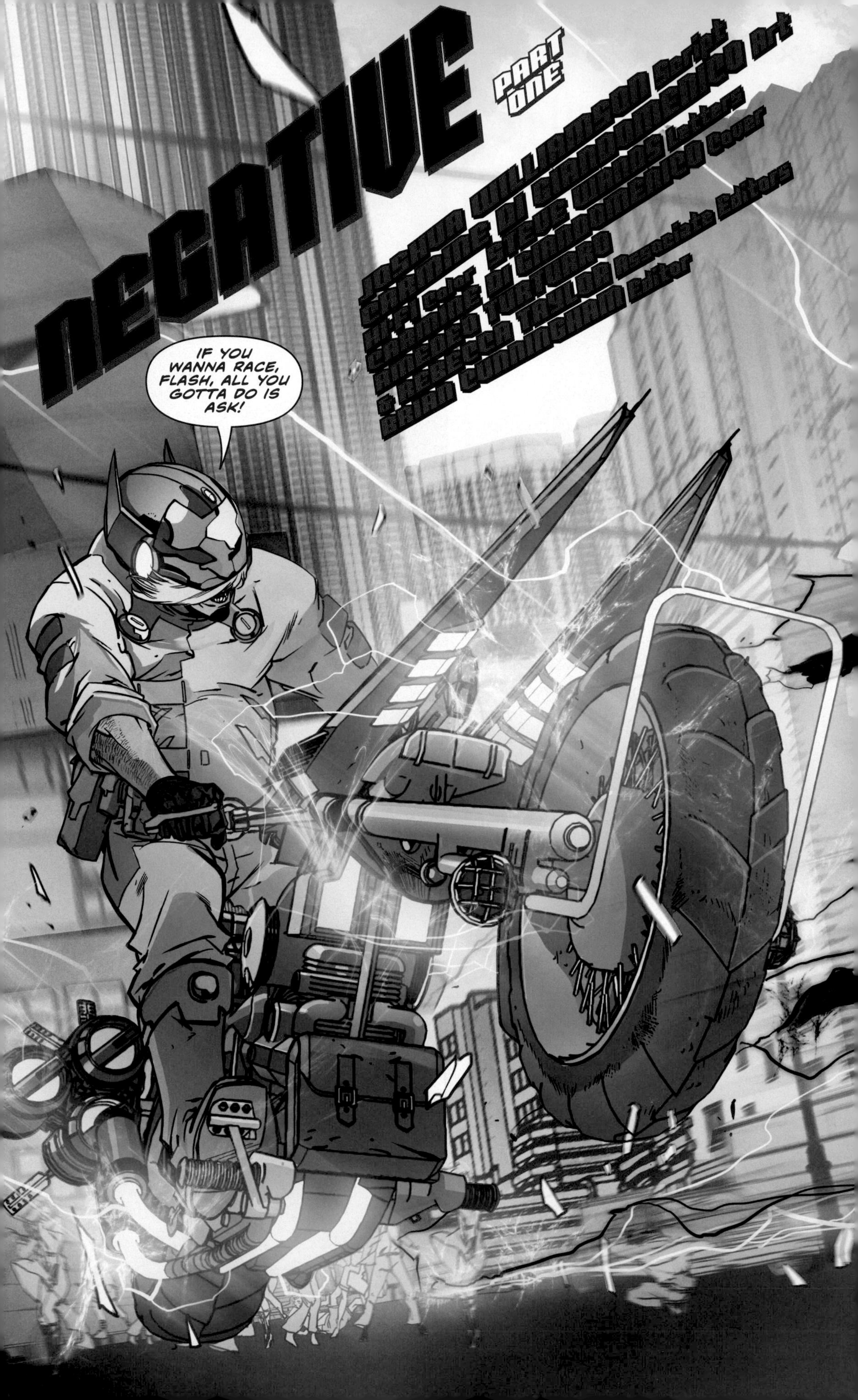
NEGATIVE PART ONE
JOSHUA WILLIAMSON Script
CARMINE DI GIANDOMENICO Art
HI-FI color STEVE WANDS letters
CARMINE DI GIANDOMENICO Cover
AMEDEO TURTURRO
& REBECCA TAYLOR Associate Editors
BRIAN CUNNINGHAM Editor
IF YOU WANNA RACE, FLASH, ALL YOU GOTTA DO IS ASK!

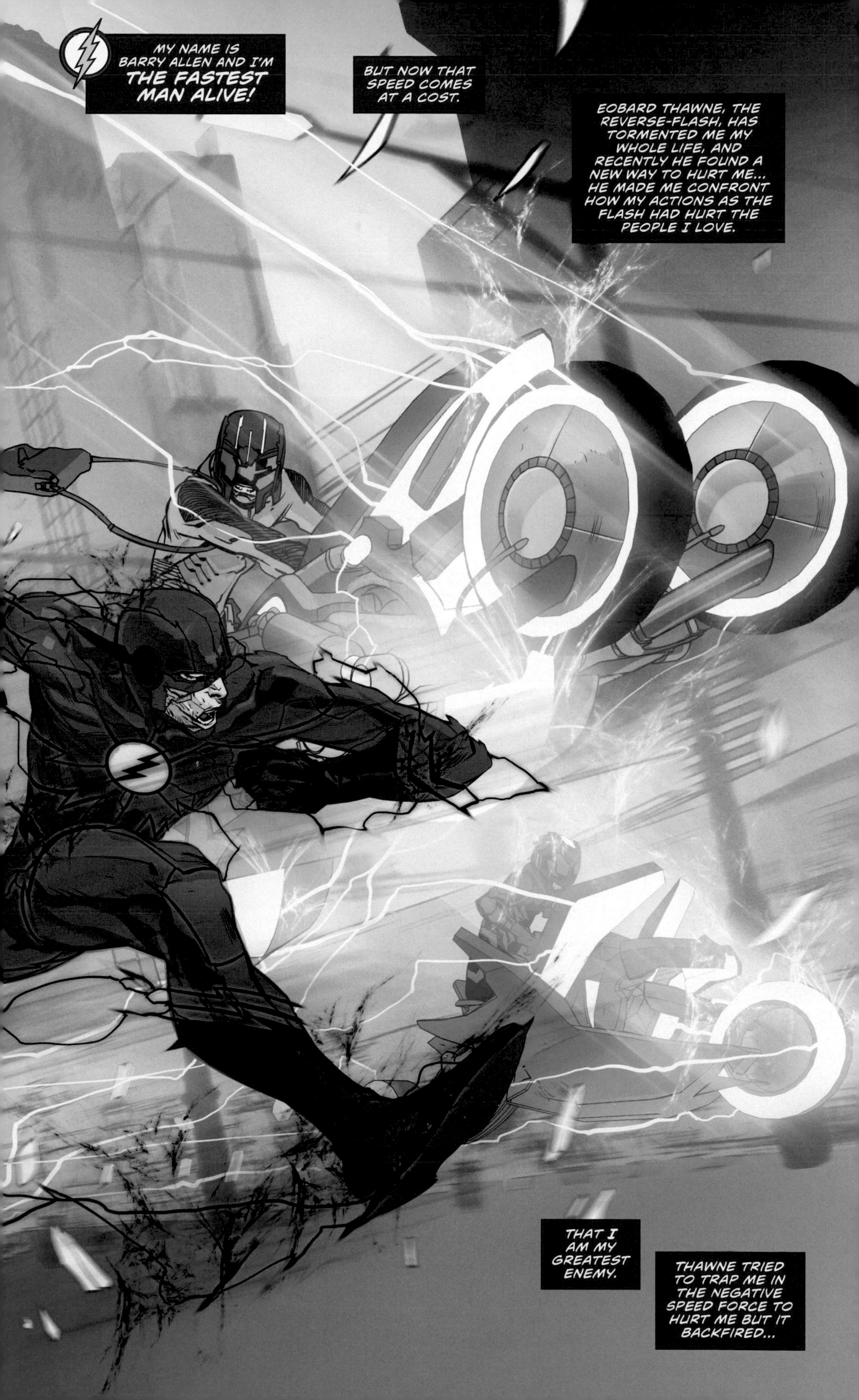
MY NAME IS BARRY ALLEN AND I'M THE FASTEST MAN ALIVE!
BUT NOW THAT SPEED COMES AT A COST.
EOBARD THAWNE, THE REVERSE-FLASH, HAS TORMENTED ME MY WHOLE LIFE, AND RECENTLY HE FOUND A NEW WAY TO HURT ME... HE MADE ME CONFRONT HOW MY ACTIONS AS THE FLASH HAD HURT THE PEOPLE I LOVE.
THAT I AM MY GREATEST ENEMY.
THAWNE TRIED TO TRAP ME IN THE NEGATIVE SPEED FORCE TO HURT ME BUT IT BACKFIRED...

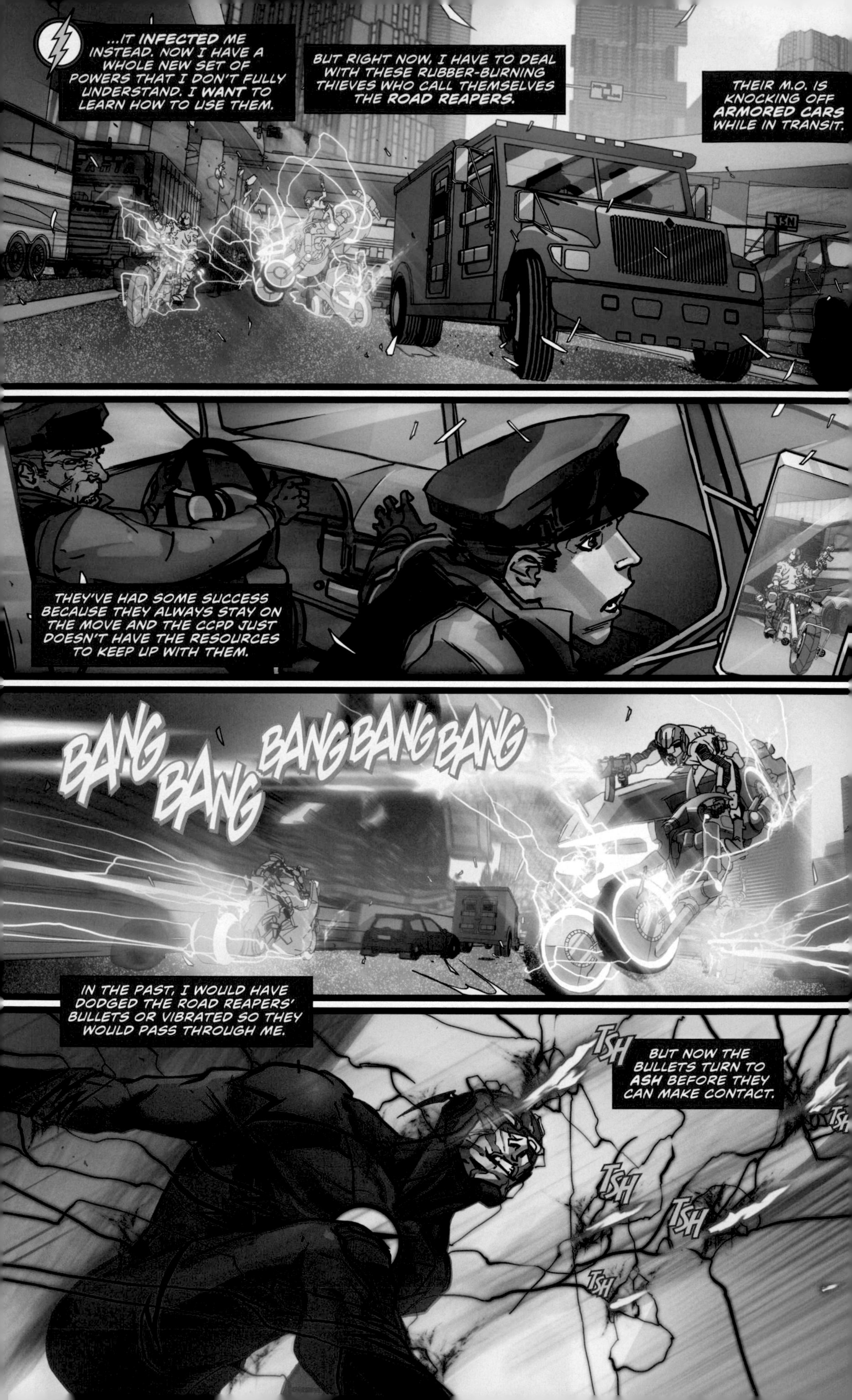
...IT INFECTED ME INSTEAD. NOW I HAVE A WHOLE NEW SET OF POWERS THAT I DON'T FULLY UNDERSTAND. I WANT TO LEARN HOW TO USE THEM.
BUT RIGHT NOW, I HAVE TO DEAL WITH THESE RUBBER-BURNING THIEVES WHO CALL THEMSELVES THE ROAD REAPERS.
THEIR M.O. IS KNOCKING OFF ARMORED CARS WHILE IN TRANSIT.
TSN
THEY'VE HAD SOME SUCCESS BECAUSE THEY ALWAYS STAY ON THE MOVE AND THE CCPD JUST DOESN'T HAVE THE RESOURCES TO KEEP UP WITH THEM.
BANG
BANG
BANG BANG BANG
IN THE PAST, I WOULD HAVE DODGED THE ROAD REAPERS' BULLETS OR VIBRATED SO THEY WOULD PASS THROUGH ME.
TSH
BUT NOW THE BULLETS TURN TO ASH BEFORE THEY CAN MAKE CONTACT.
TSH
TSH
TSH
TSH

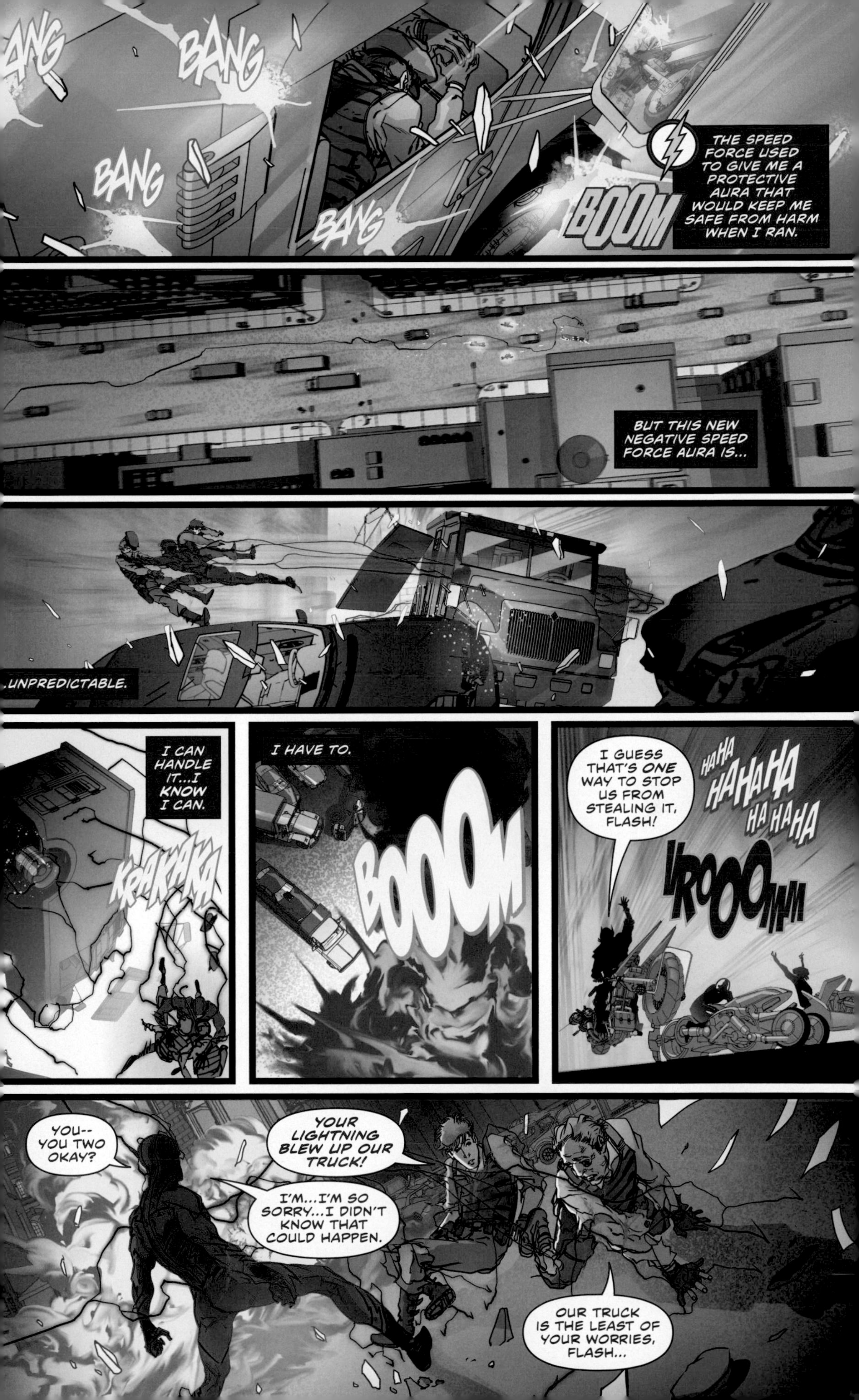

ANG
BANG
BANG
BANG
THE SPEED FORCE USED TO GIVE ME A PROTECTIVE AURA THAT WOULD KEEP ME SAFE FROM HARM WHEN I RAN.
BOOM
BUT THIS NEW NEGATIVE SPEED FORCE AURA IS...
..UNPREDICTABLE.
I CAN HANDLE IT...I KNOW I CAN.
KRAKAKA
I HAVE TO.
BOOOM
I GUESS THAT'S ONE WAY TO STOP US FROM STEALING IT, FLASH!
HAHA HAHAHA HA HAHA
VROOOMM
YOU-- YOU TWO OKAY?
YOUR LIGHTNING BLEW UP OUR TRUCK!
I'M...I'M SO SORRY...I DIDN'T KNOW THAT COULD HAPPEN.
OUR TRUCK IS THE LEAST OF YOUR WORRIES, FLASH...

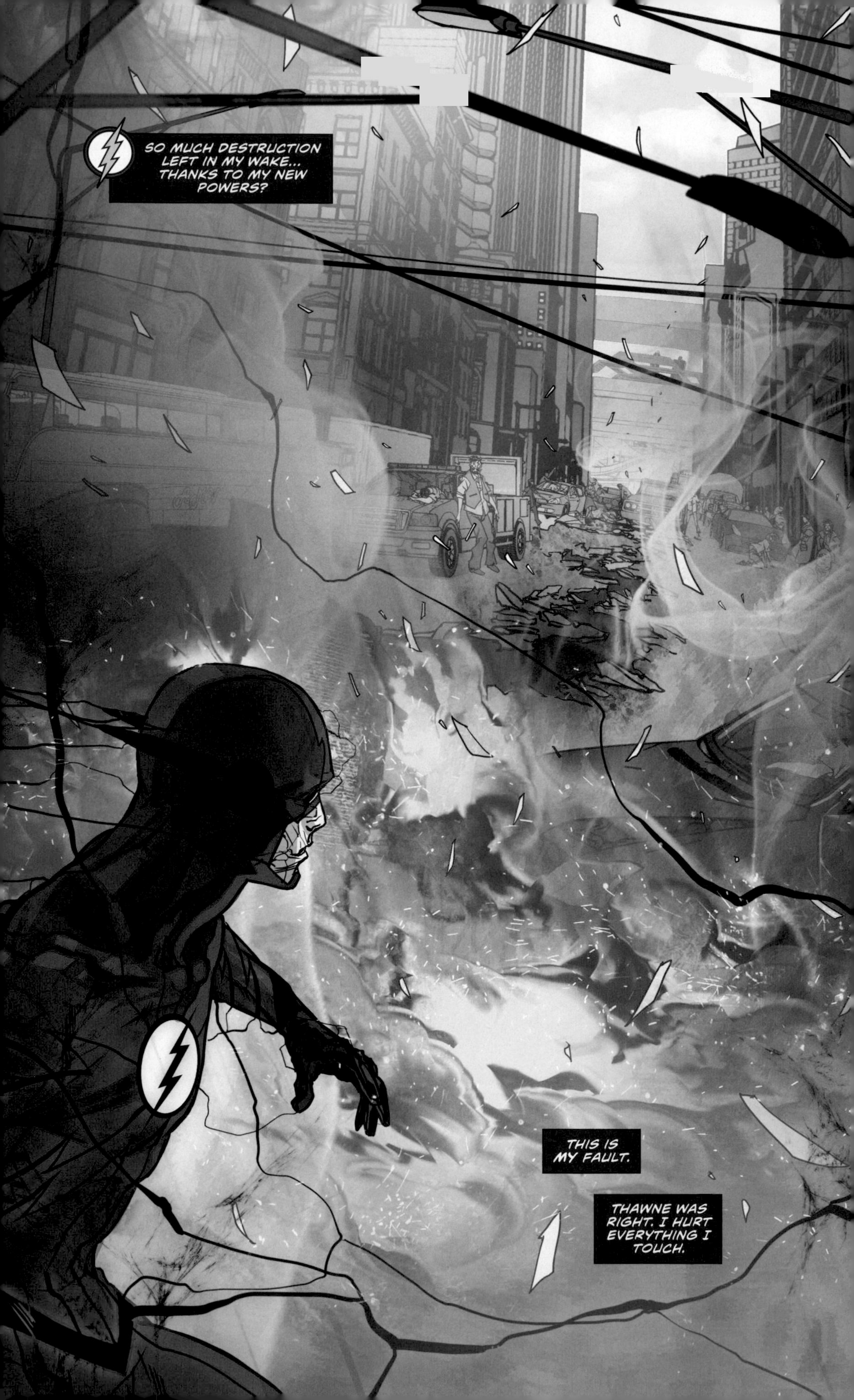
SO MUCH DESTRUCTION LEFT IN MY WAKE... THANKS TO MY NEW POWERS?
THIS IS MY FAULT.
THAWNE WAS RIGHT. I HURT EVERYTHING I TOUCH.

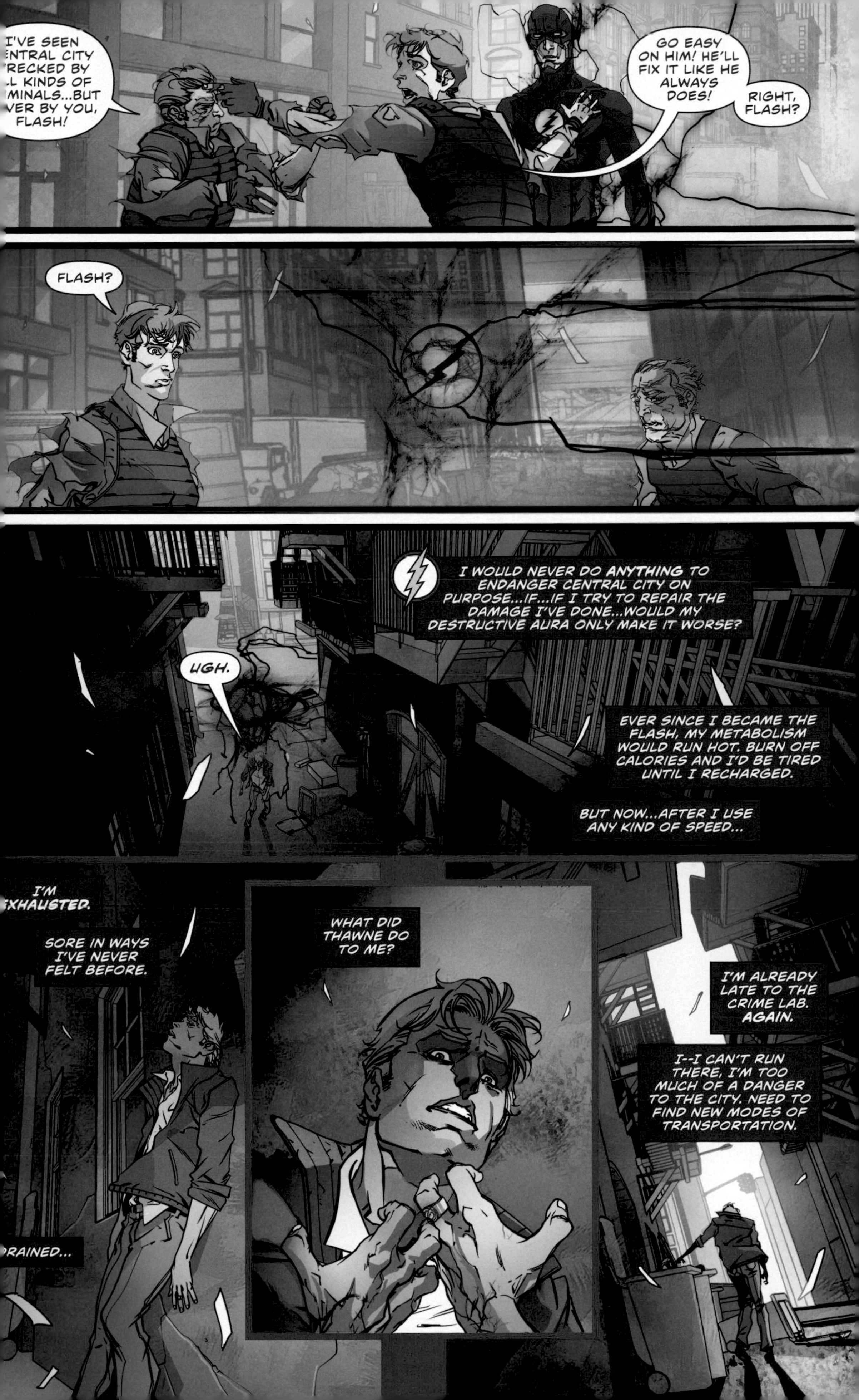
I'VE SEEN
ENTRAL CITY
RECKED BY
LL KINDS OF
MINALS...BUT
VER BY YOU,
FLASH!
GO EASY ON HIM! HE'LL FIX IT LIKE HE ALWAYS DOES!
RIGHT, FLASH?
FLASH?
I WOULD NEVER DO ANYTHING TO ENDANGER CENTRAL CITY ON PURPOSE...IF...IF I TRY TO REPAIR THE DAMAGE I'VE DONE...WOULD MY DESTRUCTIVE AURA ONLY MAKE IT WORSE?
UGH.
EVER SINCE I BECAME THE FLASH, MY METABOLISM WOULD RUN HOT. BURN OFF CALORIES AND I'D BE TIRED UNTIL I RECHARGED.
BUT NOW...AFTER I USE ANY KIND OF SPEED...
I'M
XHAUSTED.
SORE IN WAYS I'VE NEVER FELT BEFORE.
RAINED...
WHAT DID THAWNE DO TO ME?
I'M ALREADY LATE TO THE CRIME LAB. AGAIN.
I--I CAN'T RUN THERE, I'M TOO MUCH OF A DANGER TO THE CITY. NEED TO FIND NEW MODES OF TRANSPORTATION.

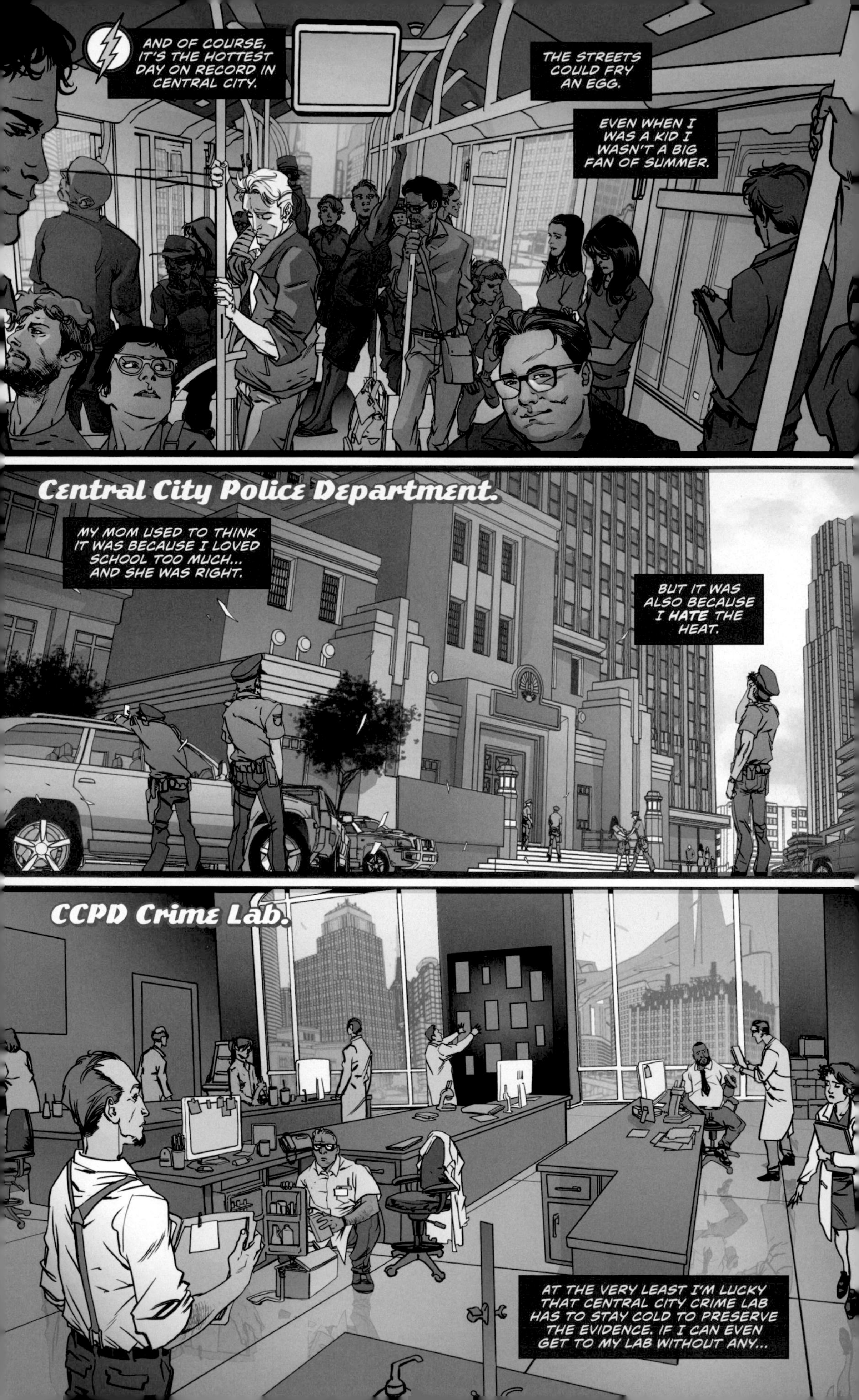
AND OF COURSE, IT'S THE HOTTEST DAY ON RECORD IN CENTRAL CITY.
THE STREETS COULD FRY AN EGG.
EVEN WHEN I WAS A KID I WASN'T A BIG FAN OF SUMMER.
Central City Police Department.
MY MOM USED TO THINK IT WAS BECAUSE I LOVED SCHOOL TOO MUCH... AND SHE WAS RIGHT.
BUT IT WAS ALSO BECAUSE I HATE THE HEAT.
CCPD Crime Lab.
AT THE VERY LEAST I'M LUCKY THAT CENTRAL CITY CRIME LAB HAS TO STAY COLD TO PRESERVE THE EVIDENCE. IF I CAN EVEN GET TO MY LAB WITHOUT ANY...

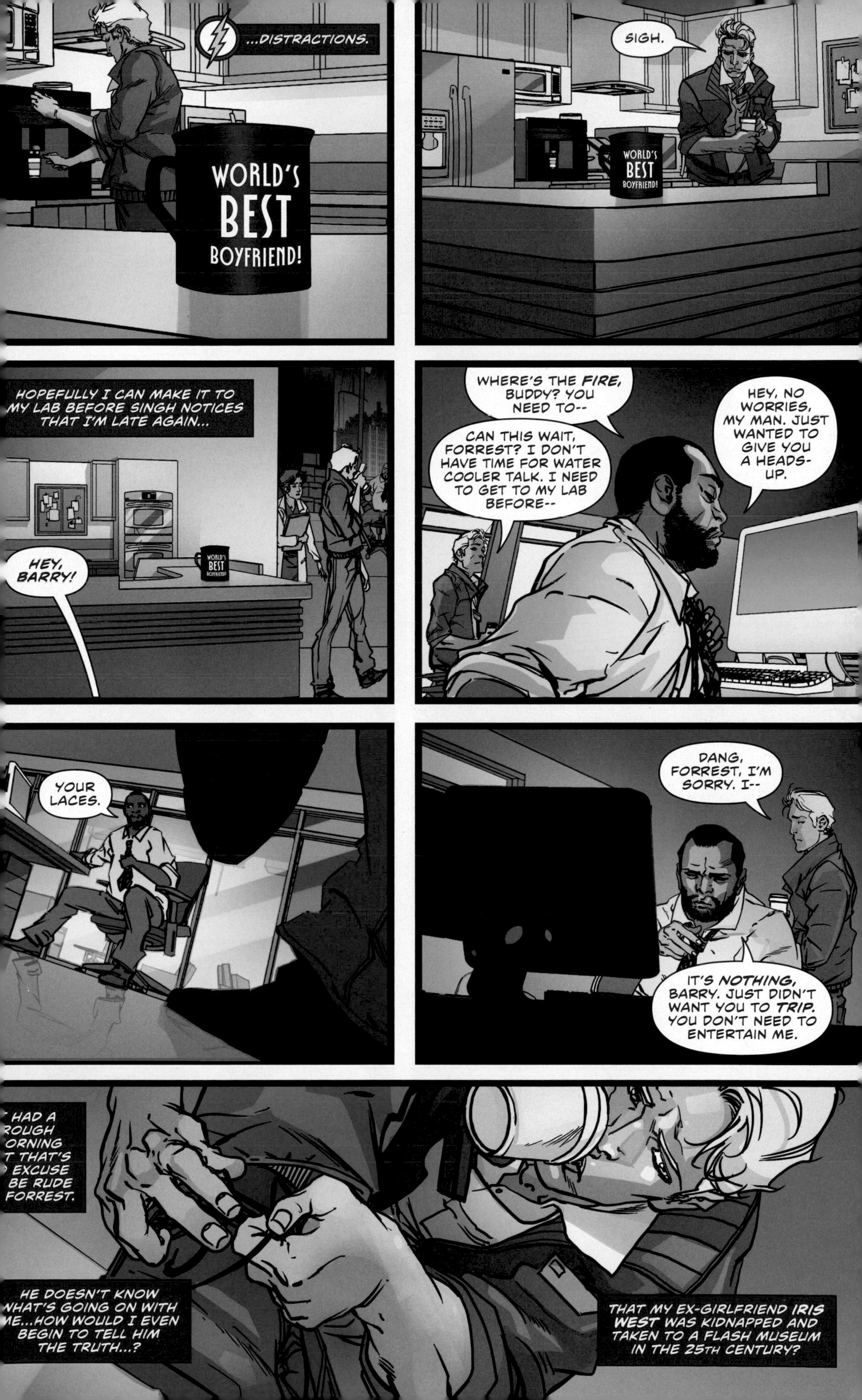
...DISTRACTIONS.
WORLD'S BEST BOYFRIEND!
SIGH.
WORLD'S BEST BOYFRIEND!
HOPEFULLY I CAN MAKE IT TO MY LAB BEFORE SINGH NOTICES THAT I'M LATE AGAIN...
HEY, BARRY!
WORLD'S BEST BOYFRIEND!
WHERE'S THE FIRE, BUDDY? YOU NEED TO--
CAN THIS WAIT, FORREST? I DON'T HAVE TIME FOR WATER COOLER TALK. I NEED TO GET TO MY LAB BEFORE--
HEY, NO WORRIES, MY MAN. JUST WANTED TO GIVE YOU A HEADS-UP.
YOUR LACES.
DANG, FORREST, I'M SORRY. I--
IT'S NOTHING, BARRY. JUST DIDN'T WANT YOU TO TRIP. YOU DON'T NEED TO ENTERTAIN ME.
HAD A ROUGH ORNING T THAT'S EXCUSE BE RUDE FORREST.
HE DOESN'T KNOW WHAT'S GOING ON WITH ME...HOW WOULD I EVEN BEGIN TO TELL HIM THE TRUTH...?
THAT MY EX-GIRLFRIEND IRIS WEST WAS KIDNAPPED AND TAKEN TO A FLASH MUSEUM IN THE 25TH CENTURY?

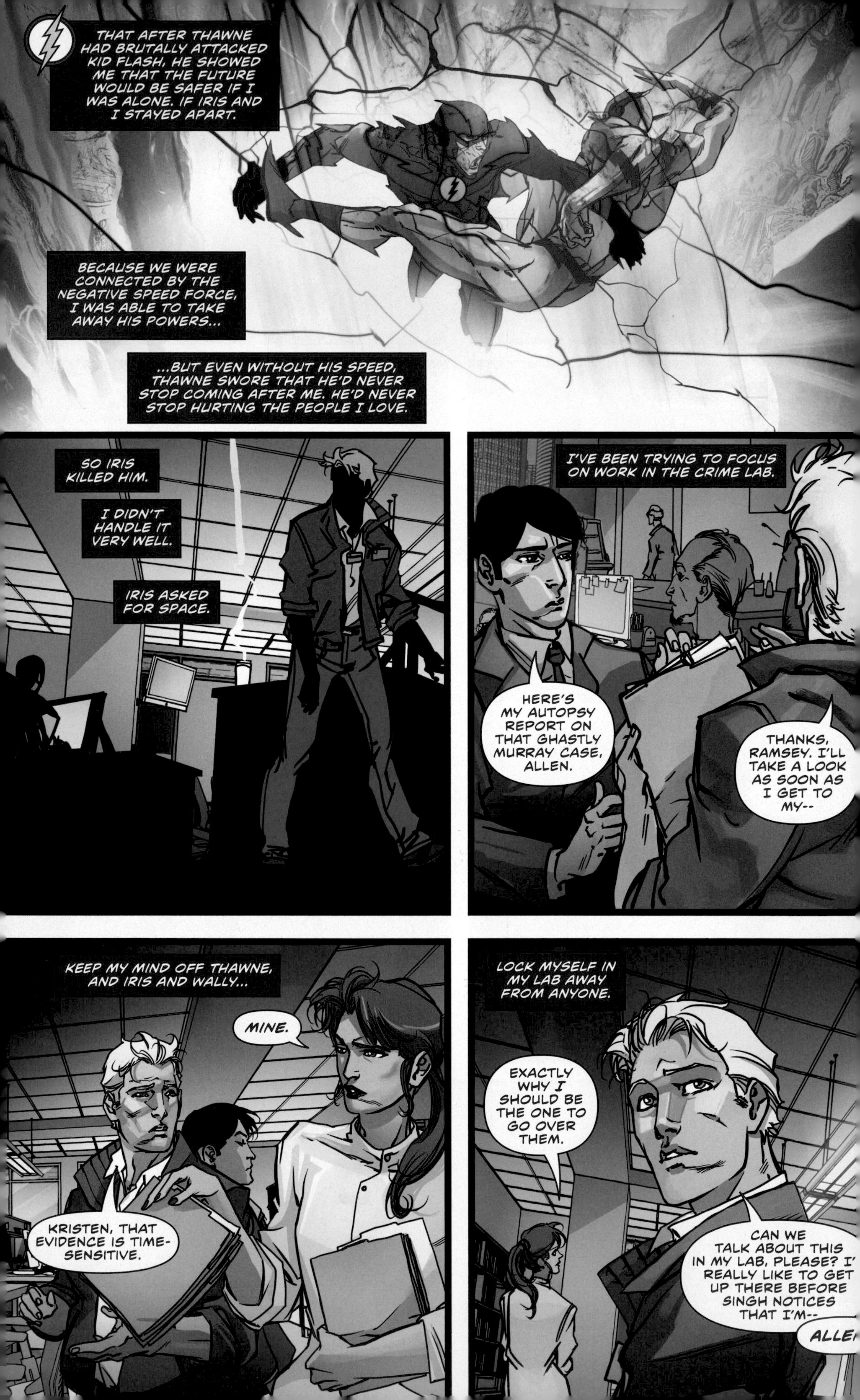
THAT AFTER THAWNE HAD BRUTALLY ATTACKED KID FLASH, HE SHOWED ME THAT THE FUTURE WOULD BE SAFER IF I WAS ALONE. IF IRIS AND I STAYED APART.
BECAUSE WE WERE CONNECTED BY THE NEGATIVE SPEED FORCE, I WAS ABLE TO TAKE AWAY HIS POWERS...
...BUT EVEN WITHOUT HIS SPEED, THAWNE SWORE THAT HE'D NEVER STOP COMING AFTER ME. HE'D NEVER STOP HURTING THE PEOPLE I LOVE.
SO IRIS KILLED HIM.
I DIDN'T HANDLE IT VERY WELL.
IRIS ASKED FOR SPACE.
I'VE BEEN TRYING TO FOCUS ON WORK IN THE CRIME LAB.
HERE'S MY AUTOPSY REPORT ON THAT GHASTLY MURRAY CASE, ALLEN.
THANKS, RAMSEY. I'LL TAKE A LOOK AS SOON AS I GET TO MY--
KEEP MY MIND OFF THAWNE, AND IRIS AND WALLY...
MINE.
KRISTEN, THAT EVIDENCE IS TIME-SENSITIVE.
LOCK MYSELF IN MY LAB AWAY FROM ANYONE.
EXACTLY WHY I SHOULD BE THE ONE TO GO OVER THEM.
CAN WE TALK ABOUT THIS IN MY LAB, PLEASE? I'D REALLY LIKE TO GET UP THERE BEFORE SINGH NOTICES THAT I'M--
ALLE

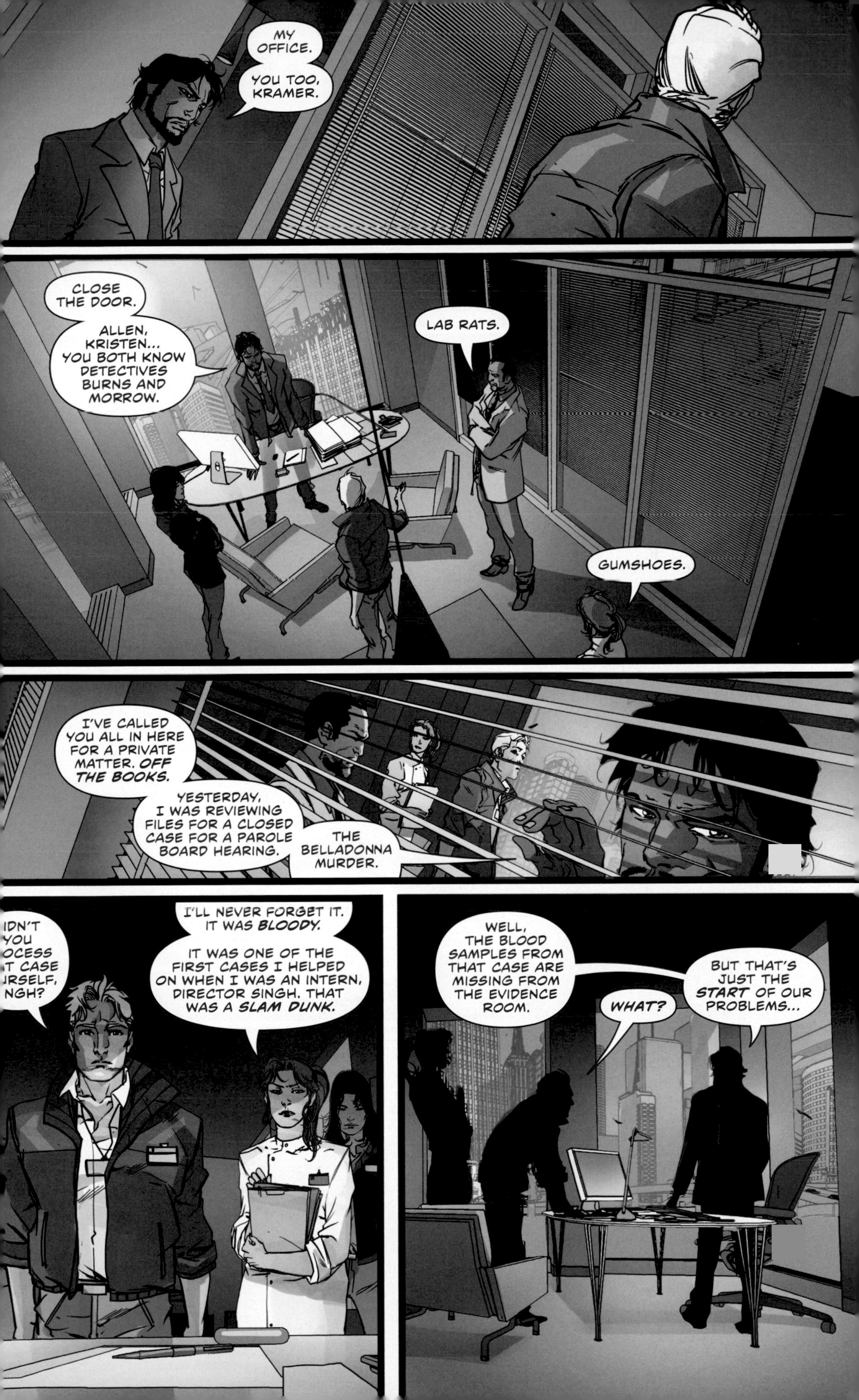
MY OFFICE.
YOU TOO, KRAMER.
CLOSE THE DOOR.
ALLEN, KRISTEN... YOU BOTH KNOW DETECTIVES BURNS AND MORROW.
LAB RATS.
GUMSHOES.
I'VE CALLED YOU ALL IN HERE FOR A PRIVATE MATTER. *OFF THE BOOKS.*
YESTERDAY, I WAS REVIEWING FILES FOR A CLOSED CASE FOR A PAROLE BOARD HEARING.
THE BELLADONNA MURDER.
IDN'T YOU OCESS T CASE RSELF, NGH?
I'LL NEVER FORGET IT. IT WAS *BLOODY.*
IT WAS ONE OF THE FIRST CASES I HELPED ON WHEN I WAS AN INTERN, DIRECTOR SINGH. THAT WAS A *SLAM DUNK.*
WELL, THE BLOOD SAMPLES FROM THAT CASE ARE MISSING FROM THE EVIDENCE ROOM.
WHAT?
BUT THAT'S JUST THE *START* OF OUR PROBLEMS...

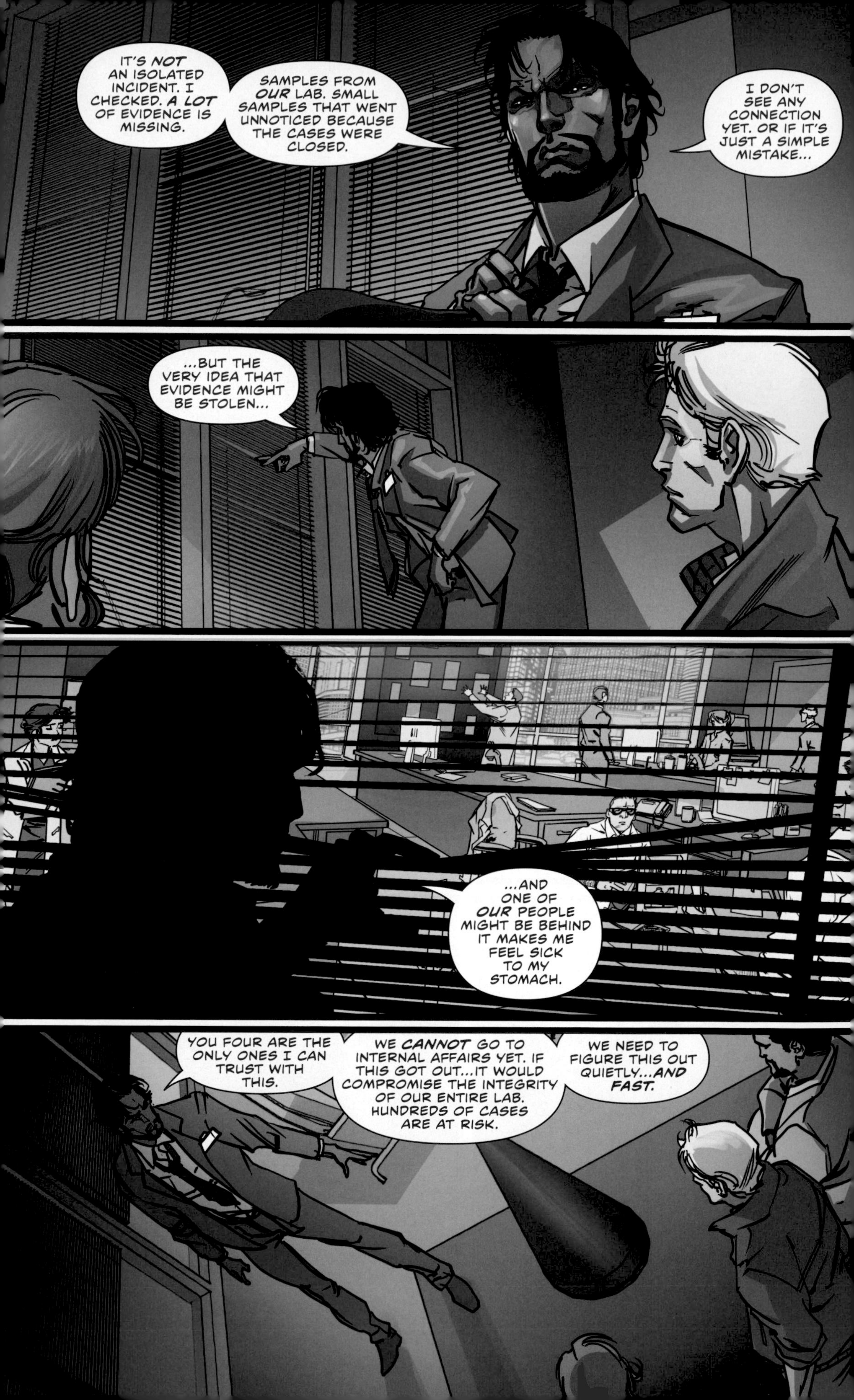
IT'S NOT AN ISOLATED INCIDENT. I CHECKED. A LOT OF EVIDENCE IS MISSING.
SAMPLES FROM OUR LAB. SMALL SAMPLES THAT WENT UNNOTICED BECAUSE THE CASES WERE CLOSED.
I DON'T SEE ANY CONNECTION YET. OR IF IT'S JUST A SIMPLE MISTAKE...
...BUT THE VERY IDEA THAT EVIDENCE MIGHT BE STOLEN...
...AND ONE OF OUR PEOPLE MIGHT BE BEHIND IT MAKES ME FEEL SICK TO MY STOMACH.
YOU FOUR ARE THE ONLY ONES I CAN TRUST WITH THIS.
WE CANNOT GO TO INTERNAL AFFAIRS YET. IF THIS GOT OUT...IT WOULD COMPROMISE THE INTEGRITY OF OUR ENTIRE LAB. HUNDREDS OF CASES ARE AT RISK.
WE NEED TO FIGURE THIS OUT QUIETLY...AND FAST.

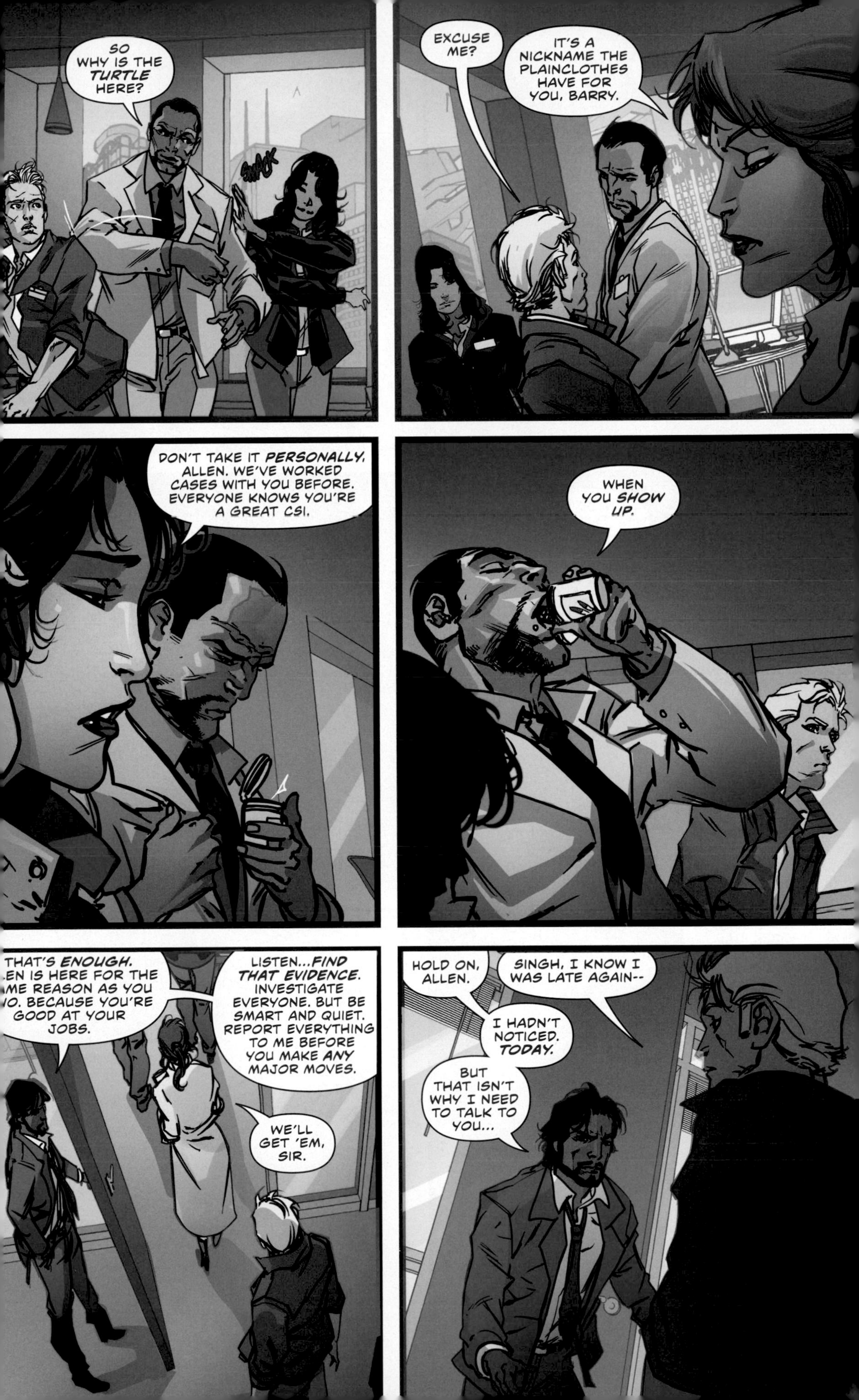
SO WHY IS THE *TURTLE* HERE?
EXCUSE ME?
IT'S A NICKNAME THE PLAINCLOTHES HAVE FOR YOU, BARRY.
DON'T TAKE IT *PERSONALLY,* ALLEN. WE'VE WORKED CASES WITH YOU BEFORE. EVERYONE KNOWS YOU'RE A GREAT CSI.
WHEN YOU *SHOW UP.*
THAT'S *ENOUGH.* EN IS HERE FOR THE ME REASON AS YOU O. BECAUSE YOU'RE GOOD AT YOUR JOBS.
LISTEN...*FIND THAT EVIDENCE.* INVESTIGATE EVERYONE. BUT BE SMART AND QUIET. REPORT EVERYTHING TO ME BEFORE YOU MAKE *ANY* MAJOR MOVES.
WE'LL GET 'EM, SIR.
HOLD ON, ALLEN.
SINGH, I KNOW I WAS LATE AGAIN--
I HADN'T NOTICED. *TODAY.*
BUT THAT ISN'T WHY I NEED TO TALK TO YOU...

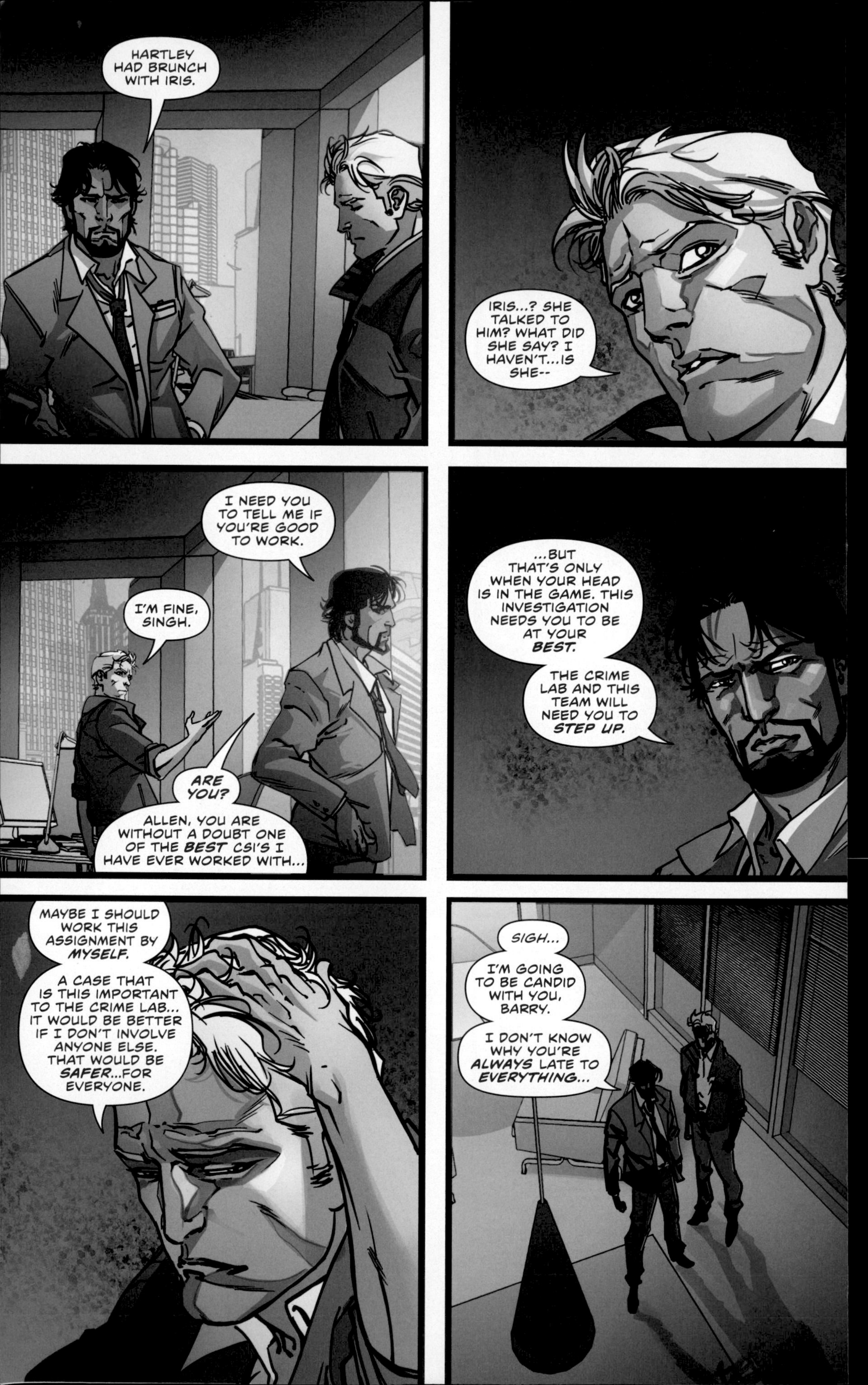
HARTLEY HAD BRUNCH WITH IRIS.
IRIS...? SHE TALKED TO HIM? WHAT DID SHE SAY? I HAVEN'T...IS SHE--
I NEED YOU TO TELL ME IF YOU'RE GOOD TO WORK.
I'M FINE, SINGH.
ARE YOU?
ALLEN, YOU ARE WITHOUT A DOUBT ONE OF THE BEST CSI'S I HAVE EVER WORKED WITH...
...BUT THAT'S ONLY WHEN YOUR HEAD IS IN THE GAME. THIS INVESTIGATION NEEDS YOU TO BE AT YOUR BEST.
THE CRIME LAB AND THIS TEAM WILL NEED YOU TO STEP UP.
MAYBE I SHOULD WORK THIS ASSIGNMENT BY MYSELF.
A CASE THAT IS THIS IMPORTANT TO THE CRIME LAB... IT WOULD BE BETTER IF I DON'T INVOLVE ANYONE ELSE. THAT WOULD BE SAFER...FOR EVERYONE.
SIGH...
I'M GOING TO BE CANDID WITH YOU, BARRY.
I DON'T KNOW WHY YOU'RE ALWAYS LATE TO EVERYTHING...

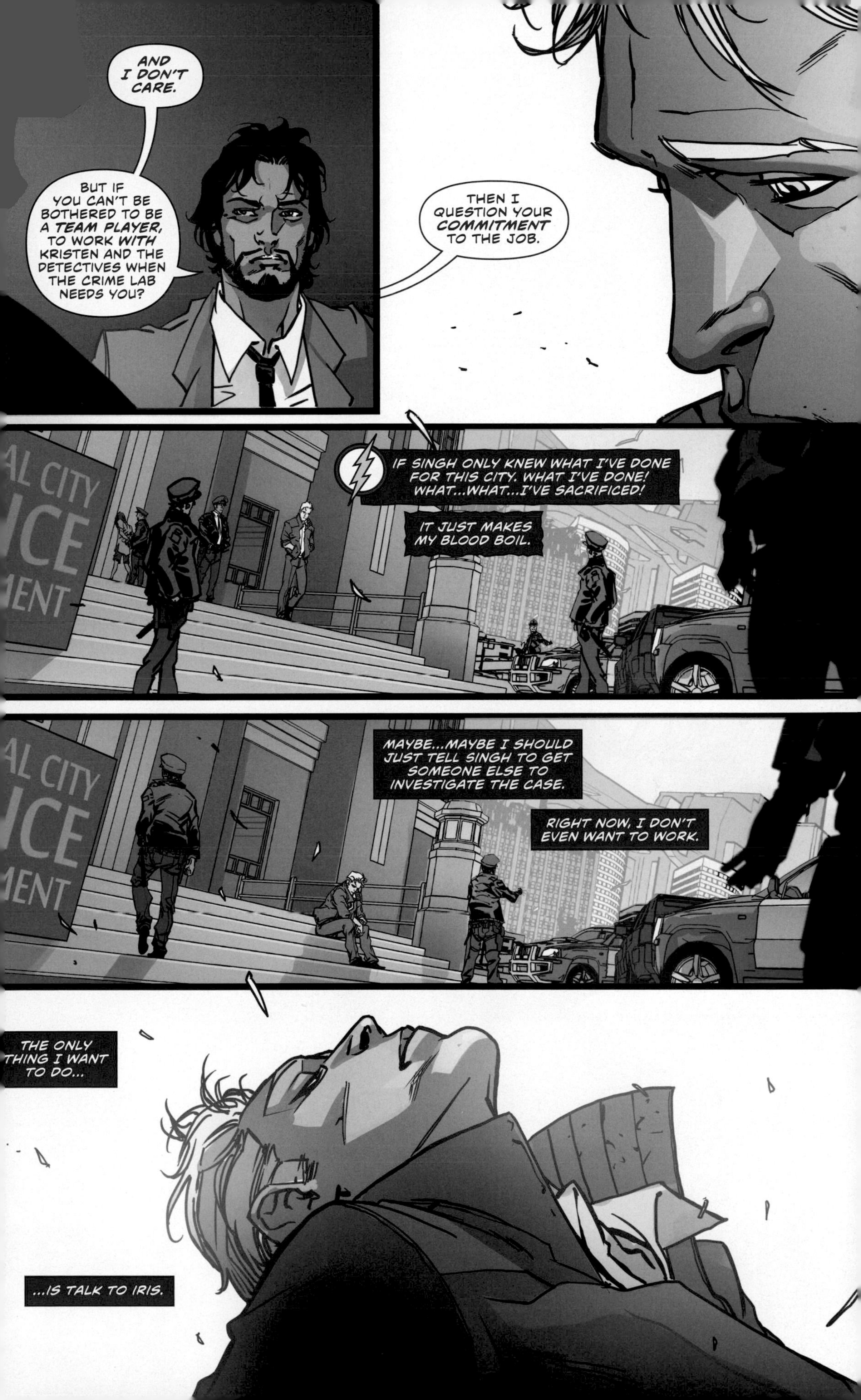

AND I DON'T CARE.
BUT IF YOU CAN'T BE BOTHERED TO BE A TEAM PLAYER, TO WORK WITH KRISTEN AND THE DETECTIVES WHEN THE CRIME LAB NEEDS YOU?
THEN I QUESTION YOUR COMMITMENT TO THE JOB.
IF SINGH ONLY KNEW WHAT I'VE DONE FOR THIS CITY. WHAT I'VE DONE! WHAT...WHAT...I'VE SACRIFICED!
IT JUST MAKES MY BLOOD BOIL.
AL CITY ICE MENT
MAYBE...MAYBE I SHOULD JUST TELL SINGH TO GET SOMEONE ELSE TO INVESTIGATE THE CASE.
RIGHT NOW, I DON'T EVEN WANT TO WORK.
THE ONLY THING I WANT TO DO...
...IS TALK TO IRIS.

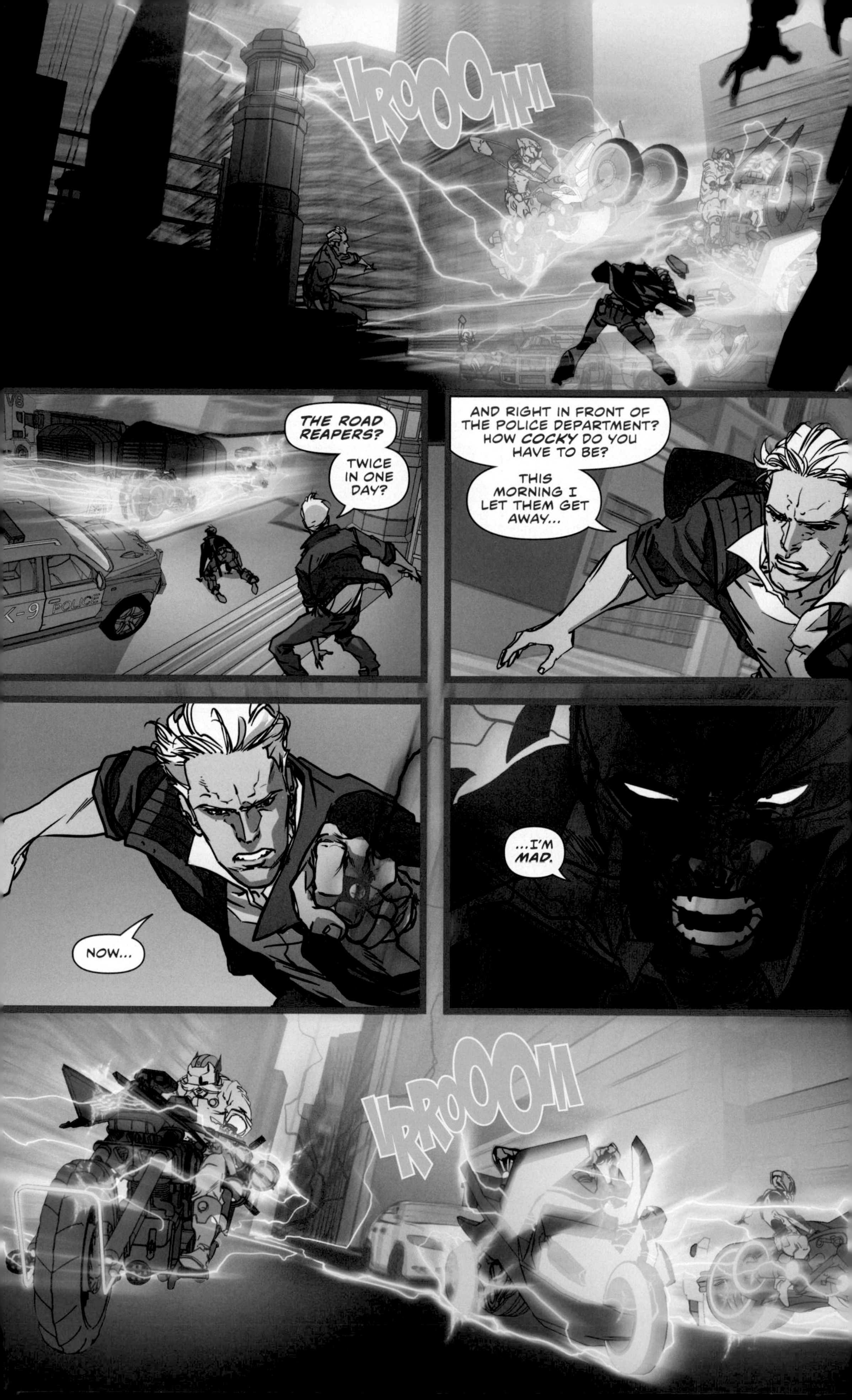
VRROOOMM
THE ROAD REAPERS?
TWICE IN ONE DAY?
AND RIGHT IN FRONT OF THE POLICE DEPARTMENT? HOW COCKY DO YOU HAVE TO BE?
THIS MORNING I LET THEM GET AWAY...
NOW...
...I'M MAD.
VRROOOM

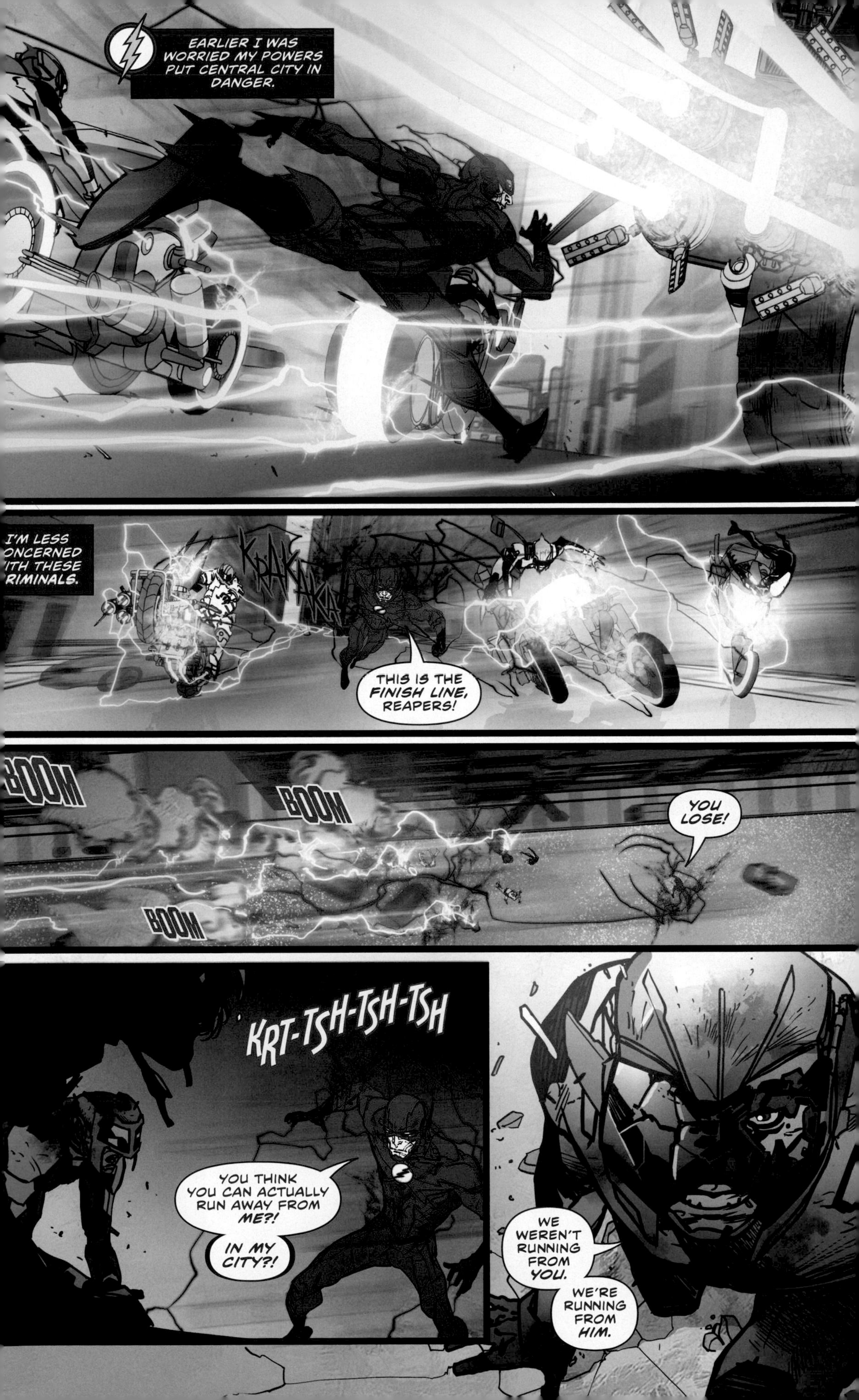
EARLIER I WAS WORRIED MY POWERS PUT CENTRAL CITY IN DANGER.
I'M LESS ONCERNED ITH THESE RIMINALS.
KRAKAKAKA
THIS IS THE FINISH LINE, REAPERS!
BOOM
BOOM
BOOM
YOU LOSE!
KRT-TSH-TSH-TSH
YOU THINK YOU CAN ACTUALLY RUN AWAY FROM ME?!
IN MY CITY?!
WE WEREN'T RUNNING FROM YOU.
WE'RE RUNNING FROM HIM.

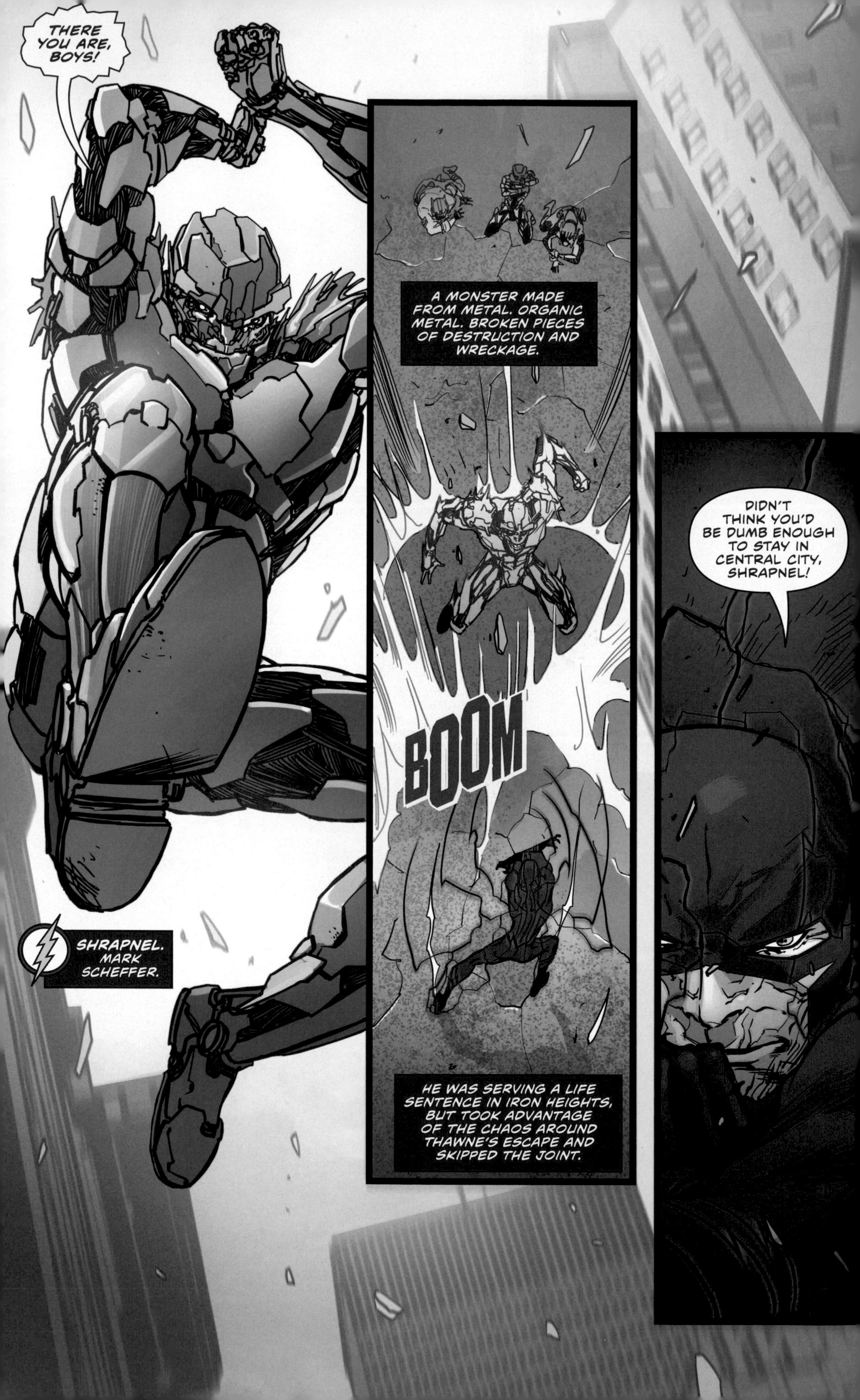
THERE YOU ARE, BOYS!
SHRAPNEL. MARK SCHEFFER.
A MONSTER MADE FROM METAL. ORGANIC METAL. BROKEN PIECES OF DESTRUCTION AND WRECKAGE.
BOOM
HE WAS SERVING A LIFE SENTENCE IN IRON HEIGHTS, BUT TOOK ADVANTAGE OF THE CHAOS AROUND THAWNE'S ESCAPE AND SKIPPED THE JOINT.
DIDN'T THINK YOU'D BE DUMB ENOUGH TO STAY IN CENTRAL CITY, SHRAPNEL!

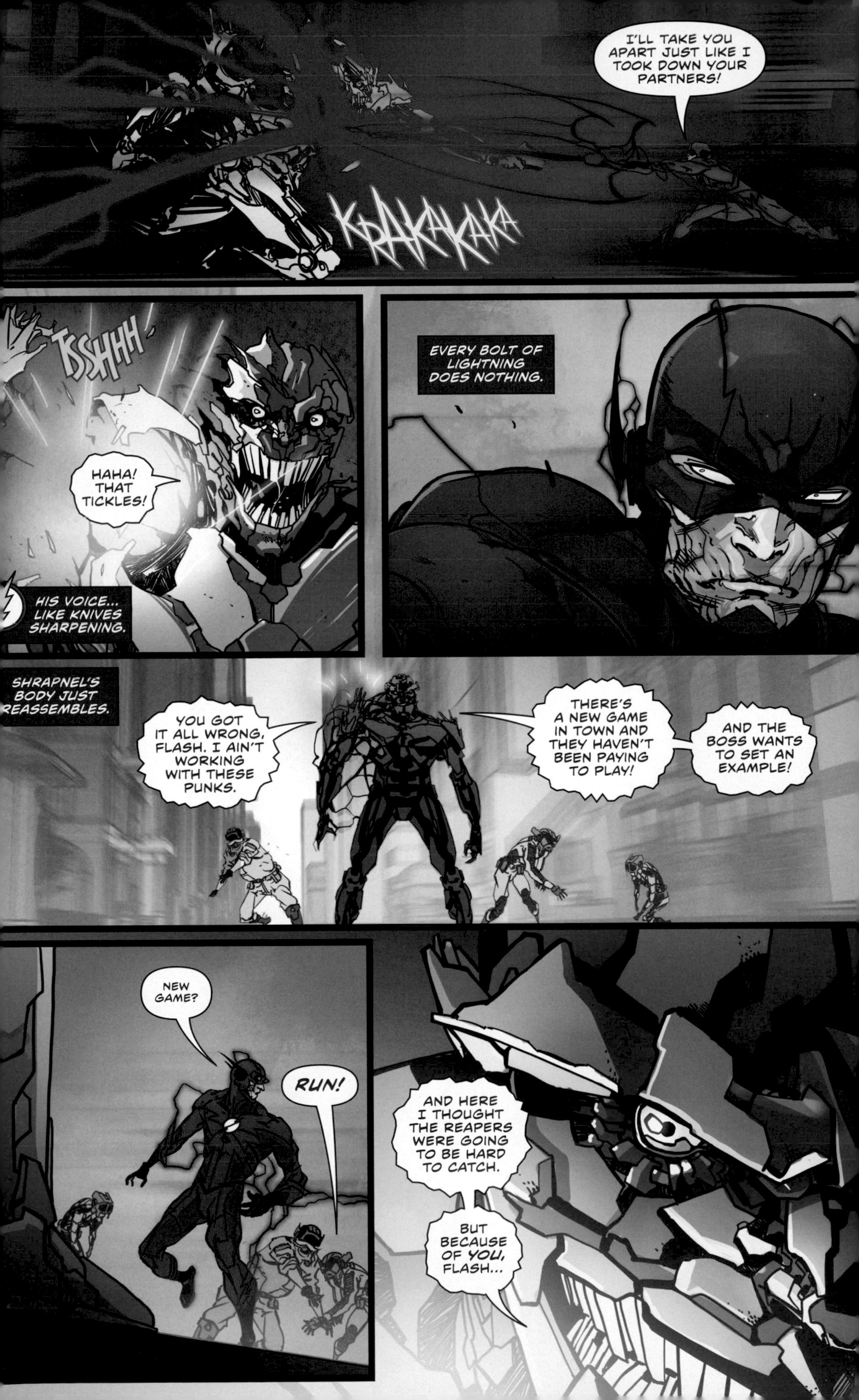
I'LL TAKE YOU APART JUST LIKE I TOOK DOWN YOUR PARTNERS!
KRAKAKAKA
TSSHHH
HAHA! THAT TICKLES!
HIS VOICE... LIKE KNIVES SHARPENING.
EVERY BOLT OF LIGHTNING DOES NOTHING.
SHRAPNEL'S BODY JUST REASSEMBLES.
YOU GOT IT ALL WRONG, FLASH. I AIN'T WORKING WITH THESE PUNKS.
THERE'S A NEW GAME IN TOWN AND THEY HAVEN'T BEEN PAYING TO PLAY!
AND THE BOSS WANTS TO SET AN EXAMPLE!
NEW GAME?
RUN!
AND HERE I THOUGHT THE REAPERS WERE GOING TO BE HARD TO CATCH.
BUT BECAUSE OF YOU, FLASH...

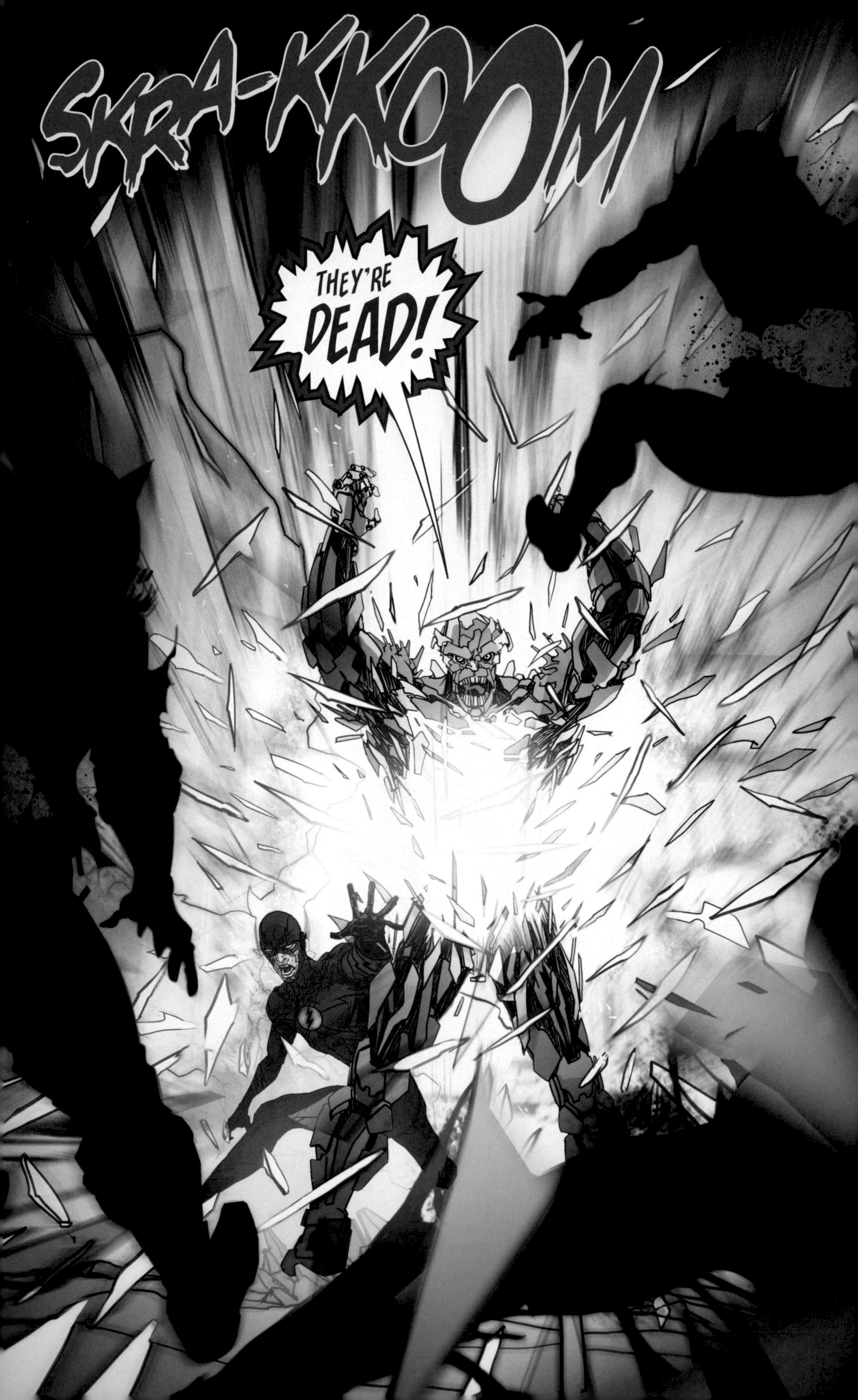
SKRA-KKOOM
THEY'RE DEAD!

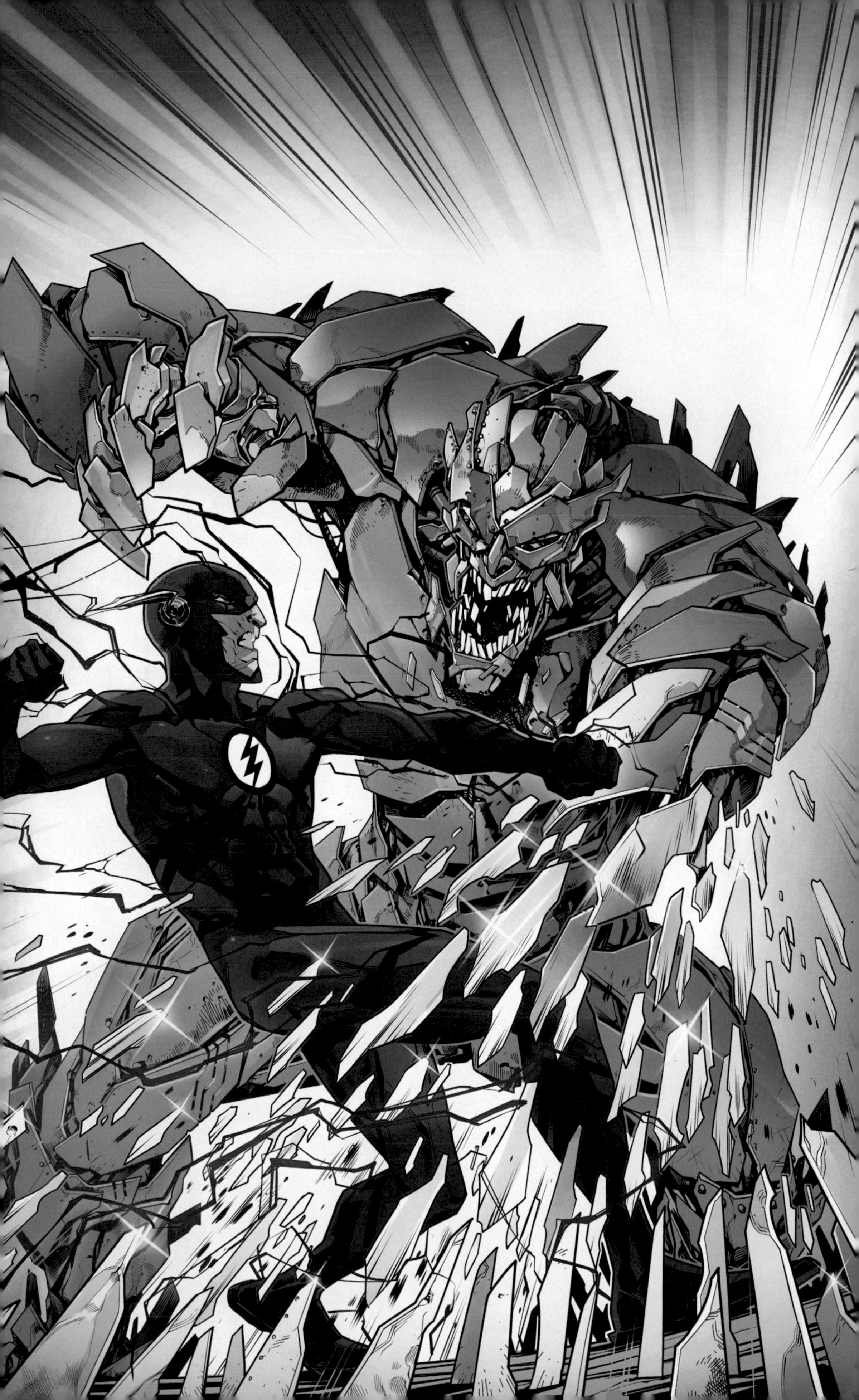

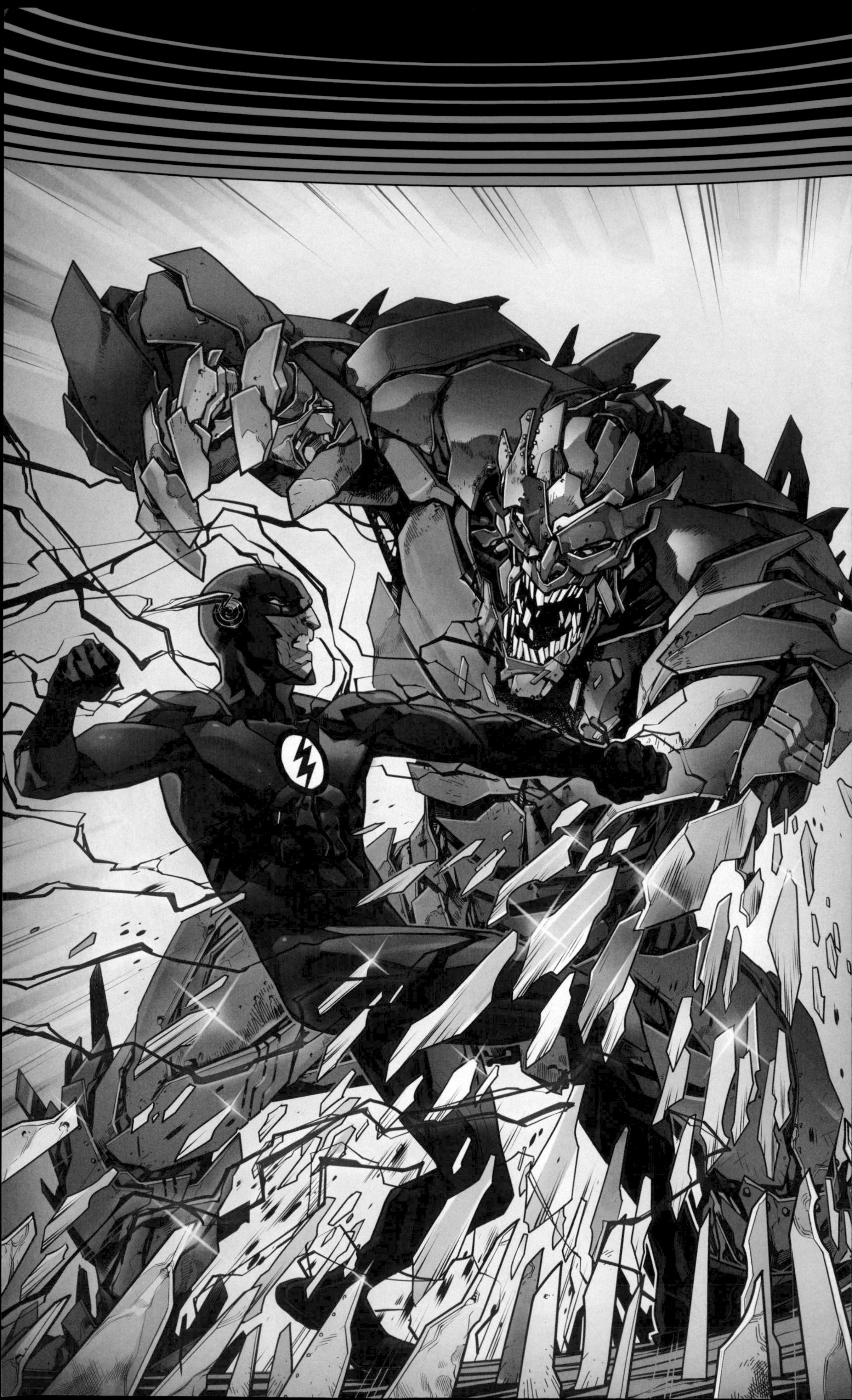

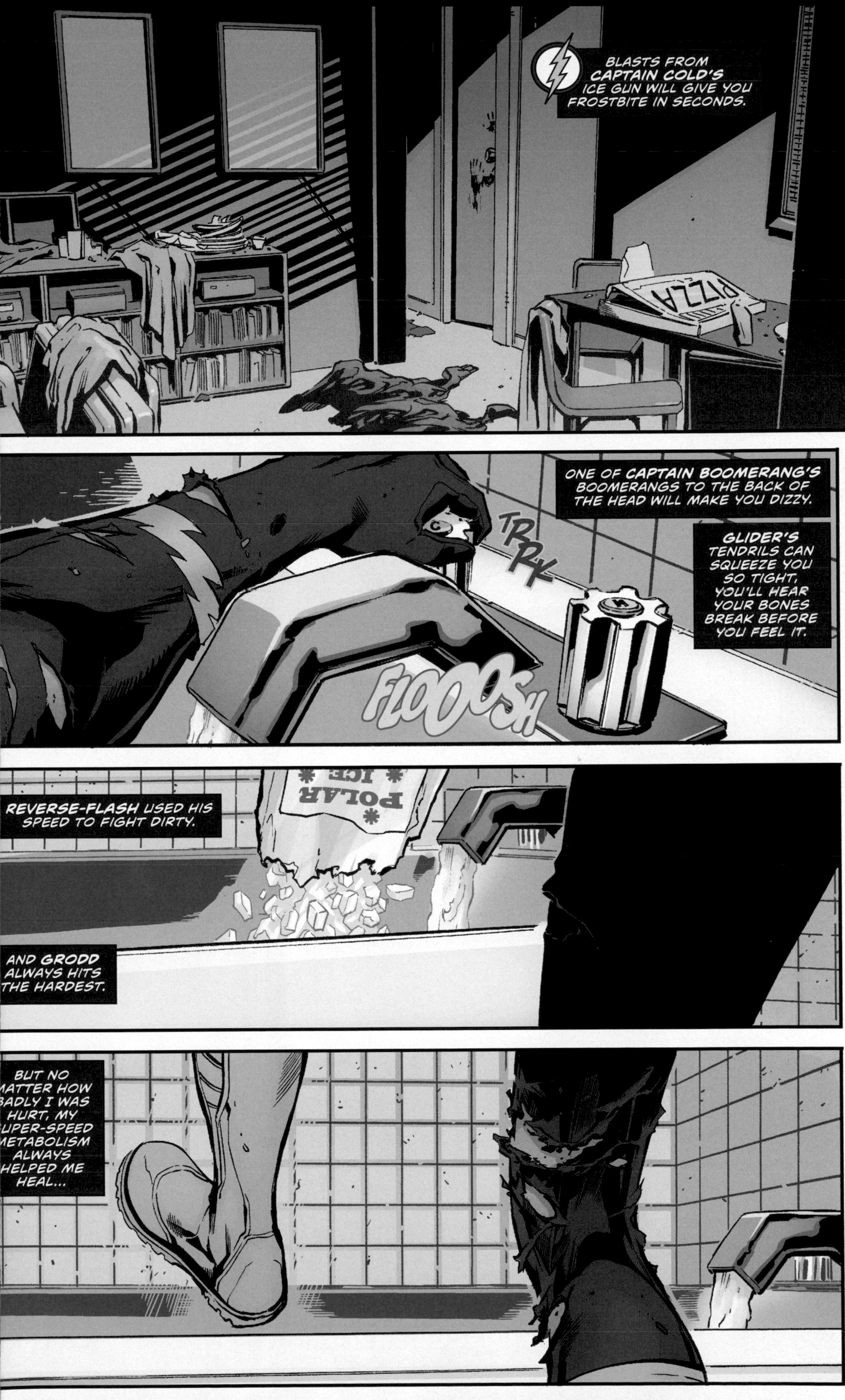

BLASTS FROM CAPTAIN COLD'S ICE GUN WILL GIVE YOU FROSTBITE IN SECONDS.
PIZZA
ONE OF CAPTAIN BOOMERANG'S BOOMERANGS TO THE BACK OF THE HEAD WILL MAKE YOU DIZZY.
TRRK
GLIDER'S TENDRILS CAN SQUEEZE YOU SO TIGHT, YOU'LL HEAR YOUR BONES BREAK BEFORE YOU FEEL IT.
FLOOOSH
REVERSE-FLASH USED HIS SPEED TO FIGHT DIRTY.
POLAR ICE
AND GRODD ALWAYS HITS THE HARDEST.
BUT NO MATTER HOW BADLY I WAS HURT, MY SUPER-SPEED METABOLISM ALWAYS HELPED ME HEAL...

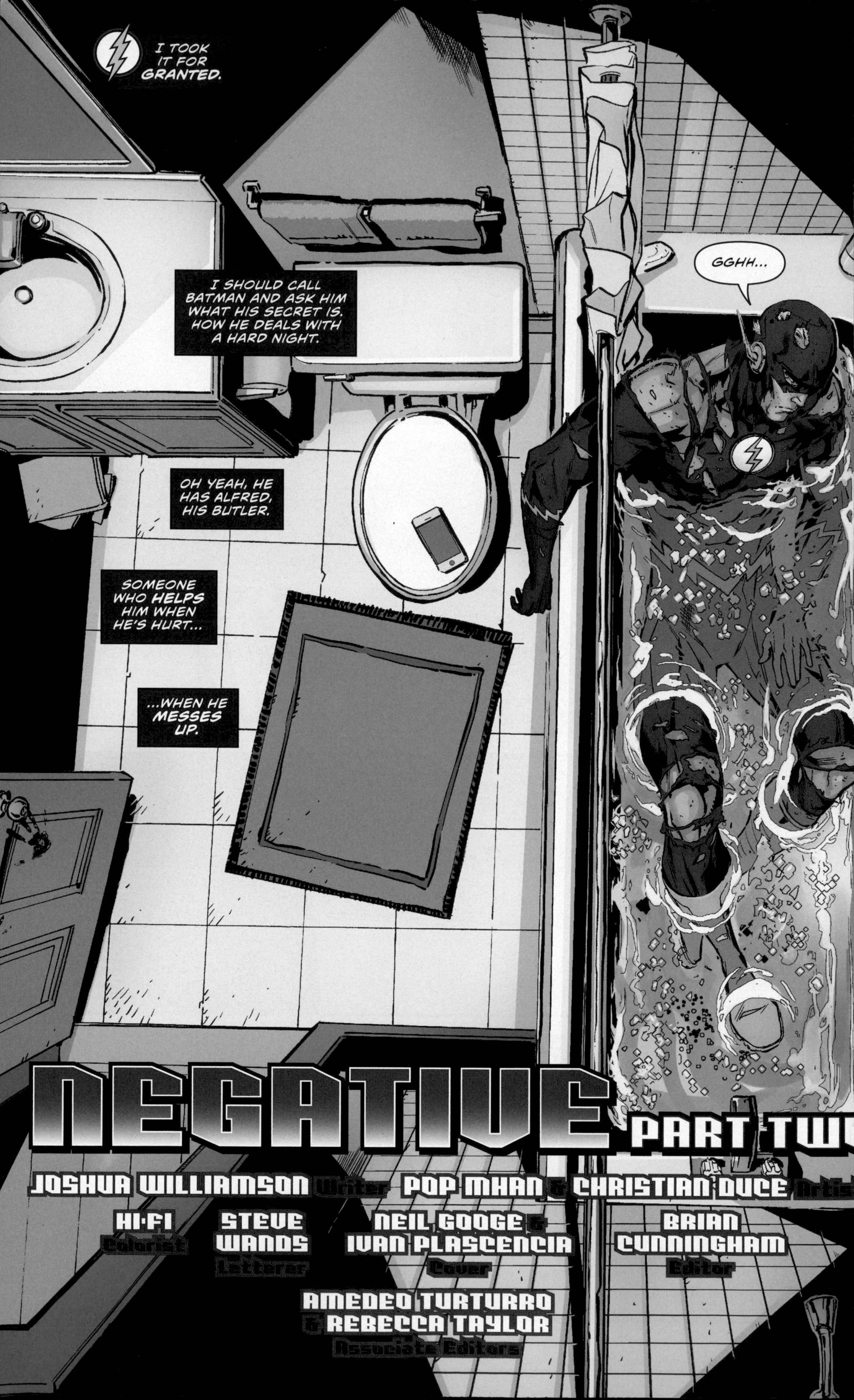
I TOOK IT FOR GRANTED.
I SHOULD CALL BATMAN AND ASK HIM WHAT HIS SECRET IS. HOW HE DEALS WITH A HARD NIGHT.
GGHH...
OH YEAH, HE HAS ALFRED, HIS BUTLER.
SOMEONE WHO HELPS HIM WHEN HE'S HURT...
...WHEN HE MESSES UP.
NEGATIVE PART TWO
JOSHUA WILLIAMSON Writer POP MHAN & CHRISTIAN DUCE Artists
HI-FI Colorist
STEVE WANDS Letterer
NEIL GOOGE & IVAN PLASCENCIA Cover
BRIAN CUNNINGHAM Editor
AMEDEO TURTURRO & REBECCA TAYLOR Associate Editors

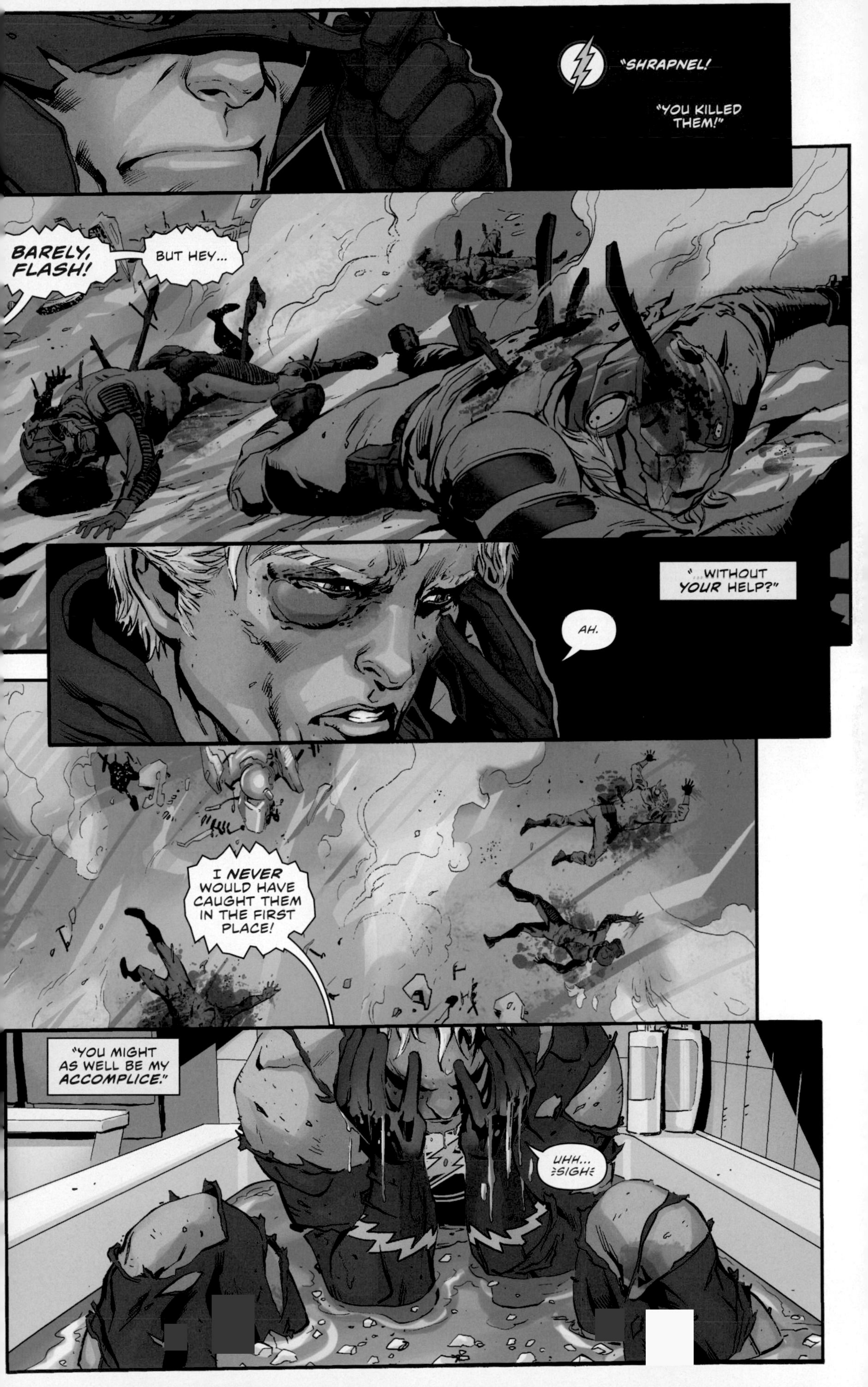
"SHRAPNEL!
"YOU KILLED THEM!"
BARELY, FLASH!
BUT HEY...
"...WITHOUT YOUR HELP?"
AH.
I NEVER WOULD HAVE CAUGHT THEM IN THE FIRST PLACE!
"YOU MIGHT AS WELL BE MY ACCOMPLICE."
UHH... SIGH

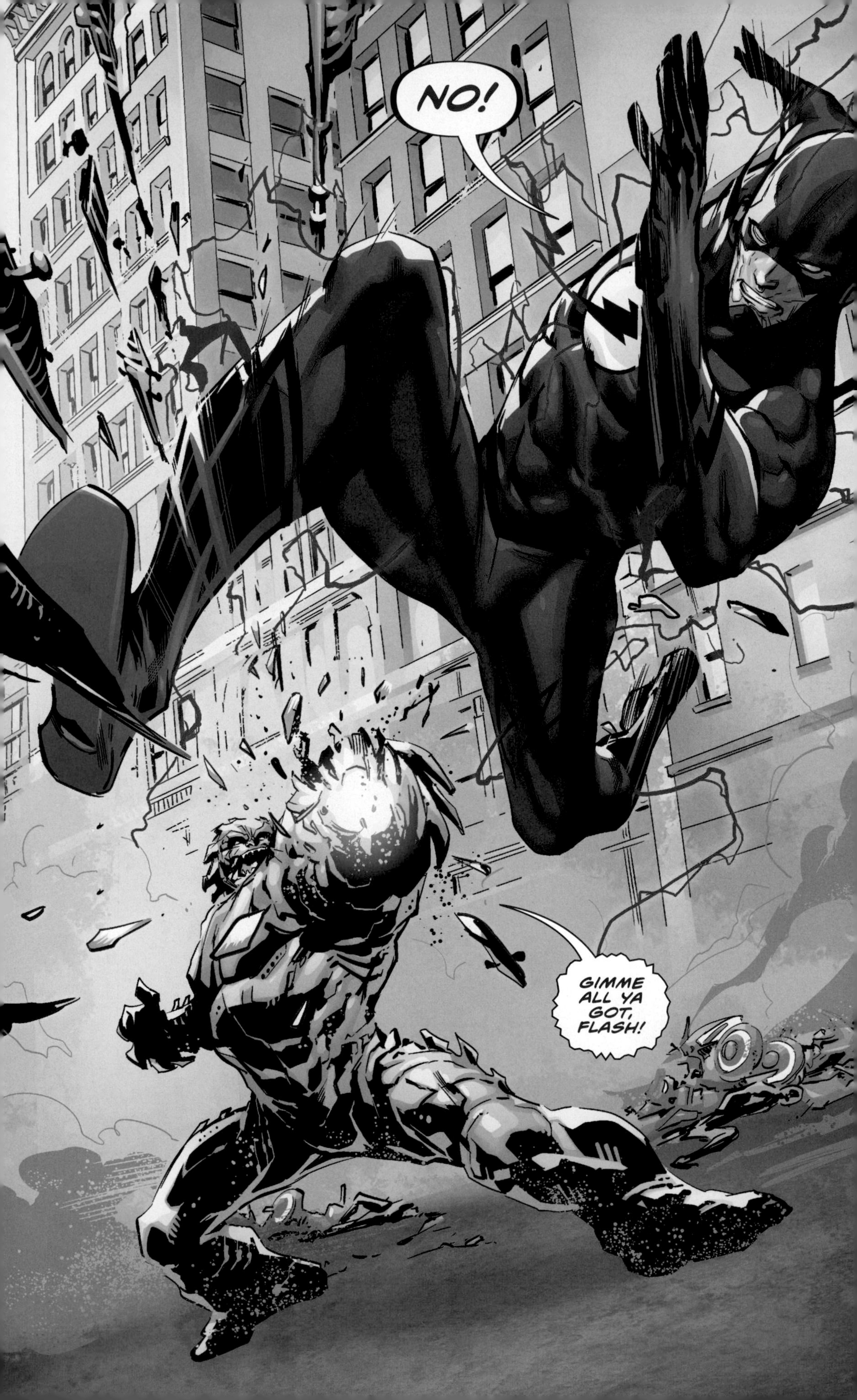
NO!
GIMME ALL YA GOT, FLASH!

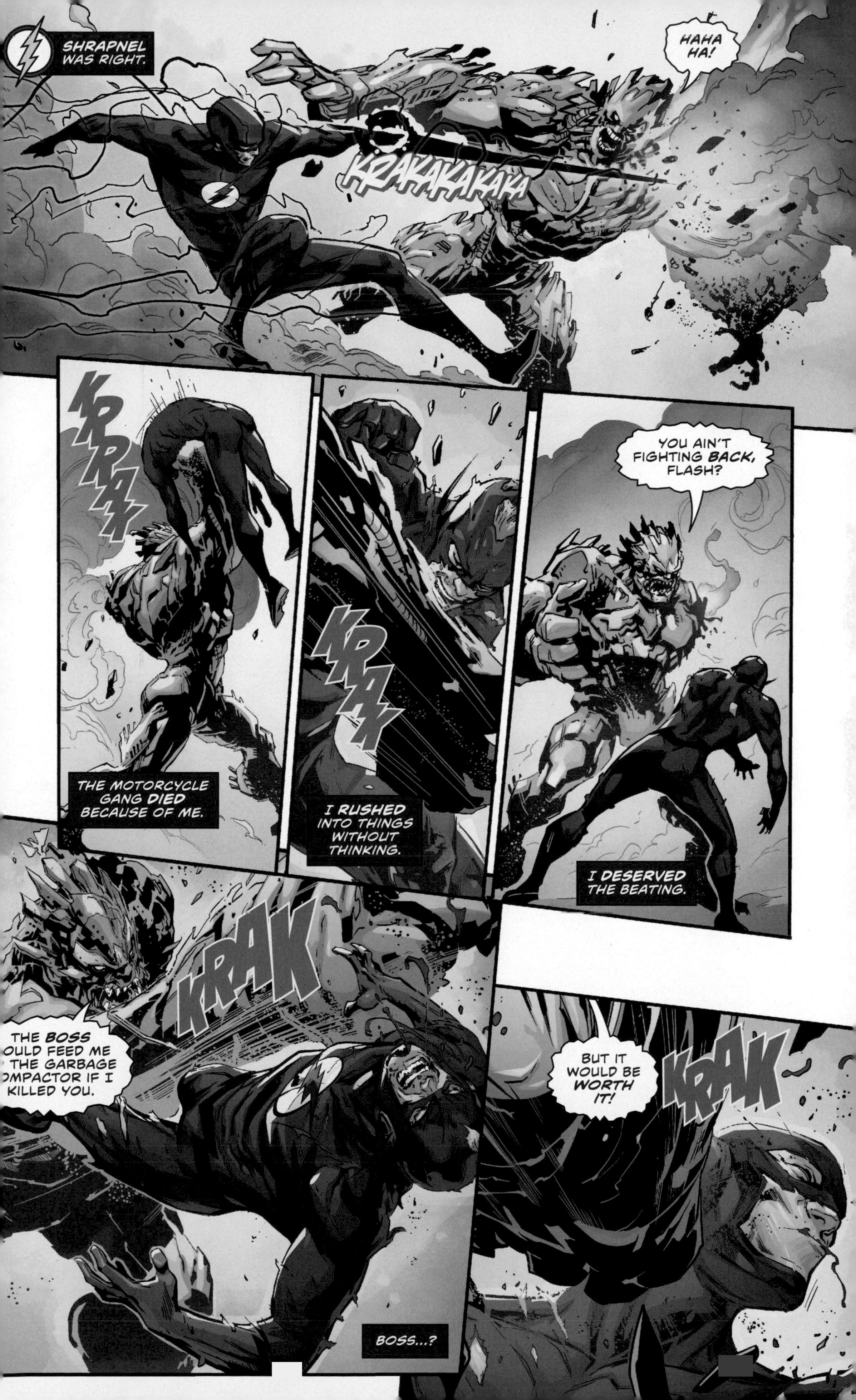
SHRAPNEL WAS RIGHT.
HAHA HA!
KRAKAKAKAKAKA
KRAK
THE MOTORCYCLE GANG DIED BECAUSE OF ME.
KRAK
I RUSHED INTO THINGS WITHOUT THINKING.
YOU AIN'T FIGHTING BACK, FLASH?
I DESERVED THE BEATING.
KRAK
THE BOSS
OULD FEED ME
THE GARBAGE
OMPACTOR IF I
KILLED YOU.
BUT IT WOULD BE WORTH IT!
KRAK
BOSS...?

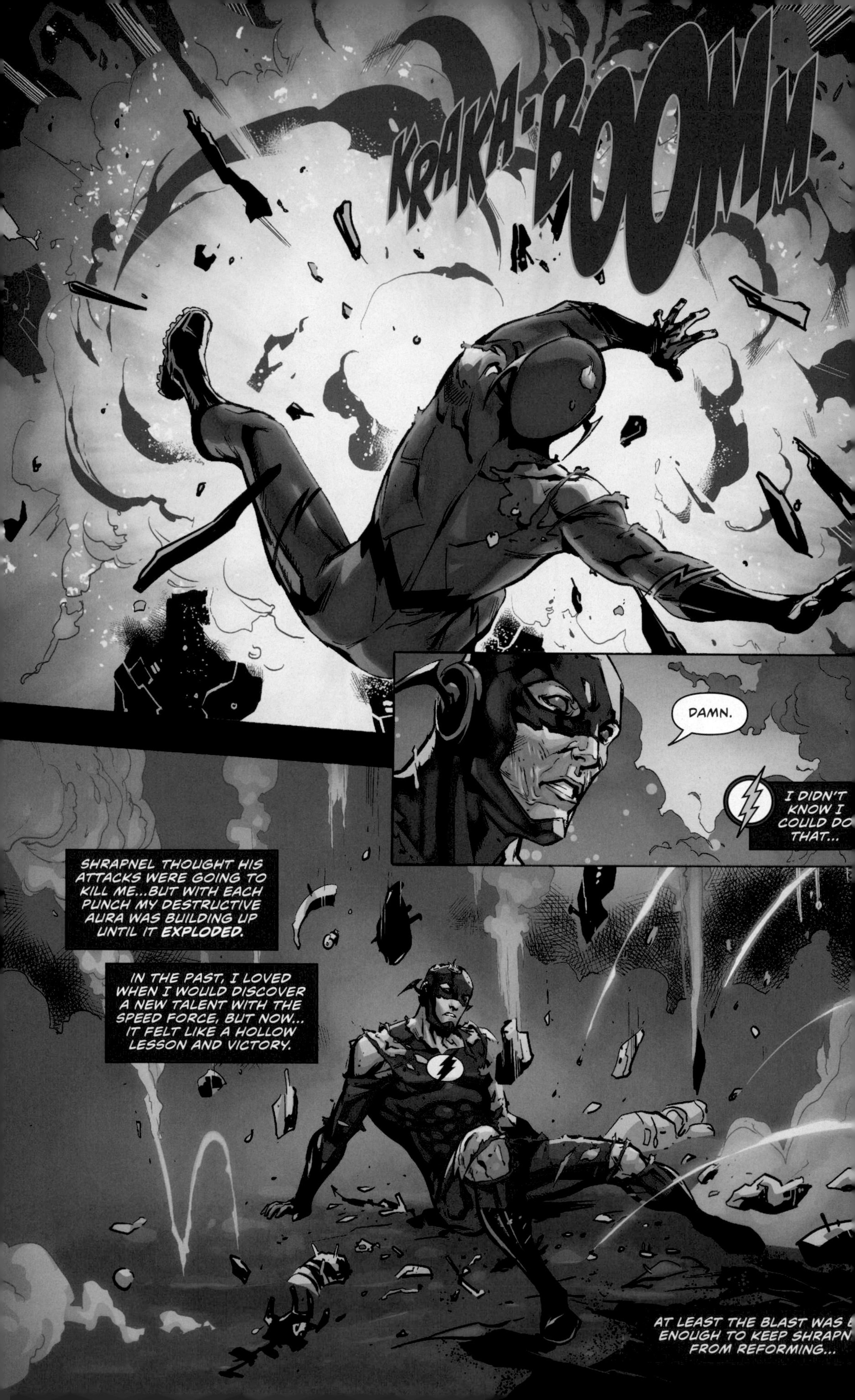
KRAKA-BOOMM
DAMN.
I DIDN'T KNOW I COULD DO THAT...
SHRAPNEL THOUGHT HIS ATTACKS WERE GOING TO KILL ME...BUT WITH EACH PUNCH MY DESTRUCTIVE AURA WAS BUILDING UP UNTIL IT **EXPLODED**.
IN THE PAST, I LOVED WHEN I WOULD DISCOVER A NEW TALENT WITH THE SPEED FORCE, BUT NOW... IT FELT LIKE A HOLLOW LESSON AND VICTORY.
AT LEAST THE BLAST WAS ENOUGH TO KEEP SHRAPN FROM REFORMING...

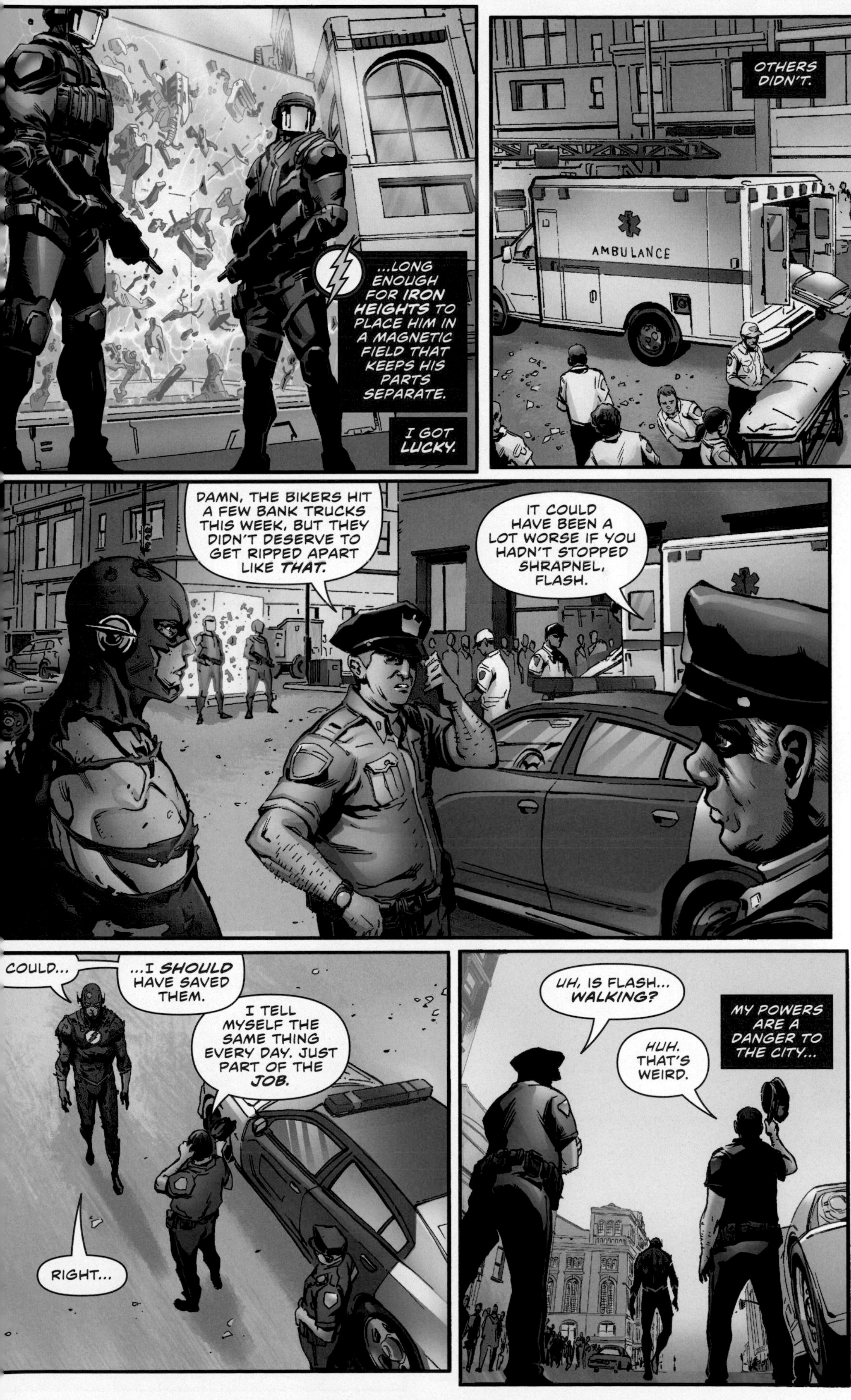
...LONG ENOUGH FOR IRON HEIGHTS TO PLACE HIM IN A MAGNETIC FIELD THAT KEEPS HIS PARTS SEPARATE.
I GOT LUCKY.
OTHERS DIDN'T.
AMBULANCE
DAMN, THE BIKERS HIT A FEW BANK TRUCKS THIS WEEK, BUT THEY DIDN'T DESERVE TO GET RIPPED APART LIKE THAT.
IT COULD HAVE BEEN A LOT WORSE IF YOU HADN'T STOPPED SHRAPNEL, FLASH.
COULD...
...I SHOULD HAVE SAVED THEM.
I TELL MYSELF THE SAME THING EVERY DAY. JUST PART OF THE JOB.
RIGHT...
UH, IS FLASH... WALKING?
HUH. THAT'S WEIRD.
MY POWERS ARE A DANGER TO THE CITY...

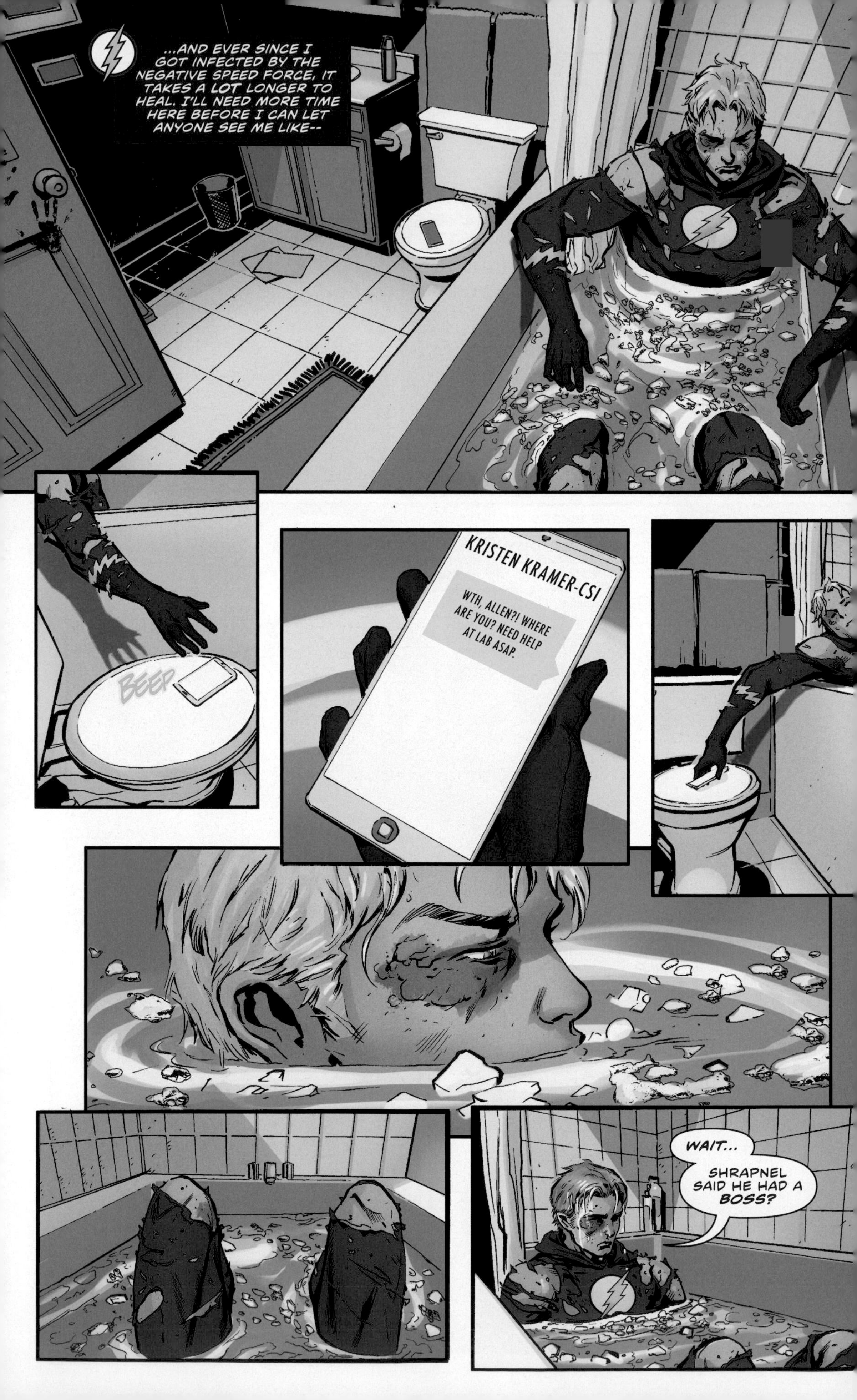
...AND EVER SINCE I GOT INFECTED BY THE NEGATIVE SPEED FORCE, IT TAKES A LOT LONGER TO HEAL. I'LL NEED MORE TIME HERE BEFORE I CAN LET ANYONE SEE ME LIKE--
BEEP
KRISTEN KRAMER-CSI
WTH, ALLEN?! WHERE ARE YOU? NEED HELP AT LAB ASAP.
WAIT...
SHRAPNEL SAID HE HAD A BOSS?

CURRENTLY INCARCERATED IRON HEIGHTS MAXIMUM SECURITY PRISON

Godspeed	Captain Cold	Mirror Master	Weather Wizard	Trickster
7_8.09 CCF	7_8.09 CCF	7_8.09 CCF	7_8.09 CCF	7_8.09 CCF

Heat Wave	Golden Glider	Tarpit	Papercut
CCF	7_8.09 CCF	7_8.09 CCF	7_8.09 CCF

ALL OF THE ROGUES ARE STILL IN IRON HEIGHTS.

WHO WAS SHRAPNEL TALKING ABOUT, THEN?

NO REPORTS ON THE WIRE. ORGANIZED CRIME IN CENTRAL CITY HAS BEEN QUIET FOR YEARS. MULTIPLE SCATTERED GANGS...NOTHING BIG.

IS THERE A NEW CRIME BOSS IN CENTRAL CITY...? MAYBE I CAN LEAN ON SHRAPNEL ABOUT--

ALLEN?!

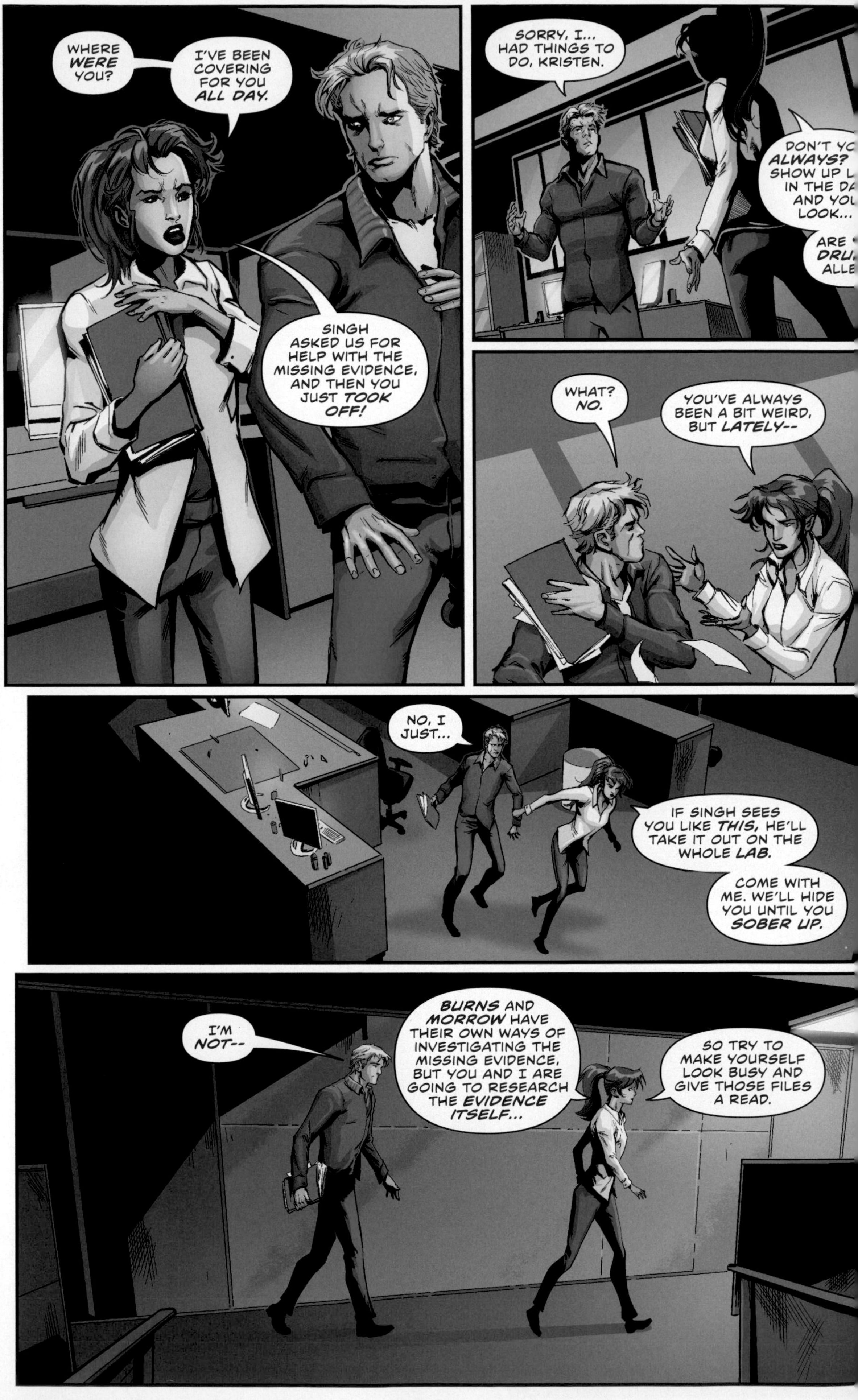
WHERE WERE YOU?
I'VE BEEN COVERING FOR YOU ALL DAY.
SINGH ASKED US FOR HELP WITH THE MISSING EVIDENCE, AND THEN YOU JUST TOOK OFF!
SORRY, I... HAD THINGS TO DO, KRISTEN.
DON'T YO ALWAYS? SHOW UP L IN THE DA AND YOU LOOK...
ARE DRU ALLE
WHAT? NO.
YOU'VE ALWAYS BEEN A BIT WEIRD, BUT LATELY--
NO, I JUST...
IF SINGH SEES YOU LIKE THIS, HE'LL TAKE IT OUT ON THE WHOLE LAB.
COME WITH ME. WE'LL HIDE YOU UNTIL YOU SOBER UP.
I'M NOT--
BURNS AND MORROW HAVE THEIR OWN WAYS OF INVESTIGATING THE MISSING EVIDENCE, BUT YOU AND I ARE GOING TO RESEARCH THE EVIDENCE ITSELF...
SO TRY TO MAKE YOURSELF LOOK BUSY AND GIVE THOSE FILES A READ.

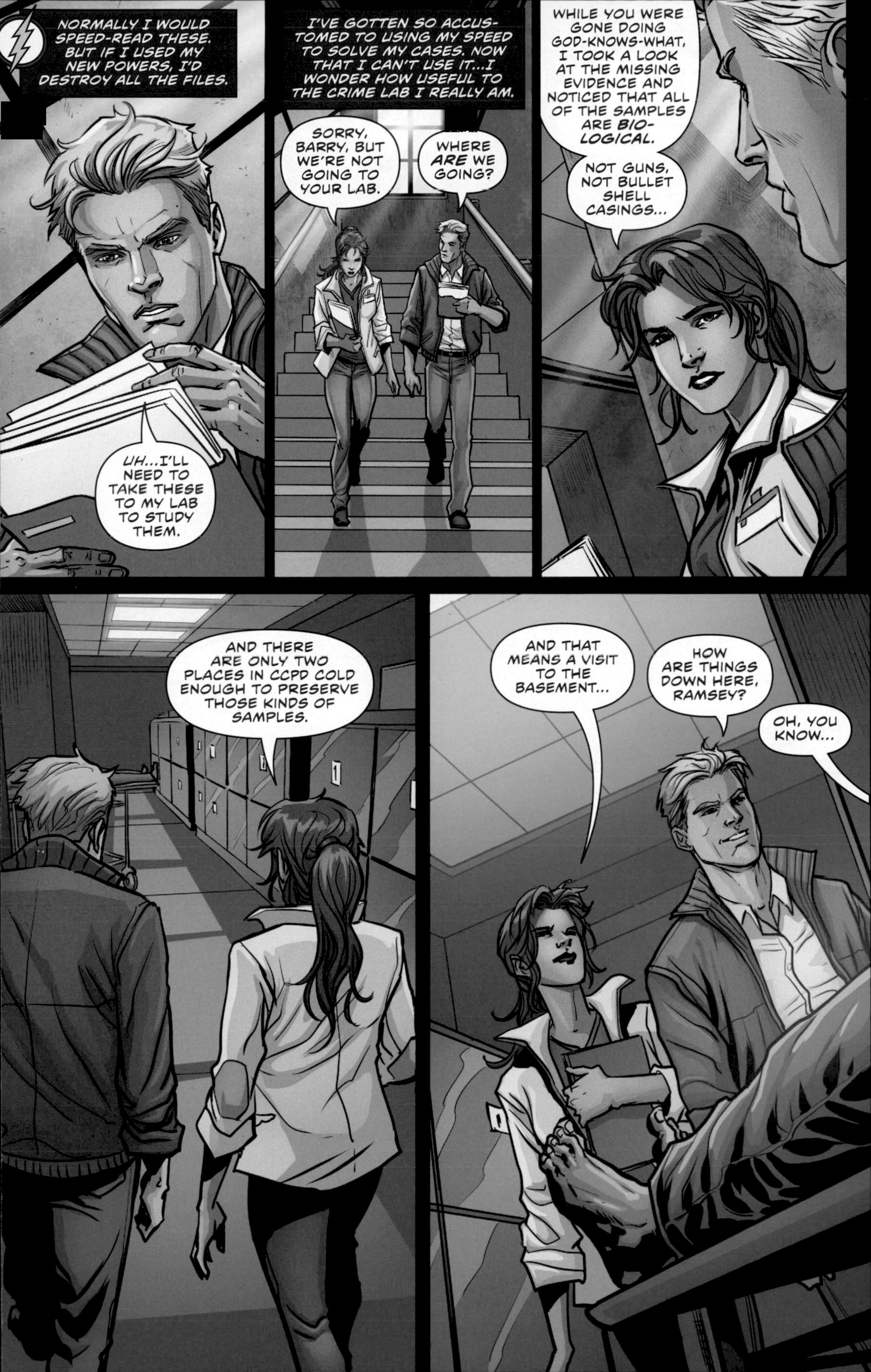

NORMALLY I WOULD SPEED-READ THESE. BUT IF I USED MY NEW POWERS, I'D DESTROY ALL THE FILES.
UH...I'LL NEED TO TAKE THESE TO MY LAB TO STUDY THEM.
I'VE GOTTEN SO ACCUSTOMED TO USING MY SPEED TO SOLVE MY CASES. NOW THAT I CAN'T USE IT...I WONDER HOW USEFUL TO THE CRIME LAB I REALLY AM.
SORRY, BARRY, BUT WE'RE NOT GOING TO YOUR LAB.
WHERE *ARE* WE GOING?
WHILE YOU WERE GONE DOING GOD-KNOWS-WHAT, I TOOK A LOOK AT THE MISSING EVIDENCE AND NOTICED THAT ALL OF THE SAMPLES ARE *BIOLOGICAL.*
NOT GUNS, NOT BULLET SHELL CASINGS...
AND THERE ARE ONLY TWO PLACES IN CCPD COLD ENOUGH TO PRESERVE THOSE KINDS OF SAMPLES.
AND THAT MEANS A VISIT TO THE BASEMENT...
HOW ARE THINGS DOWN HERE, RAMSEY?
OH, YOU KNOW...

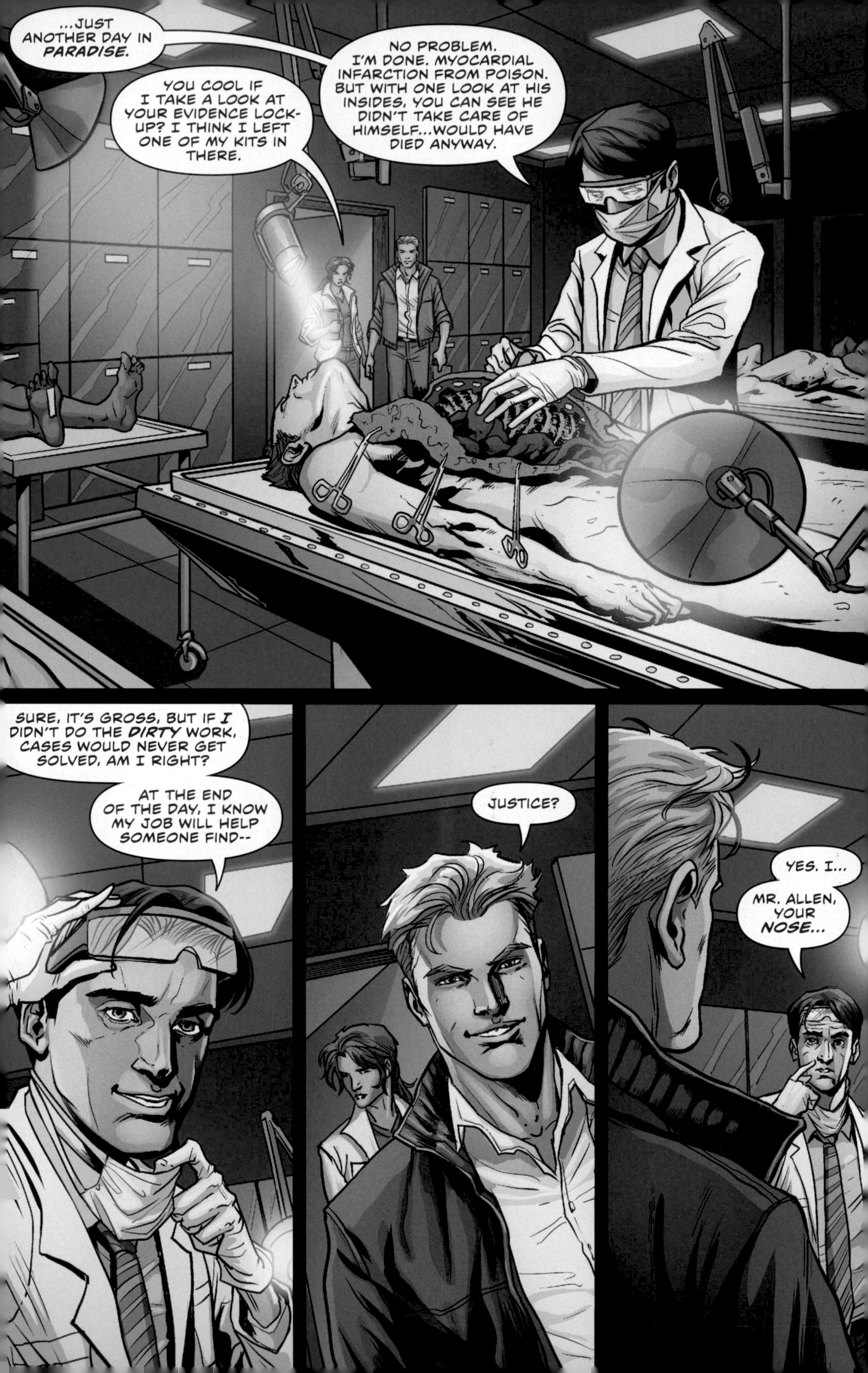
...JUST ANOTHER DAY IN *PARADISE.*
NO PROBLEM. I'M DONE. MYOCARDIAL INFARCTION FROM POISON. BUT WITH ONE LOOK AT HIS INSIDES, YOU CAN SEE HE DIDN'T TAKE CARE OF HIMSELF...WOULD HAVE DIED ANYWAY.
YOU COOL IF I TAKE A LOOK AT YOUR EVIDENCE LOCK-UP? I THINK I LEFT ONE OF MY KITS IN THERE.
SURE, IT'S GROSS, BUT IF *I* DIDN'T DO THE *DIRTY* WORK, CASES WOULD NEVER GET SOLVED, AM I RIGHT?
AT THE END OF THE DAY, I KNOW MY JOB WILL HELP SOMEONE FIND--
JUSTICE?
YES. I...
MR. ALLEN, YOUR *NOSE*...

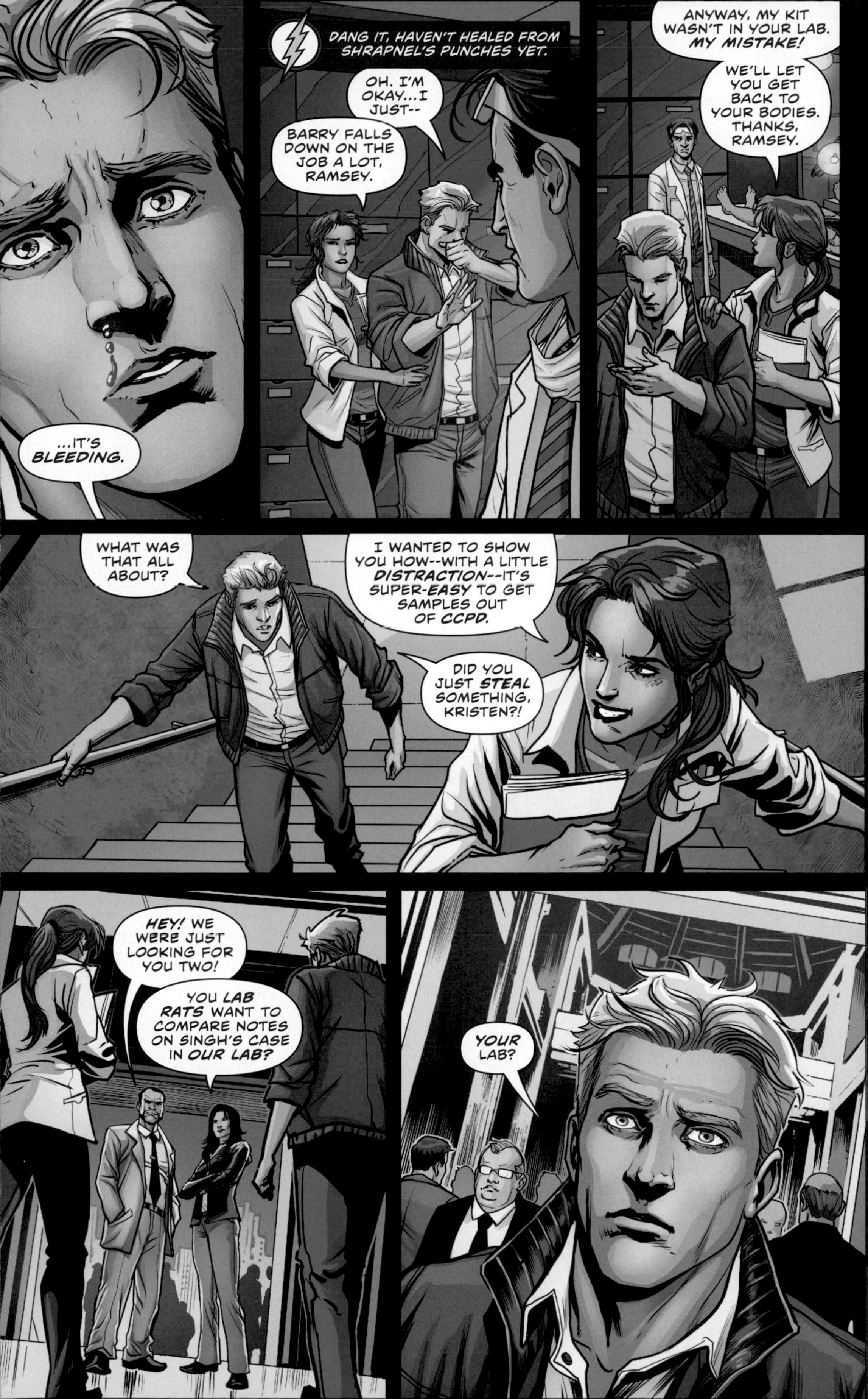
...IT'S BLEEDING.
DANG IT, HAVEN'T HEALED FROM SHRAPNEL'S PUNCHES YET.
OH. I'M OKAY...I JUST--
BARRY FALLS DOWN ON THE JOB A LOT, RAMSEY.
ANYWAY, MY KIT WASN'T IN YOUR LAB. MY MISTAKE!
WE'LL LET YOU GET BACK TO YOUR BODIES. THANKS, RAMSEY.
WHAT WAS THAT ALL ABOUT?
I WANTED TO SHOW YOU HOW--WITH A LITTLE DISTRACTION--IT'S SUPER-EASY TO GET SAMPLES OUT OF CCPD.
DID YOU JUST STEAL SOMETHING, KRISTEN?!
HEY! WE WERE JUST LOOKING FOR YOU TWO!
YOU LAB RATS WANT TO COMPARE NOTES ON SINGH'S CASE IN OUR LAB?
YOUR LAB?

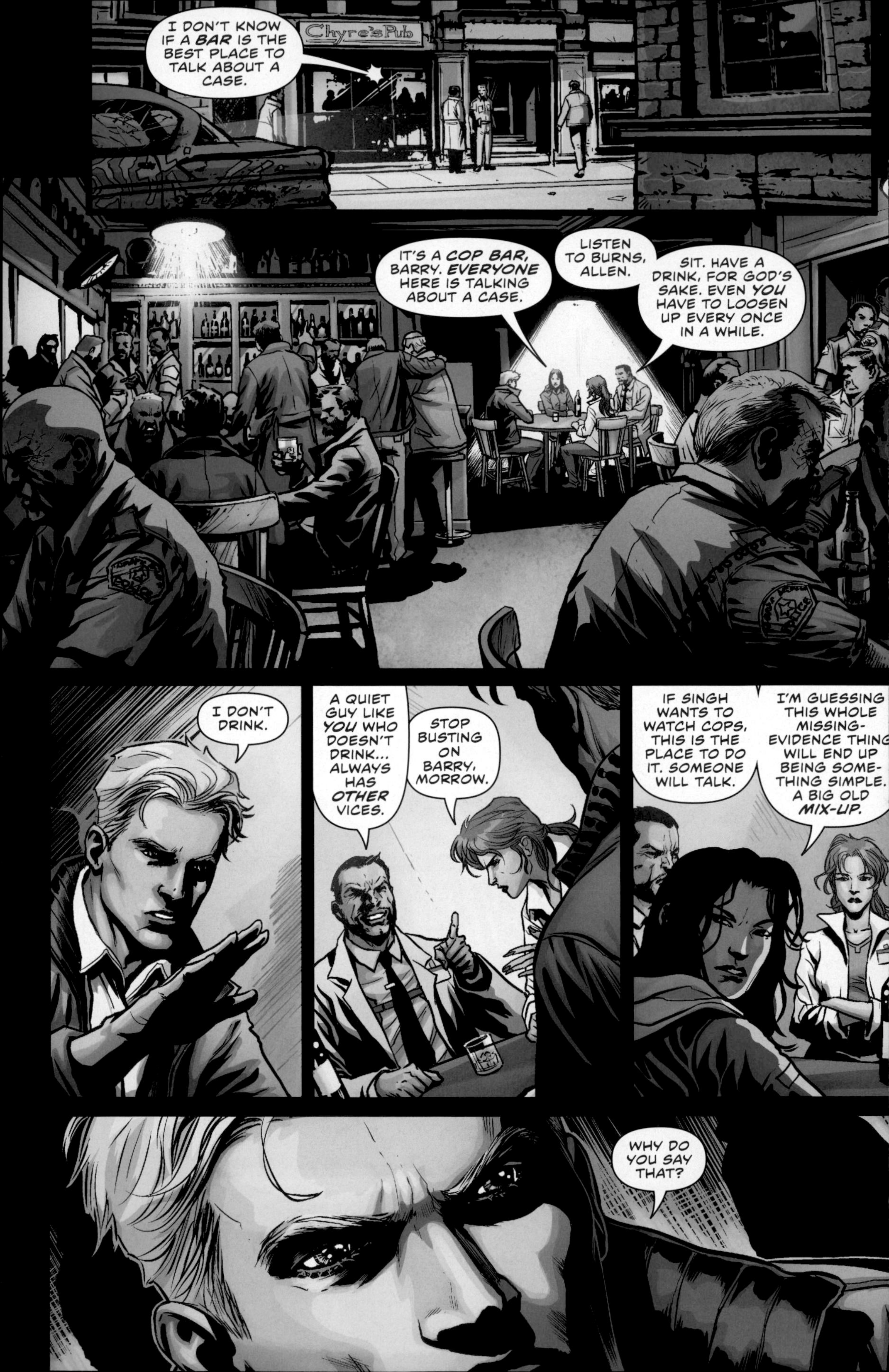
Chyre's Pub
I DON'T KNOW IF A BAR IS THE BEST PLACE TO TALK ABOUT A CASE.
IT'S A COP BAR, BARRY. EVERYONE HERE IS TALKING ABOUT A CASE.
LISTEN TO BURNS, ALLEN.
SIT. HAVE A DRINK, FOR GOD'S SAKE. EVEN YOU HAVE TO LOOSEN UP EVERY ONCE IN A WHILE.
I DON'T DRINK.
A QUIET GUY LIKE YOU WHO DOESN'T DRINK... ALWAYS HAS OTHER VICES.
STOP BUSTING ON BARRY, MORROW.
IF SINGH WANTS TO WATCH COPS, THIS IS THE PLACE TO DO IT. SOMEONE WILL TALK.
I'M GUESSING THIS WHOLE MISSING-EVIDENCE THING WILL END UP BEING SOME-THING SIMPLE. A BIG OLD MIX-UP.
WHY DO YOU SAY THAT?

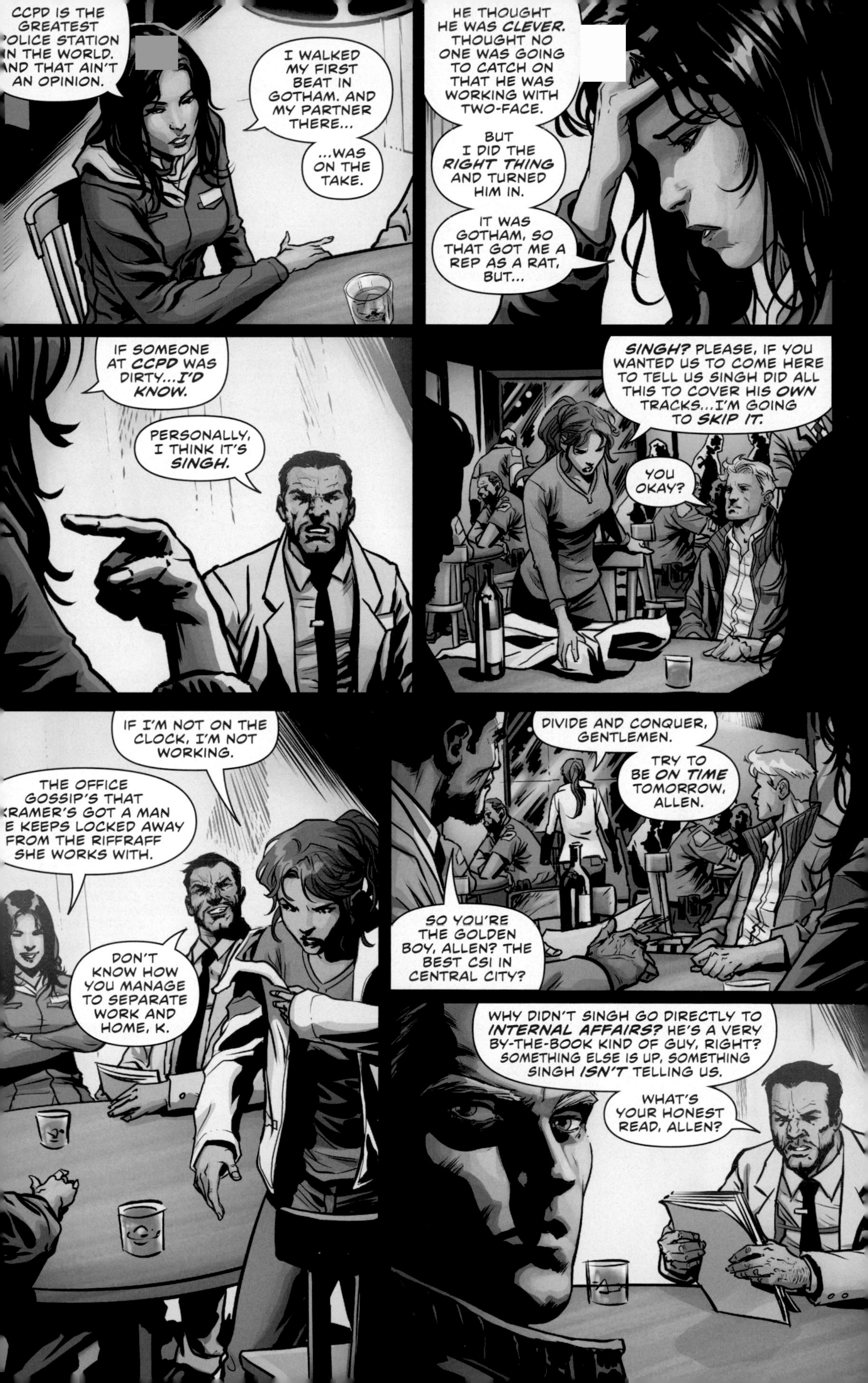
CCPD IS THE GREATEST POLICE STATION IN THE WORLD. AND THAT AIN'T AN OPINION.
I WALKED MY FIRST BEAT IN GOTHAM. AND MY PARTNER THERE...
...WAS ON THE TAKE.
HE THOUGHT HE WAS CLEVER. THOUGHT NO ONE WAS GOING TO CATCH ON THAT HE WAS WORKING WITH TWO-FACE.
BUT I DID THE RIGHT THING AND TURNED HIM IN.
IT WAS GOTHAM, SO THAT GOT ME A REP AS A RAT, BUT...
IF SOMEONE AT CCPD WAS DIRTY...I'D KNOW.
PERSONALLY, I THINK IT'S SINGH.
SINGH? PLEASE, IF YOU WANTED US TO COME HERE TO TELL US SINGH DID ALL THIS TO COVER HIS OWN TRACKS...I'M GOING TO SKIP IT.
YOU OKAY?
IF I'M NOT ON THE CLOCK, I'M NOT WORKING.
THE OFFICE GOSSIP'S THAT KRAMER'S GOT A MAN HE KEEPS LOCKED AWAY FROM THE RIFFRAFF SHE WORKS WITH.
DON'T KNOW HOW YOU MANAGE TO SEPARATE WORK AND HOME, K.
DIVIDE AND CONQUER, GENTLEMEN.
TRY TO BE ON TIME TOMORROW, ALLEN.
SO YOU'RE THE GOLDEN BOY, ALLEN? THE BEST CSI IN CENTRAL CITY?
WHY DIDN'T SINGH GO DIRECTLY TO INTERNAL AFFAIRS? HE'S A VERY BY-THE-BOOK KIND OF GUY, RIGHT? SOMETHING ELSE IS UP, SOMETHING SINGH ISN'T TELLING US.
WHAT'S YOUR HONEST READ, ALLEN?

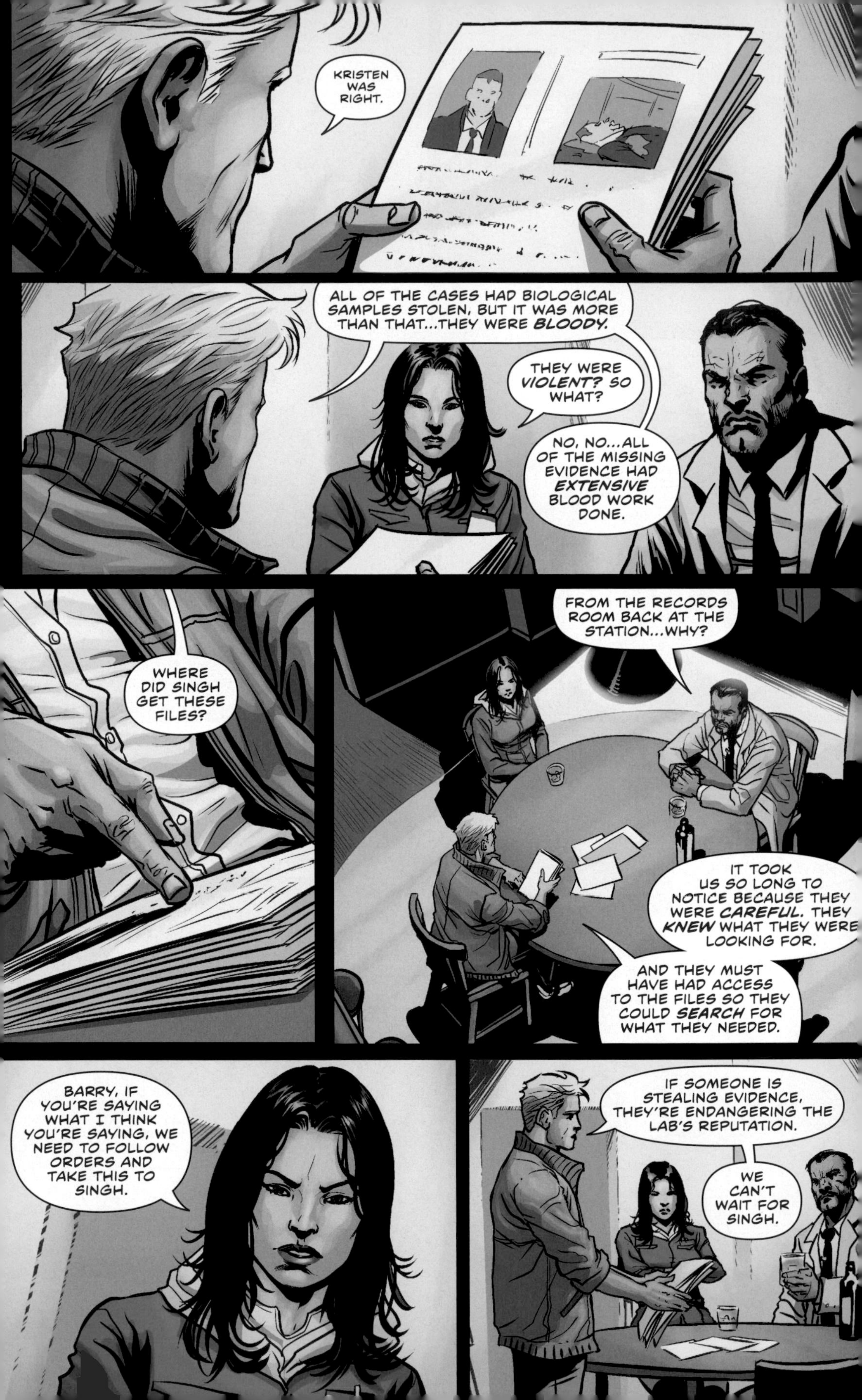
KRISTEN WAS RIGHT.
ALL OF THE CASES HAD BIOLOGICAL SAMPLES STOLEN, BUT IT WAS MORE THAN THAT...THEY WERE BLOODY.
THEY WERE VIOLENT? SO WHAT?
NO, NO...ALL OF THE MISSING EVIDENCE HAD EXTENSIVE BLOOD WORK DONE.
WHERE DID SINGH GET THESE FILES?
FROM THE RECORDS ROOM BACK AT THE STATION...WHY?
IT TOOK US SO LONG TO NOTICE BECAUSE THEY WERE CAREFUL. THEY KNEW WHAT THEY WERE LOOKING FOR.
AND THEY MUST HAVE HAD ACCESS TO THE FILES SO THEY COULD SEARCH FOR WHAT THEY NEEDED.
BARRY, IF YOU'RE SAYING WHAT I THINK YOU'RE SAYING, WE NEED TO FOLLOW ORDERS AND TAKE THIS TO SINGH.
IF SOMEONE IS STEALING EVIDENCE, THEY'RE ENDANGERING THE LAB'S REPUTATION.
WE CAN'T WAIT FOR SINGH.

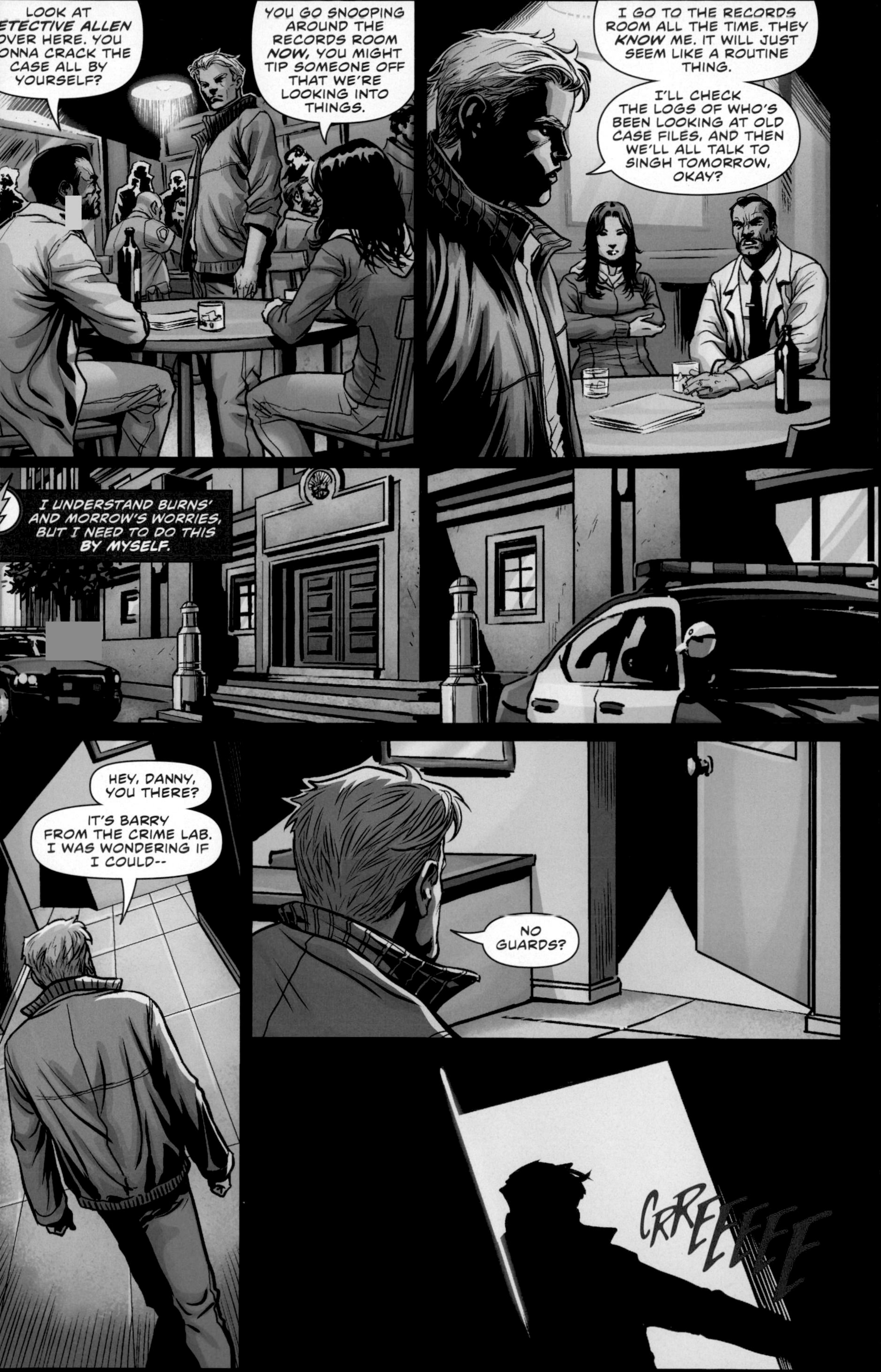

LOOK AT ETECTIVE ALLEN OVER HERE. YOU ONNA CRACK THE CASE ALL BY YOURSELF?
YOU GO SNOOPING AROUND THE RECORDS ROOM NOW, YOU MIGHT TIP SOMEONE OFF THAT WE'RE LOOKING INTO THINGS.
I GO TO THE RECORDS ROOM ALL THE TIME. THEY KNOW ME. IT WILL JUST SEEM LIKE A ROUTINE THING.
I'LL CHECK THE LOGS OF WHO'S BEEN LOOKING AT OLD CASE FILES, AND THEN WE'LL ALL TALK TO SINGH TOMORROW, OKAY?
I UNDERSTAND BURNS' AND MORROW'S WORRIES, BUT I NEED TO DO THIS BY MYSELF.
HEY, DANNY, YOU THERE?
IT'S BARRY FROM THE CRIME LAB. I WAS WONDERING IF I COULD--
NO GUARDS?
CRREEEEE

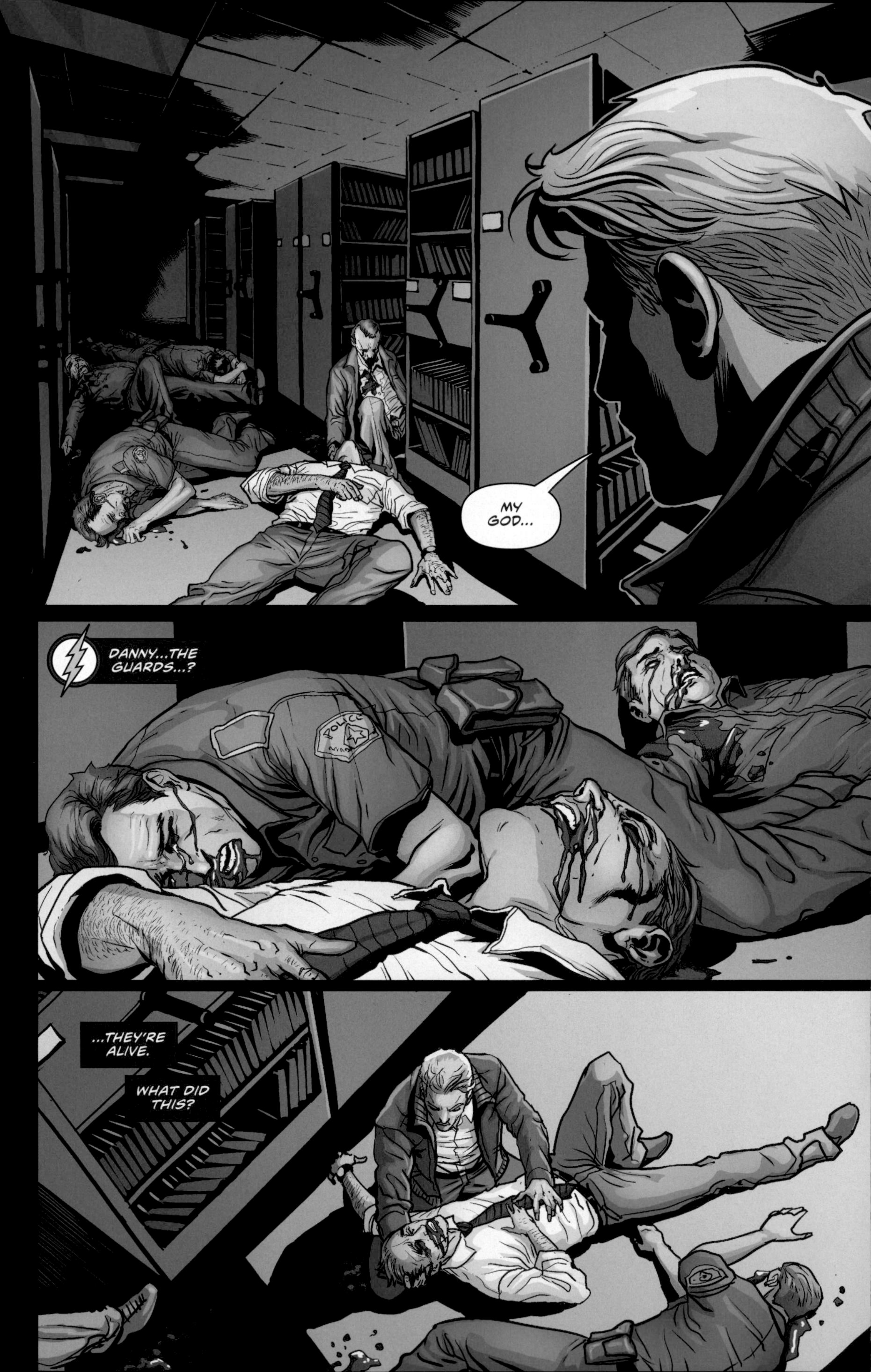
MY GOD...
DANNY...THE GUARDS...?
...THEY'RE ALIVE.
WHAT DID THIS?

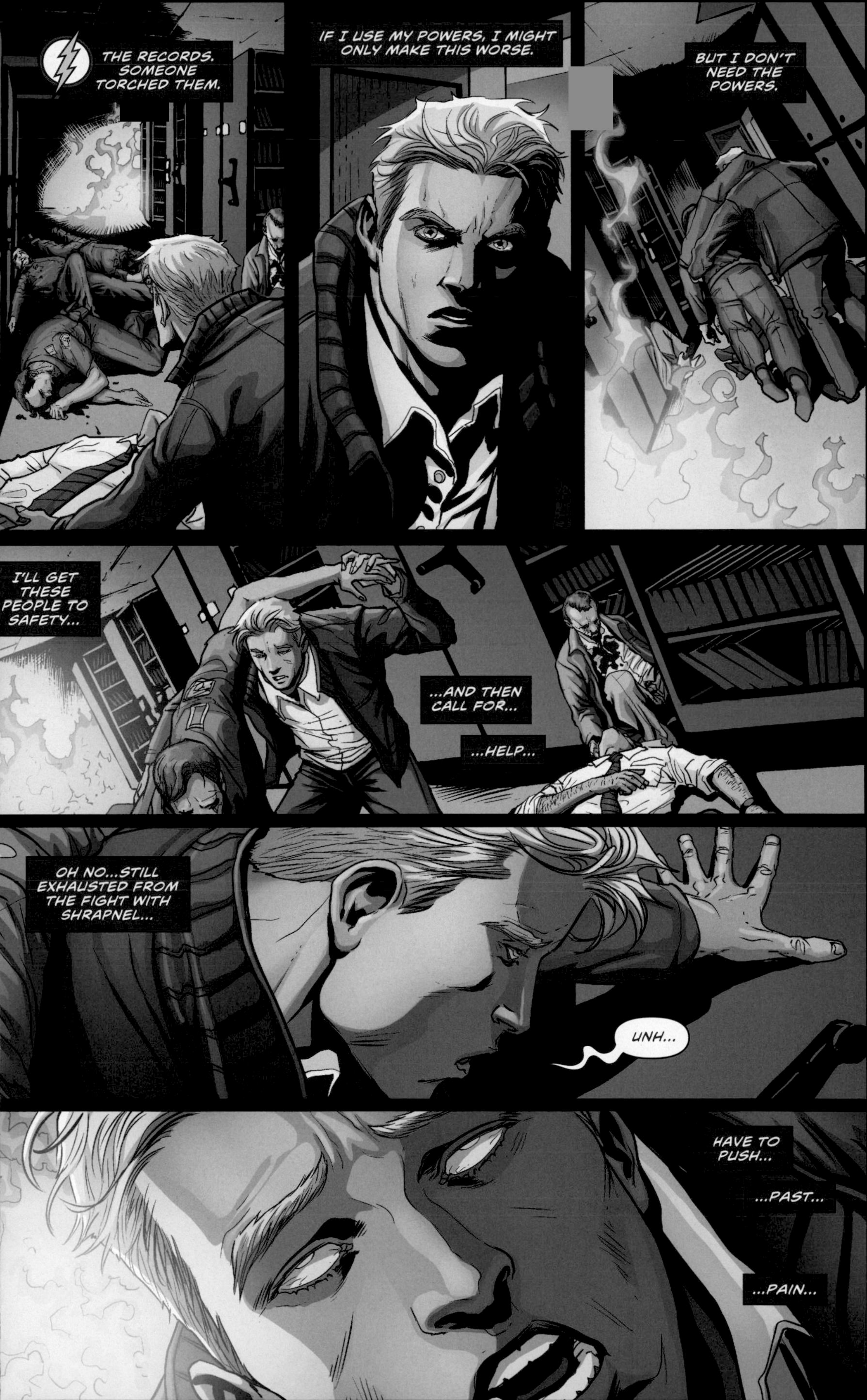
THE RECORDS. SOMEONE TORCHED THEM.
IF I USE MY POWERS, I MIGHT ONLY MAKE THIS WORSE.
BUT I DON'T NEED THE POWERS.
I'LL GET THESE PEOPLE TO SAFETY...
...AND THEN CALL FOR...
...HELP...
OH NO...STILL EXHAUSTED FROM THE FIGHT WITH SHRAPNEL...
UNH...
HAVE TO PUSH...
...PAST...
...PAIN...

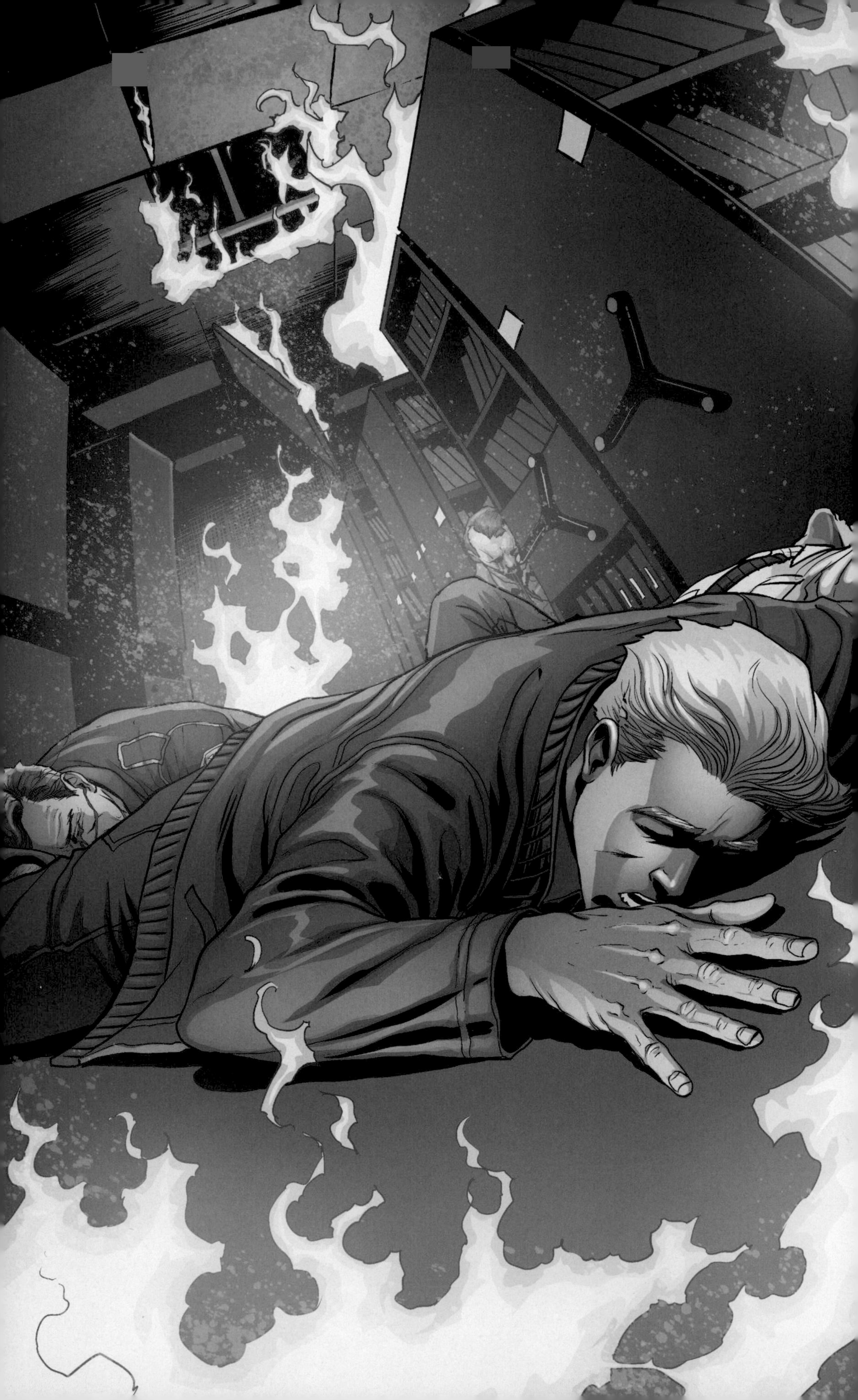

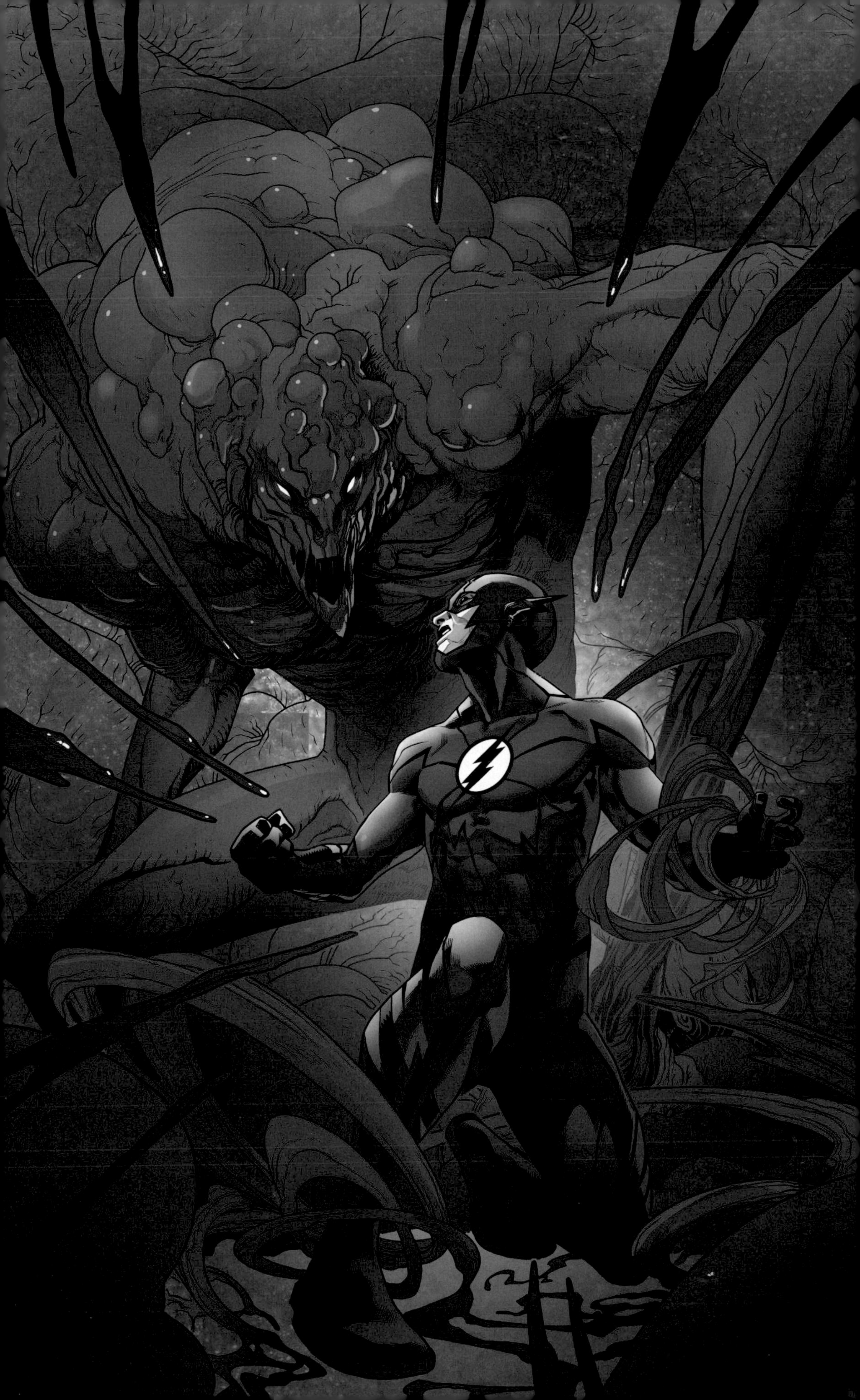

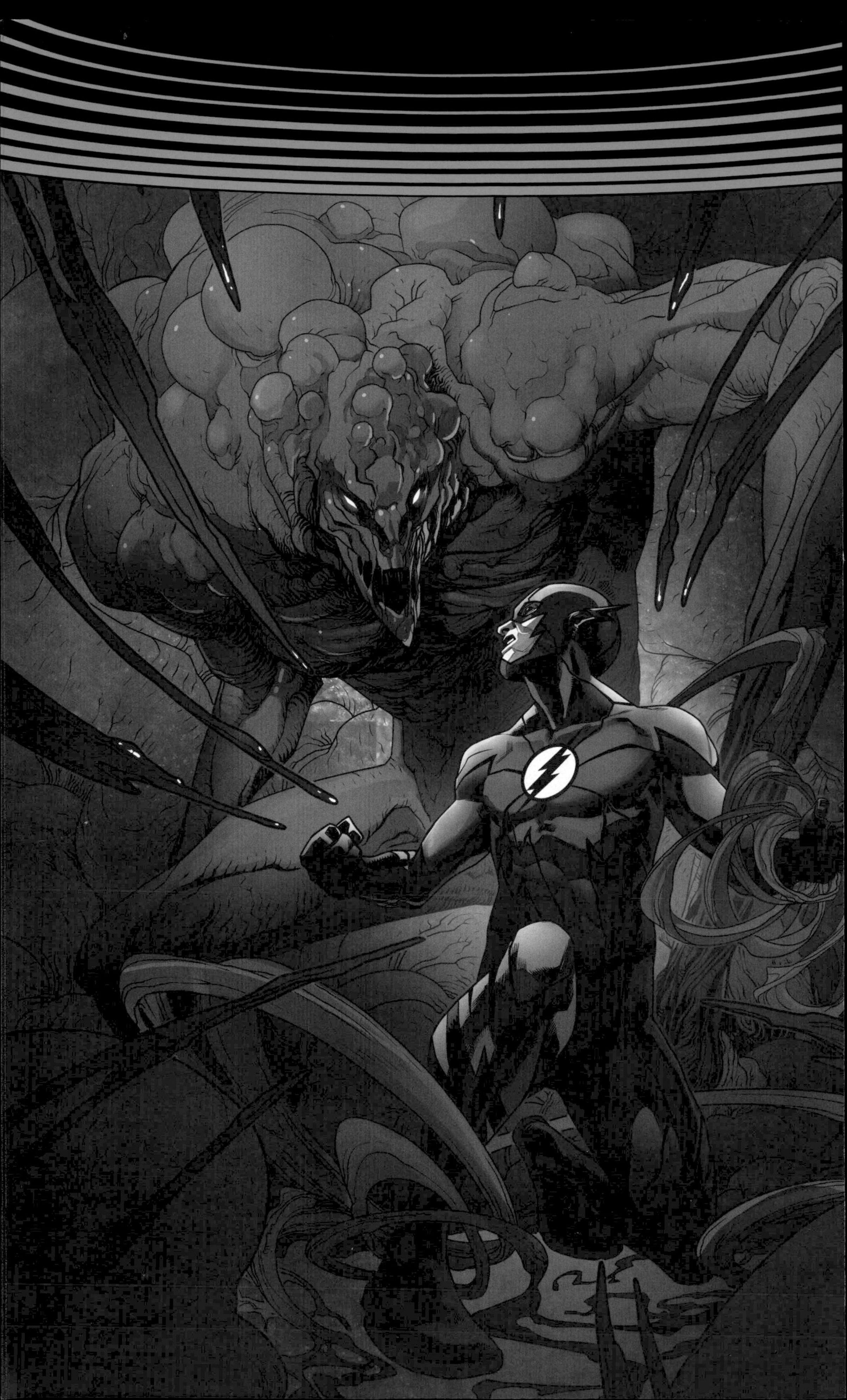

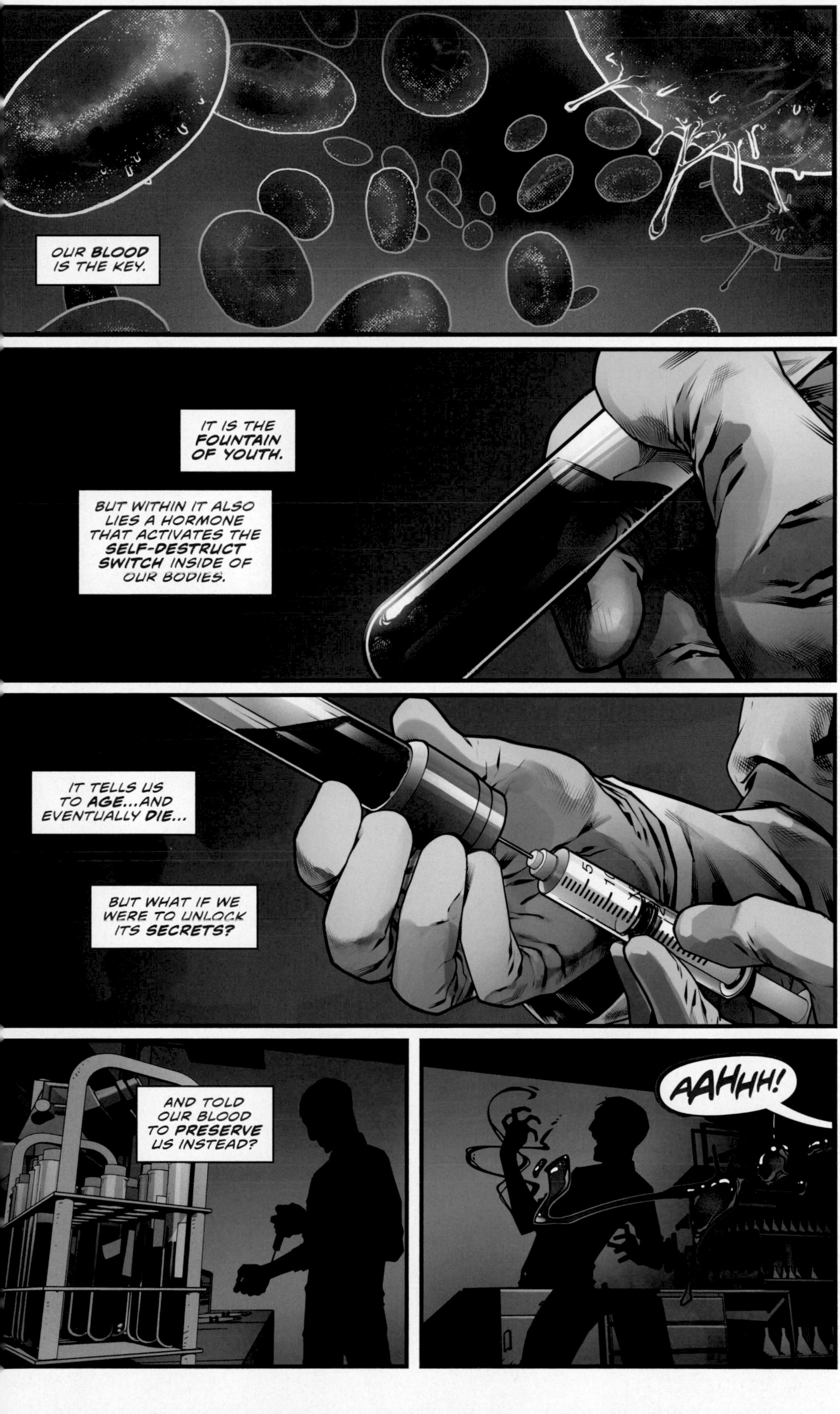
OUR BLOOD IS THE KEY.
IT IS THE FOUNTAIN OF YOUTH.
BUT WITHIN IT ALSO LIES A HORMONE THAT ACTIVATES THE SELF-DESTRUCT SWITCH INSIDE OF OUR BODIES.
IT TELLS US TO AGE...AND EVENTUALLY DIE...
BUT WHAT IF WE WERE TO UNLOCK ITS SECRETS?
AND TOLD OUR BLOOD TO PRESERVE US INSTEAD?
AAHHH!

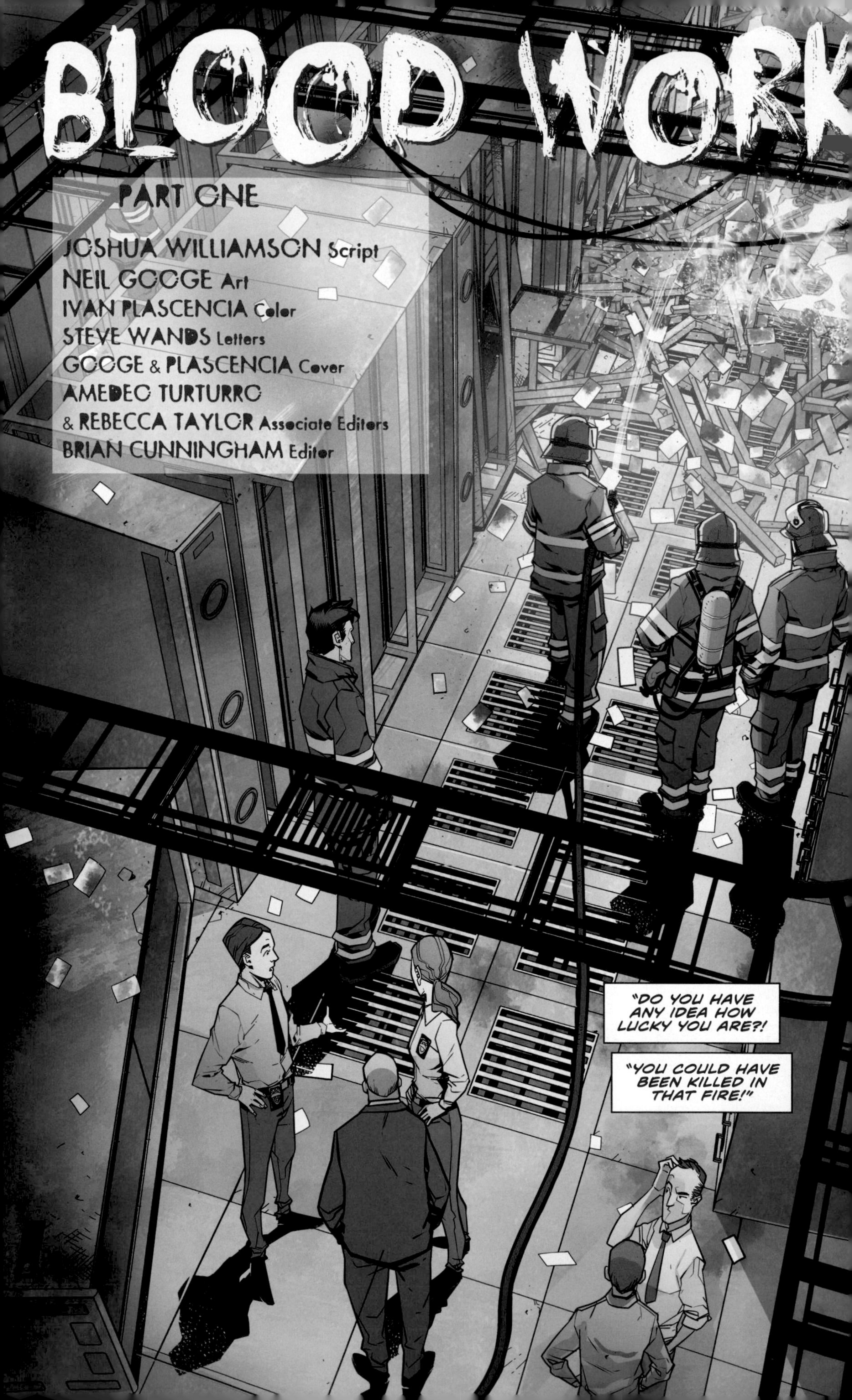
BLOOD WORK
PART ONE
JOSHUA WILLIAMSON Script
NEIL GOOGE Art
IVAN PLASCENCIA Color
STEVE WANDS Letters
GOOGE & PLASCENCIA Cover
AMEDEO TURTURRO
& REBECCA TAYLOR Associate Editors
BRIAN CUNNINGHAM Editor
"DO YOU HAVE ANY IDEA HOW LUCKY YOU ARE?!
"YOU COULD HAVE BEEN KILLED IN THAT FIRE!"

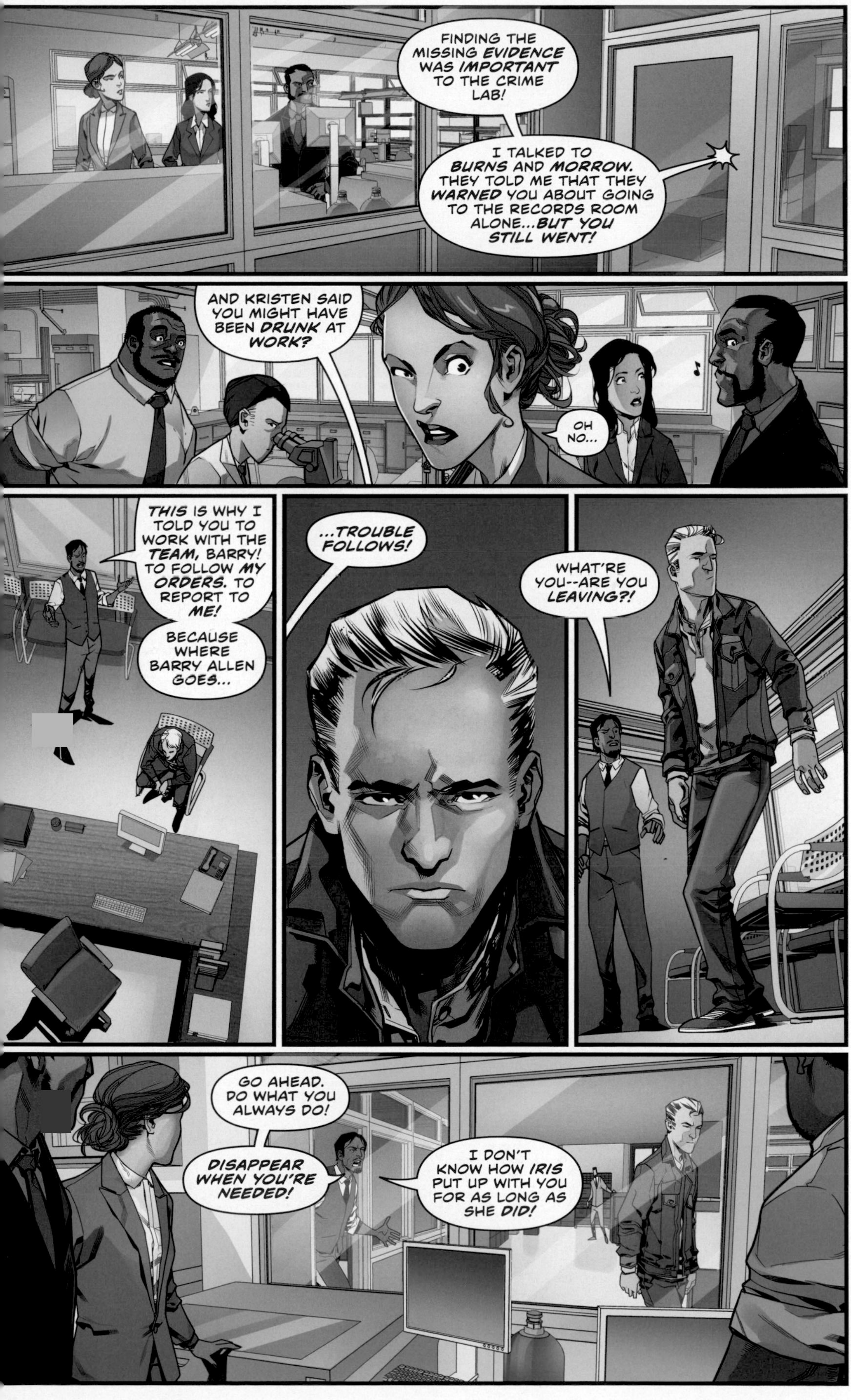
FINDING THE MISSING EVIDENCE WAS IMPORTANT TO THE CRIME LAB!
I TALKED TO BURNS AND MORROW. THEY TOLD ME THAT THEY WARNED YOU ABOUT GOING TO THE RECORDS ROOM ALONE...BUT YOU STILL WENT!
AND KRISTEN SAID YOU MIGHT HAVE BEEN DRUNK AT WORK?
OH NO...
THIS IS WHY I TOLD YOU TO WORK WITH THE TEAM, BARRY! TO FOLLOW MY ORDERS. TO REPORT TO ME!
BECAUSE WHERE BARRY ALLEN GOES...
...TROUBLE FOLLOWS!
WHAT'RE YOU--ARE YOU LEAVING?!
GO AHEAD. DO WHAT YOU ALWAYS DO!
DISAPPEAR WHEN YOU'RE NEEDED!
I DON'T KNOW HOW IRIS PUT UP WITH YOU FOR AS LONG AS SHE DID!

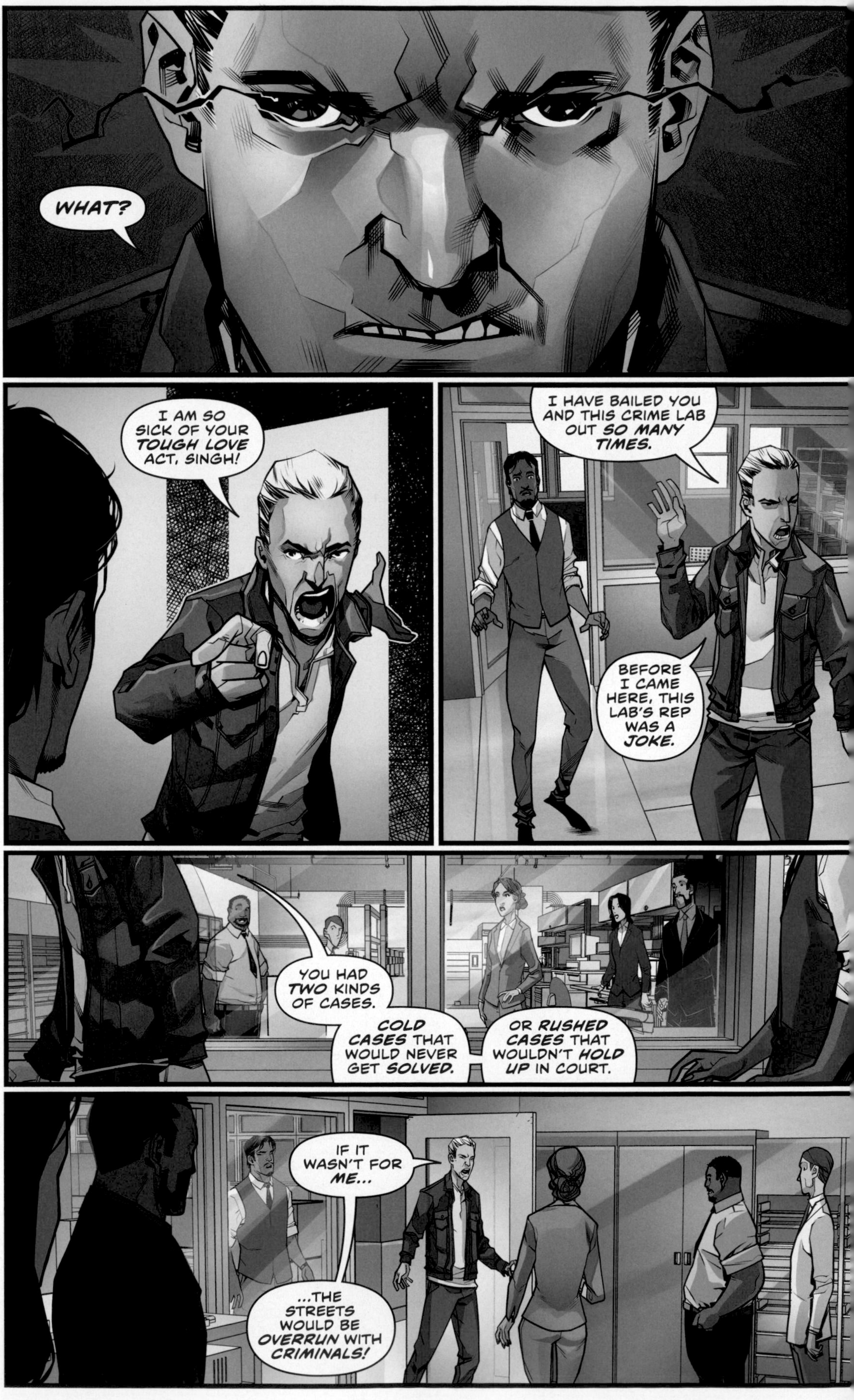
WHAT?
I AM SO SICK OF YOUR TOUGH LOVE ACT, SINGH!
I HAVE BAILED YOU AND THIS CRIME LAB OUT SO MANY TIMES.
BEFORE I CAME HERE, THIS LAB'S REP WAS A JOKE.
YOU HAD TWO KINDS OF CASES.
COLD CASES THAT WOULD NEVER GET SOLVED.
OR RUSHED CASES THAT WOULDN'T HOLD UP IN COURT.
IF IT WASN'T FOR ME...
...THE STREETS WOULD BE OVERRUN WITH CRIMINALS!

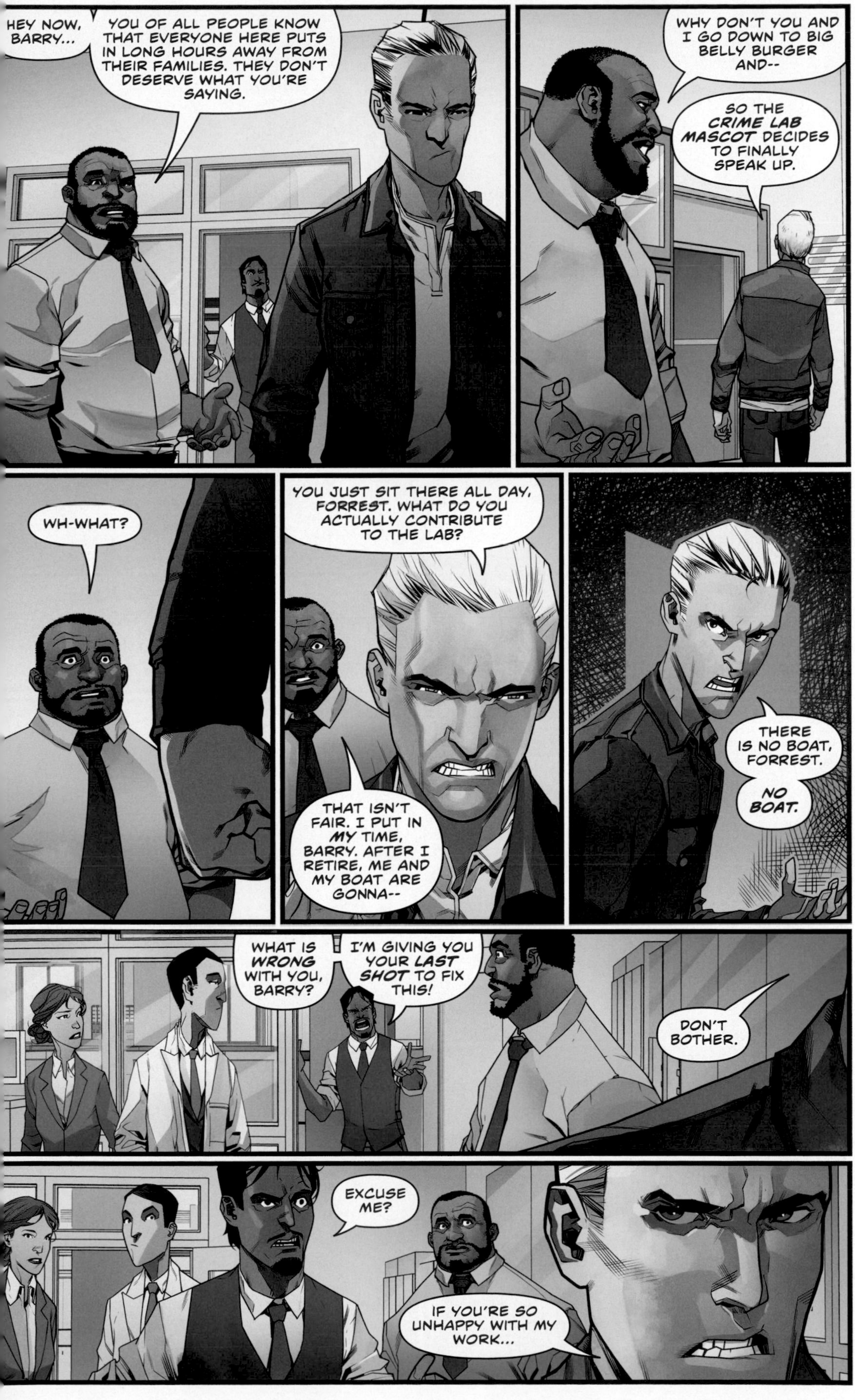
HEY NOW, BARRY...
YOU OF ALL PEOPLE KNOW THAT EVERYONE HERE PUTS IN LONG HOURS AWAY FROM THEIR FAMILIES. THEY DON'T DESERVE WHAT YOU'RE SAYING.
WHY DON'T YOU AND I GO DOWN TO BIG BELLY BURGER AND--
SO THE *CRIME LAB MASCOT* DECIDES TO FINALLY SPEAK UP.
WH-WHAT?
YOU JUST SIT THERE ALL DAY, FORREST. WHAT DO YOU ACTUALLY CONTRIBUTE TO THE LAB?
THAT ISN'T FAIR. I PUT IN *MY* TIME, BARRY. AFTER I RETIRE, ME AND MY BOAT ARE GONNA--
THERE IS NO BOAT, FORREST.
NO BOAT.
WHAT IS *WRONG* WITH YOU, BARRY?
I'M GIVING YOU YOUR *LAST SHOT* TO FIX THIS!
DON'T BOTHER.
EXCUSE ME?
IF YOU'RE SO UNHAPPY WITH MY WORK...

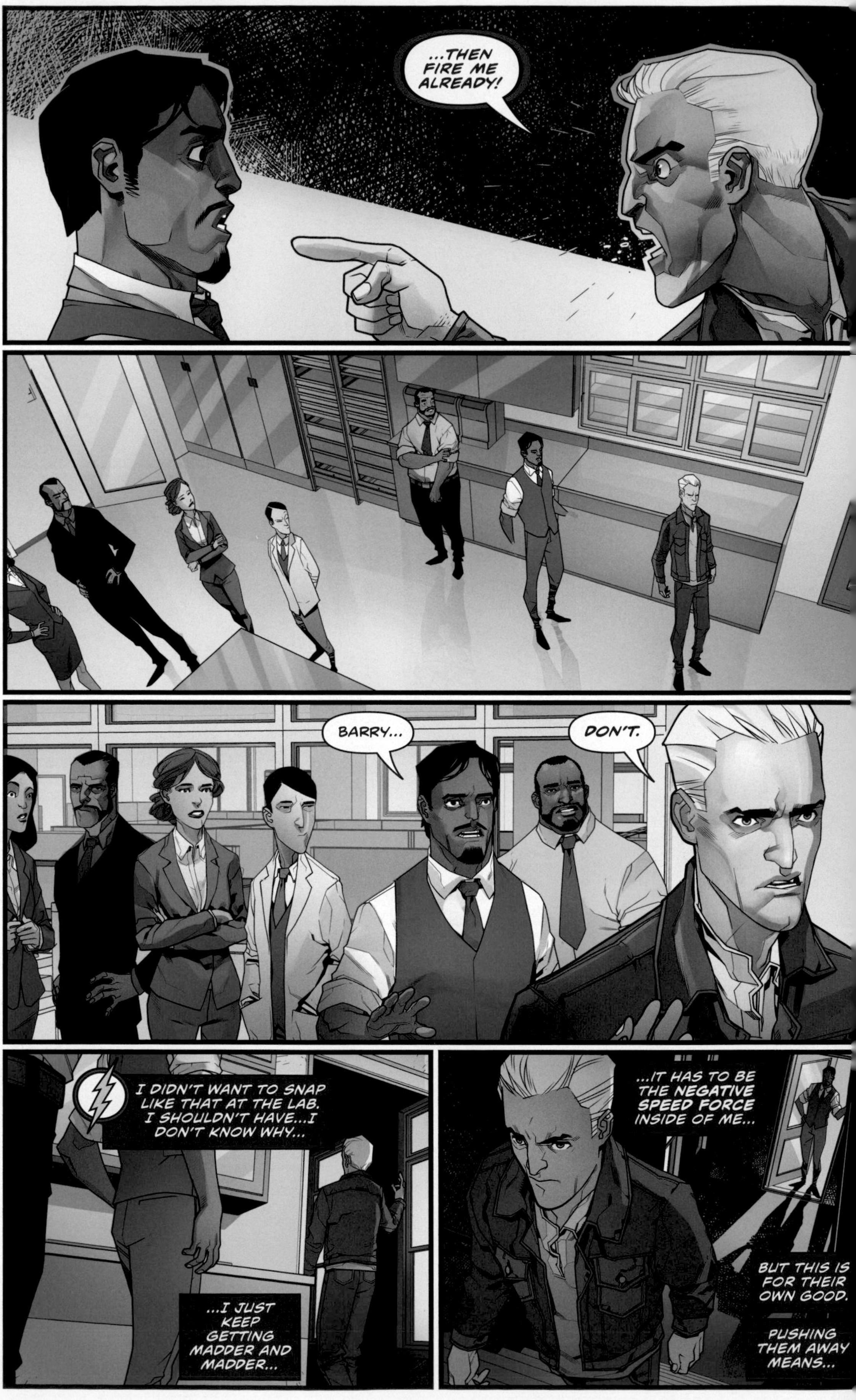
...THEN FIRE ME ALREADY!
BARRY...
DON'T.
I DIDN'T WANT TO SNAP LIKE THAT AT THE LAB. I SHOULDN'T HAVE...I DON'T KNOW WHY...
...I JUST KEEP GETTING MADDER AND MADDER...
...IT HAS TO BE THE NEGATIVE SPEED FORCE INSIDE OF ME...
BUT THIS IS FOR THEIR OWN GOOD.
PUSHING THEM AWAY MEANS...

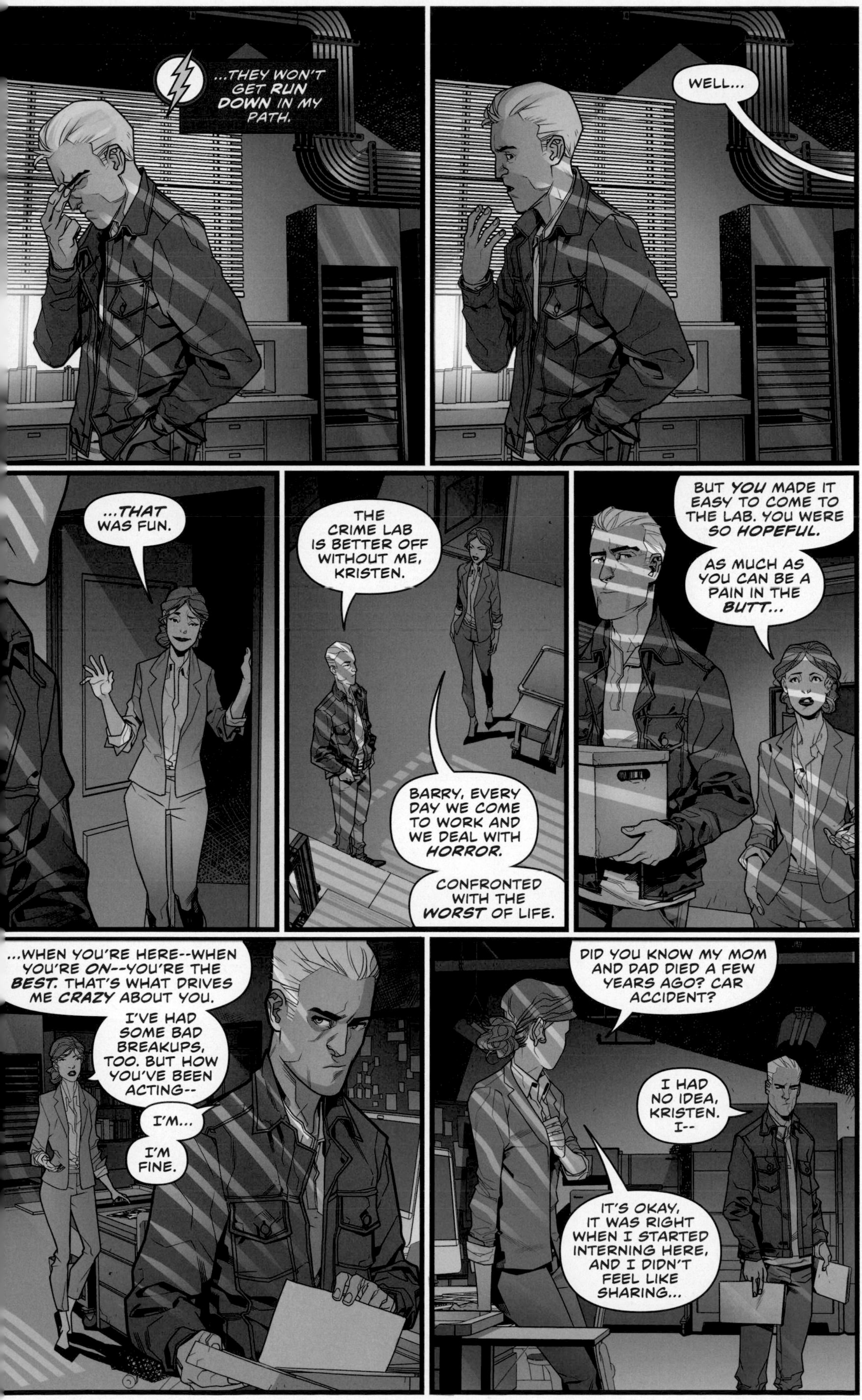
...THEY WON'T GET RUN DOWN IN MY PATH.
WELL...
...THAT WAS FUN.
THE CRIME LAB IS BETTER OFF WITHOUT ME, KRISTEN.
BARRY, EVERY DAY WE COME TO WORK AND WE DEAL WITH HORROR.
CONFRONTED WITH THE WORST OF LIFE.
BUT YOU MADE IT EASY TO COME TO THE LAB. YOU WERE SO HOPEFUL.
AS MUCH AS YOU CAN BE A PAIN IN THE BUTT...
...WHEN YOU'RE HERE--WHEN YOU'RE ON--YOU'RE THE BEST. THAT'S WHAT DRIVES ME CRAZY ABOUT YOU.
I'VE HAD SOME BAD BREAKUPS, TOO. BUT HOW YOU'VE BEEN ACTING--
I'M...
I'M FINE.
DID YOU KNOW MY MOM AND DAD DIED A FEW YEARS AGO? CAR ACCIDENT?
I HAD NO IDEA, KRISTEN. I--
IT'S OKAY, IT WAS RIGHT WHEN I STARTED INTERNING HERE, AND I DIDN'T FEEL LIKE SHARING...

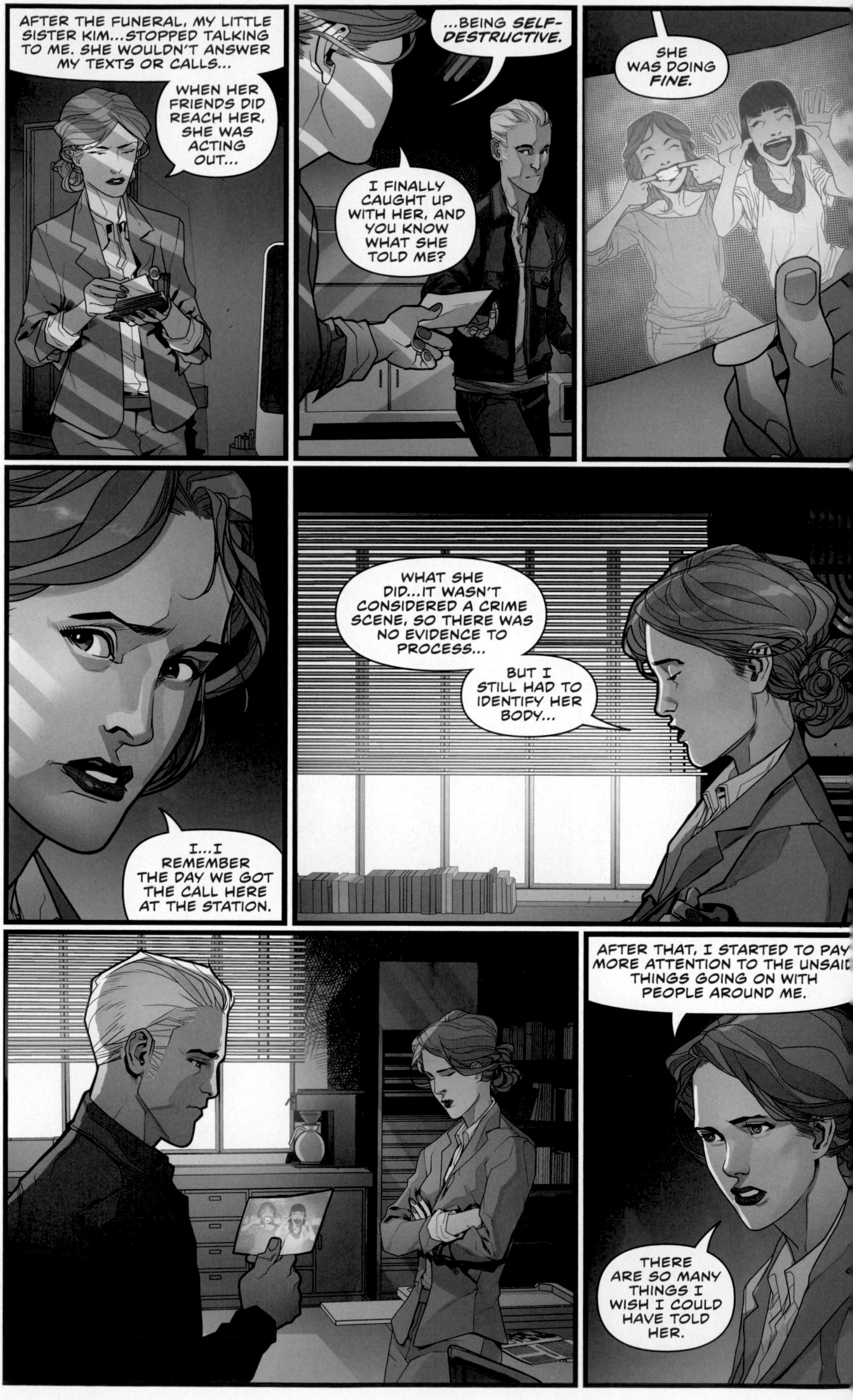
AFTER THE FUNERAL, MY LITTLE SISTER KIM...STOPPED TALKING TO ME. SHE WOULDN'T ANSWER MY TEXTS OR CALLS...
WHEN HER FRIENDS DID REACH HER, SHE WAS ACTING OUT...
...BEING SELF-DESTRUCTIVE.
I FINALLY CAUGHT UP WITH HER, AND YOU KNOW WHAT SHE TOLD ME?
SHE WAS DOING FINE.
I...I REMEMBER THE DAY WE GOT THE CALL HERE AT THE STATION.
WHAT SHE DID...IT WASN'T CONSIDERED A CRIME SCENE, SO THERE WAS NO EVIDENCE TO PROCESS...
BUT I STILL HAD TO IDENTIFY HER BODY...
AFTER THAT, I STARTED TO PAY MORE ATTENTION TO THE UNSAID THINGS GOING ON WITH PEOPLE AROUND ME.
THERE ARE SO MANY THINGS I WISH I COULD HAVE TOLD HER.

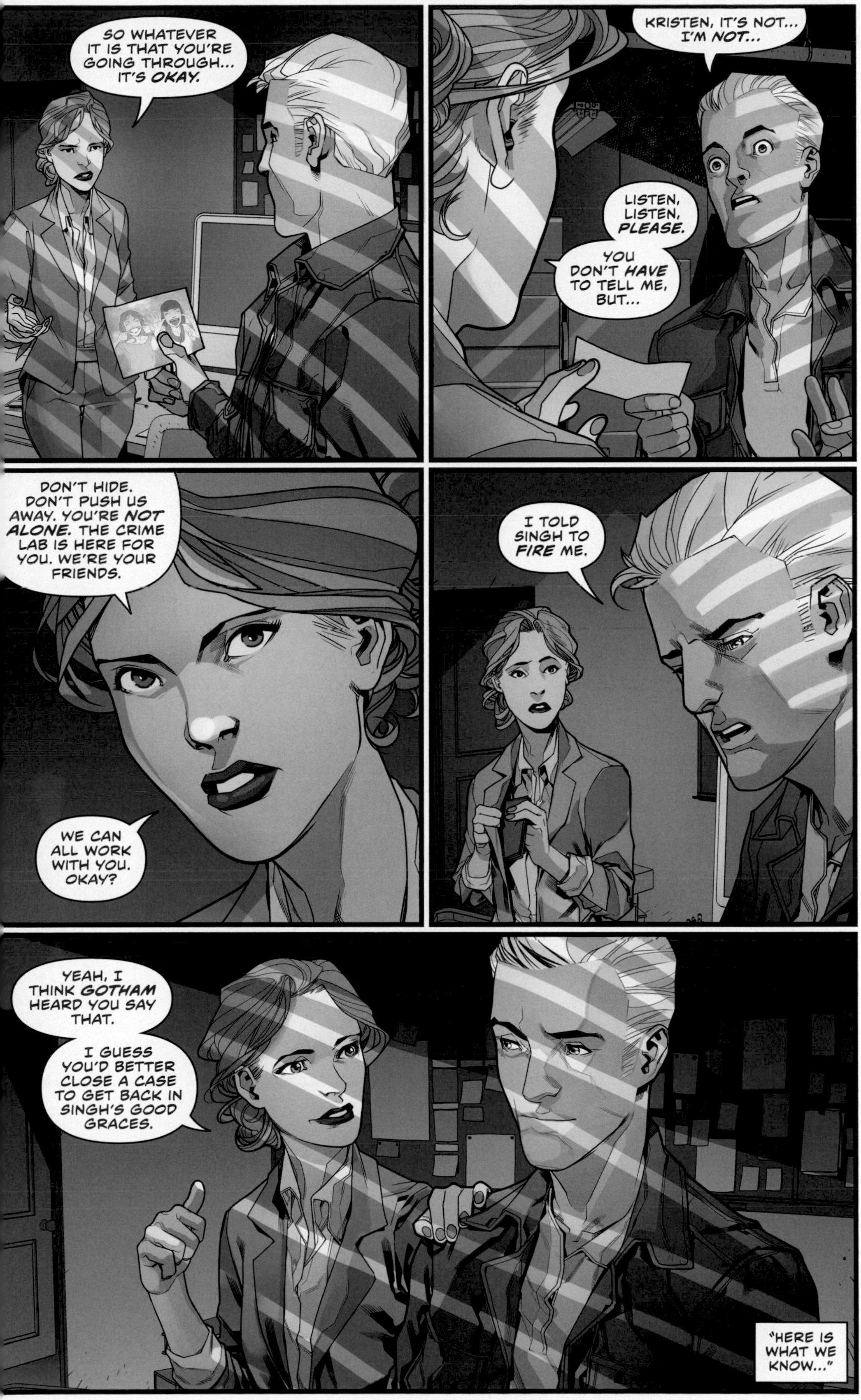
SO WHATEVER IT IS THAT YOU'RE GOING THROUGH... IT'S OKAY.
KRISTEN, IT'S NOT... I'M NOT...
LISTEN, LISTEN, PLEASE.
YOU DON'T HAVE TO TELL ME, BUT...
DON'T HIDE. DON'T PUSH US AWAY. YOU'RE NOT ALONE. THE CRIME LAB IS HERE FOR YOU. WE'RE YOUR FRIENDS.
WE CAN ALL WORK WITH YOU. OKAY?
I TOLD SINGH TO FIRE ME.
YEAH, I THINK GOTHAM HEARD YOU SAY THAT.
I GUESS YOU'D BETTER CLOSE A CASE TO GET BACK IN SINGH'S GOOD GRACES.
"HERE IS WHAT WE KNOW..."

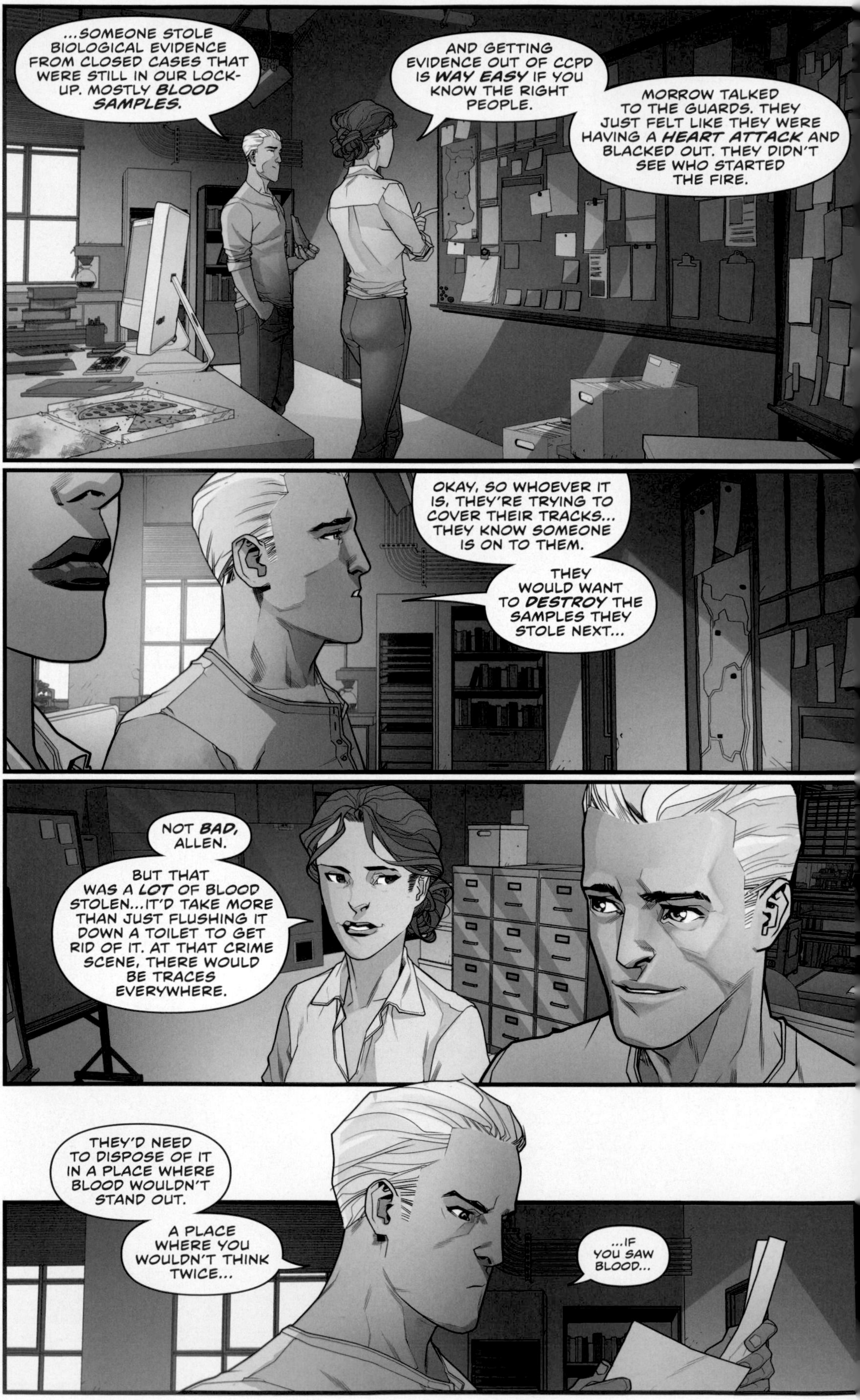
...SOMEONE STOLE BIOLOGICAL EVIDENCE FROM CLOSED CASES THAT WERE STILL IN OUR LOCK-UP. MOSTLY *BLOOD SAMPLES.*
AND GETTING EVIDENCE OUT OF CCPD IS *WAY EASY* IF YOU KNOW THE RIGHT PEOPLE.
MORROW TALKED TO THE GUARDS. THEY JUST FELT LIKE THEY WERE HAVING A *HEART ATTACK* AND BLACKED OUT. THEY DIDN'T SEE WHO STARTED THE FIRE.
OKAY, SO WHOEVER IT IS, THEY'RE TRYING TO COVER THEIR TRACKS... THEY KNOW SOMEONE IS ON TO THEM.
THEY WOULD WANT TO *DESTROY* THE SAMPLES THEY STOLE NEXT...
NOT *BAD,* ALLEN.
BUT THAT WAS A *LOT* OF BLOOD STOLEN...IT'D TAKE MORE THAN JUST FLUSHING IT DOWN A TOILET TO GET RID OF IT. AT THAT CRIME SCENE, THERE WOULD BE TRACES EVERYWHERE.
THEY'D NEED TO DISPOSE OF IT IN A PLACE WHERE BLOOD WOULDN'T STAND OUT.
A PLACE WHERE YOU WOULDN'T THINK TWICE...
...IF YOU SAW BLOOD...

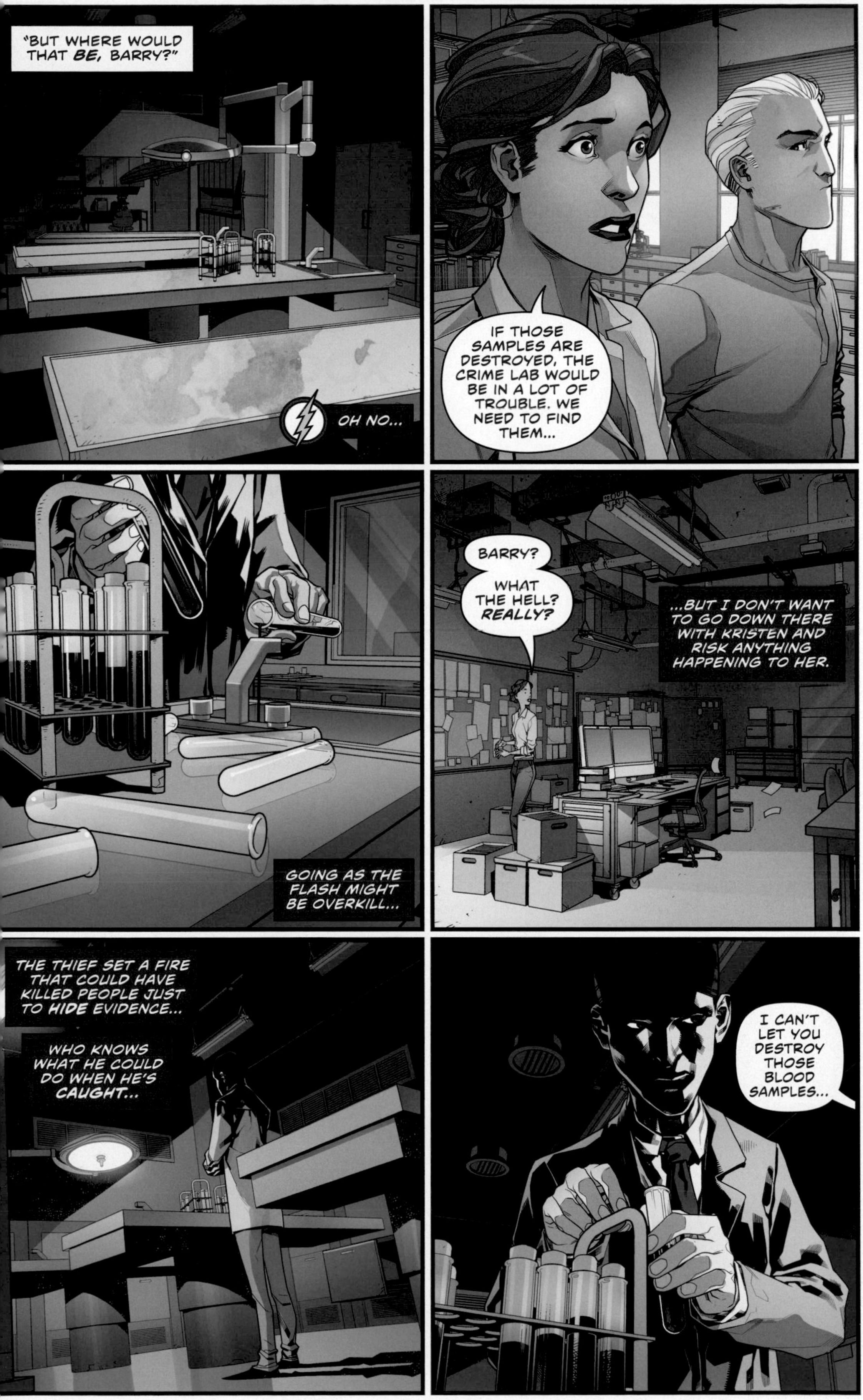
"BUT WHERE WOULD THAT BE, BARRY?"
OH NO...
IF THOSE SAMPLES ARE DESTROYED, THE CRIME LAB WOULD BE IN A LOT OF TROUBLE. WE NEED TO FIND THEM...
GOING AS THE FLASH MIGHT BE OVERKILL...
BARRY?
WHAT THE HELL? REALLY?
...BUT I DON'T WANT TO GO DOWN THERE WITH KRISTEN AND RISK ANYTHING HAPPENING TO HER.
THE THIEF SET A FIRE THAT COULD HAVE KILLED PEOPLE JUST TO HIDE EVIDENCE...
WHO KNOWS WHAT HE COULD DO WHEN HE'S CAUGHT...
I CAN'T LET YOU DESTROY THOSE BLOOD SAMPLES...

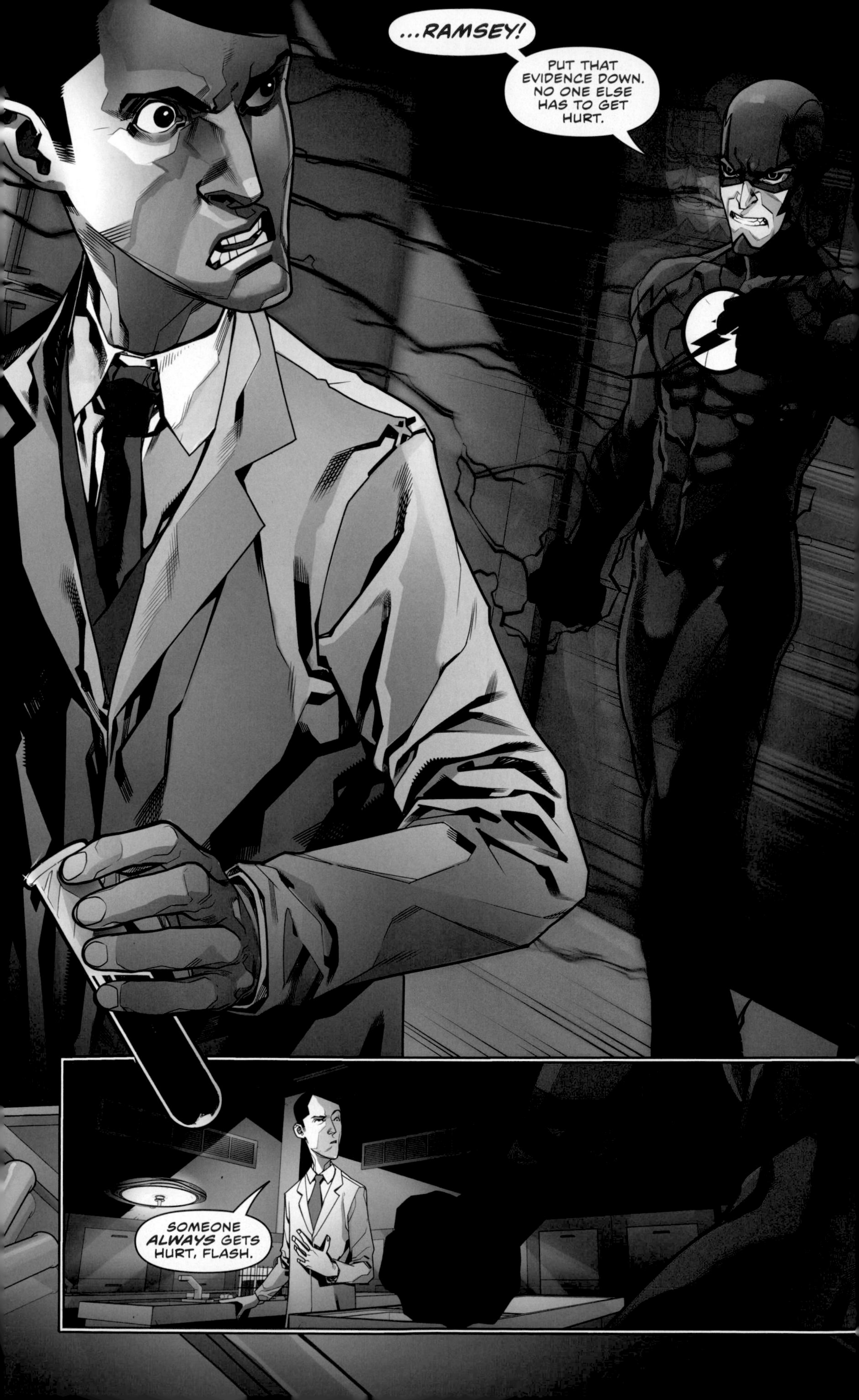
...RAMSEY!
PUT THAT EVIDENCE DOWN. NO ONE ELSE HAS TO GET HURT.
SOMEONE ALWAYS GETS HURT, FLASH.

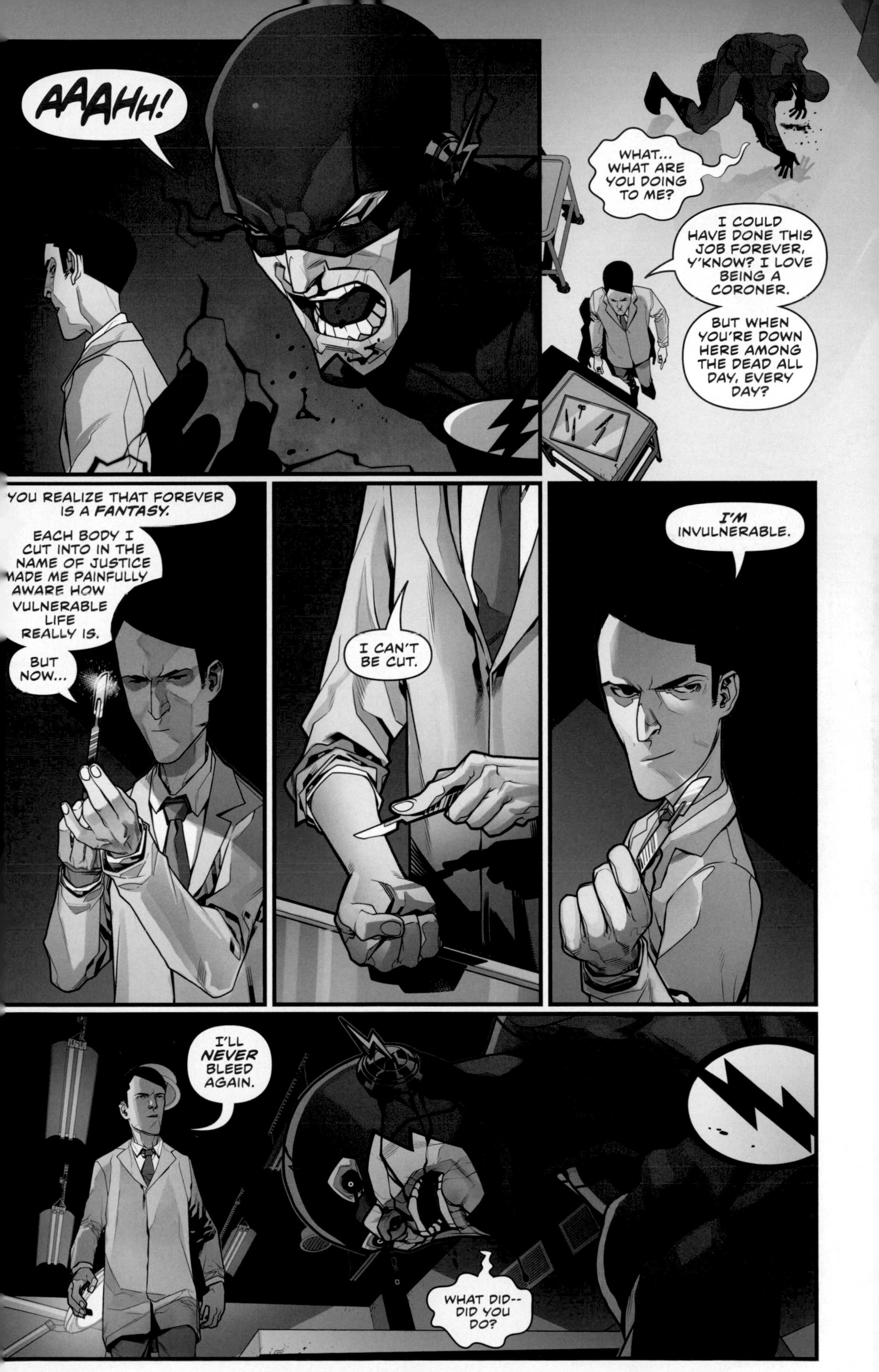
AAAHH!
WHAT... WHAT ARE YOU DOING TO ME?
I COULD HAVE DONE THIS JOB FOREVER, Y'KNOW? I LOVE BEING A CORONER.
BUT WHEN YOU'RE DOWN HERE AMONG THE DEAD ALL DAY, EVERY DAY?
YOU REALIZE THAT FOREVER IS A FANTASY.
EACH BODY I CUT INTO IN THE NAME OF JUSTICE MADE ME PAINFULLY AWARE HOW VULNERABLE LIFE REALLY IS.
BUT NOW...
I CAN'T BE CUT.
I'M INVULNERABLE.
I'LL NEVER BLEED AGAIN.
WHAT DID-- DID YOU DO?

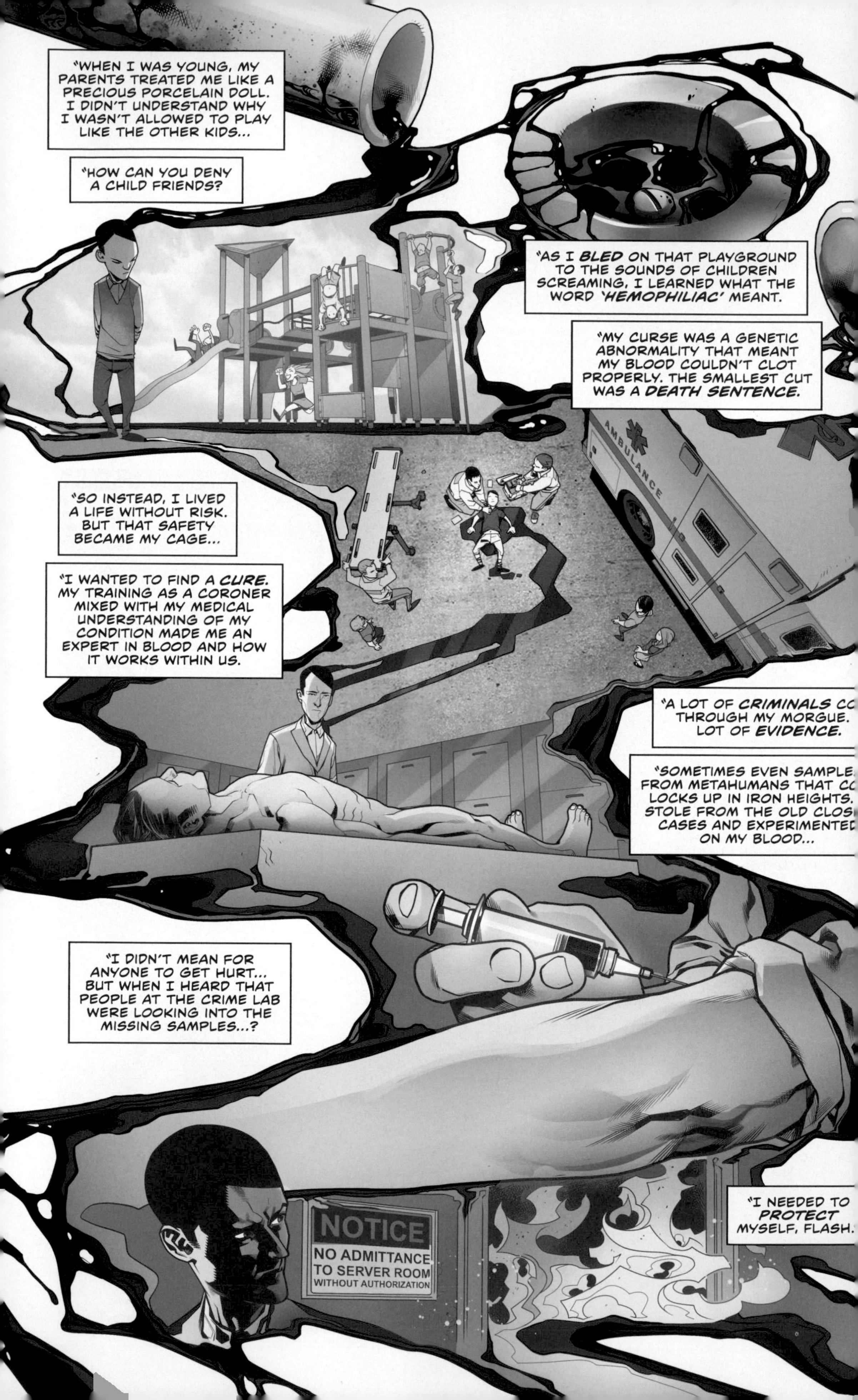
"WHEN I WAS YOUNG, MY PARENTS TREATED ME LIKE A PRECIOUS PORCELAIN DOLL. I DIDN'T UNDERSTAND WHY I WASN'T ALLOWED TO PLAY LIKE THE OTHER KIDS...
"HOW CAN YOU DENY A CHILD FRIENDS?
"AS I BLED ON THAT PLAYGROUND TO THE SOUNDS OF CHILDREN SCREAMING, I LEARNED WHAT THE WORD 'HEMOPHILIAC' MEANT.
"MY CURSE WAS A GENETIC ABNORMALITY THAT MEANT MY BLOOD COULDN'T CLOT PROPERLY. THE SMALLEST CUT WAS A DEATH SENTENCE.
AMBULANCE
"SO INSTEAD, I LIVED A LIFE WITHOUT RISK. BUT THAT SAFETY BECAME MY CAGE...
"I WANTED TO FIND A CURE. MY TRAINING AS A CORONER MIXED WITH MY MEDICAL UNDERSTANDING OF MY CONDITION MADE ME AN EXPERT IN BLOOD AND HOW IT WORKS WITHIN US.
"A LOT OF CRIMINALS CO THROUGH MY MORGUE. LOT OF EVIDENCE.
"SOMETIMES EVEN SAMPLE FROM METAHUMANS THAT CC LOCKS UP IN IRON HEIGHTS. STOLE FROM THE OLD CLOS CASES AND EXPERIMENTEI ON MY BLOOD...
"I DIDN'T MEAN FOR ANYONE TO GET HURT... BUT WHEN I HEARD THAT PEOPLE AT THE CRIME LAB WERE LOOKING INTO THE MISSING SAMPLES...?
NOTICE
NO ADMITTANCE TO SERVER ROOM WITHOUT AUTHORIZATION
"I NEEDED TO PROTECT MYSELF, FLASH.

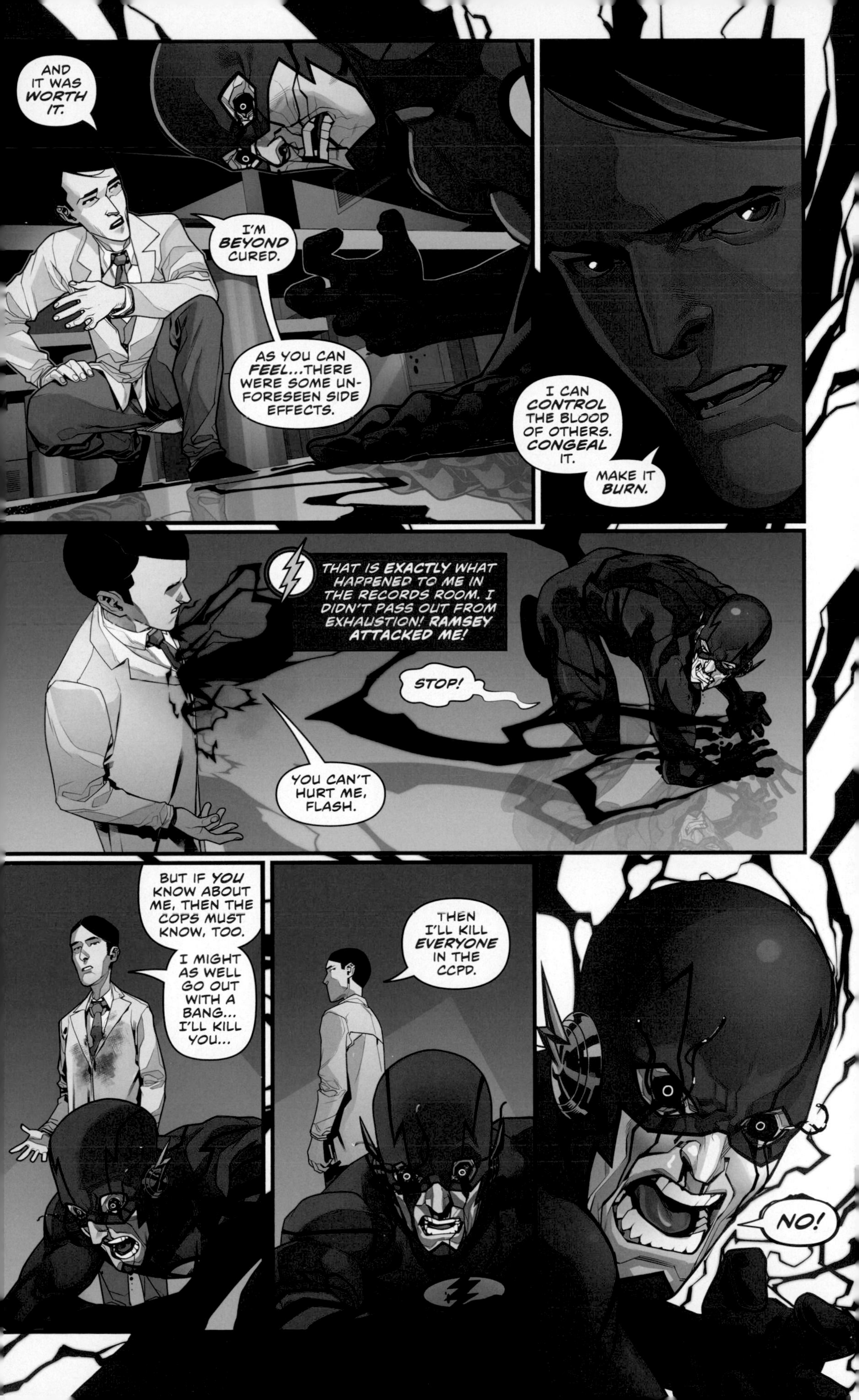
AND IT WAS WORTH IT.
I'M BEYOND CURED.
AS YOU CAN FEEL...THERE WERE SOME UN-FORESEEN SIDE EFFECTS.
I CAN CONTROL THE BLOOD OF OTHERS. CONGEAL IT.
MAKE IT BURN.
THAT IS EXACTLY WHAT HAPPENED TO ME IN THE RECORDS ROOM. I DIDN'T PASS OUT FROM EXHAUSTION! RAMSEY ATTACKED ME!
STOP!
YOU CAN'T HURT ME, FLASH.
BUT IF YOU KNOW ABOUT ME, THEN THE COPS MUST KNOW, TOO.
I MIGHT AS WELL GO OUT WITH A BANG... I'LL KILL YOU...
THEN I'LL KILL EVERYONE IN THE CCPD.
NO!

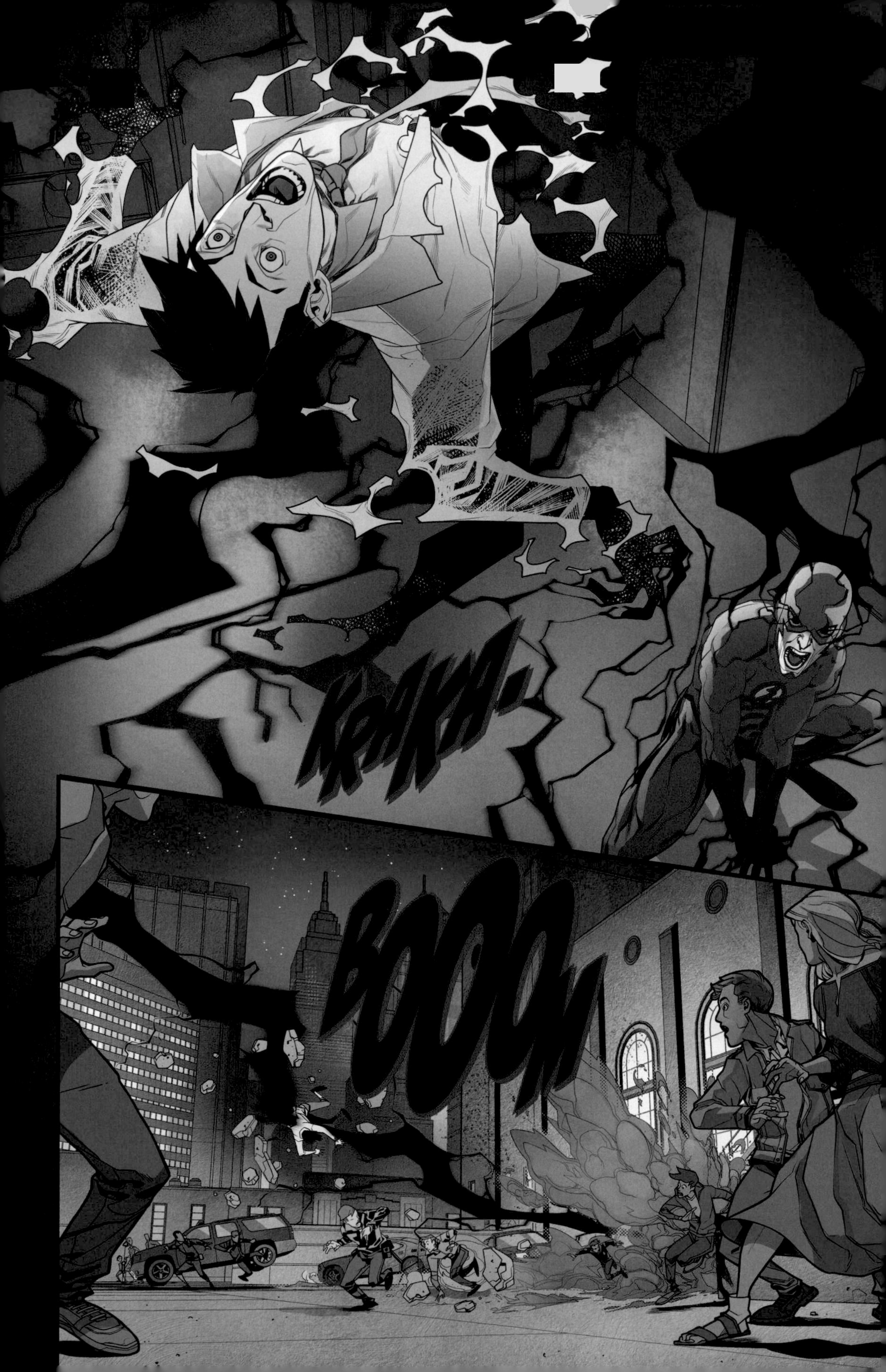
KRAKA-
BOOOM

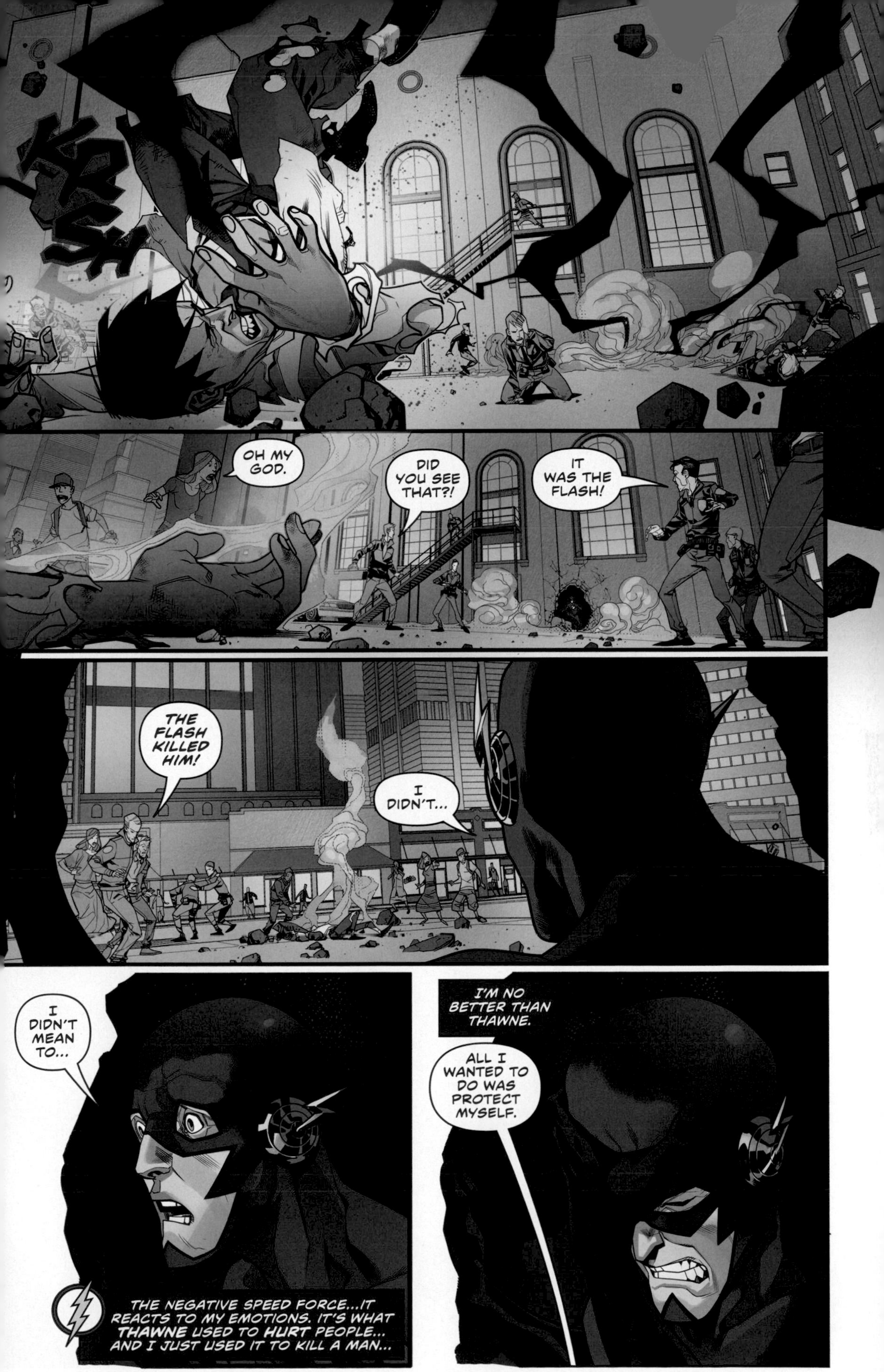
KRSH
OH MY GOD.
DID YOU SEE THAT?!
IT WAS THE FLASH!
THE FLASH KILLED HIM!
I DIDN'T...
I DIDN'T MEAN TO...
THE NEGATIVE SPEED FORCE...IT REACTS TO MY EMOTIONS. IT'S WHAT THAWNE USED TO HURT PEOPLE... AND I JUST USED IT TO KILL A MAN...
I'M NO BETTER THAN THAWNE.
ALL I WANTED TO DO WAS PROTECT MYSELF.

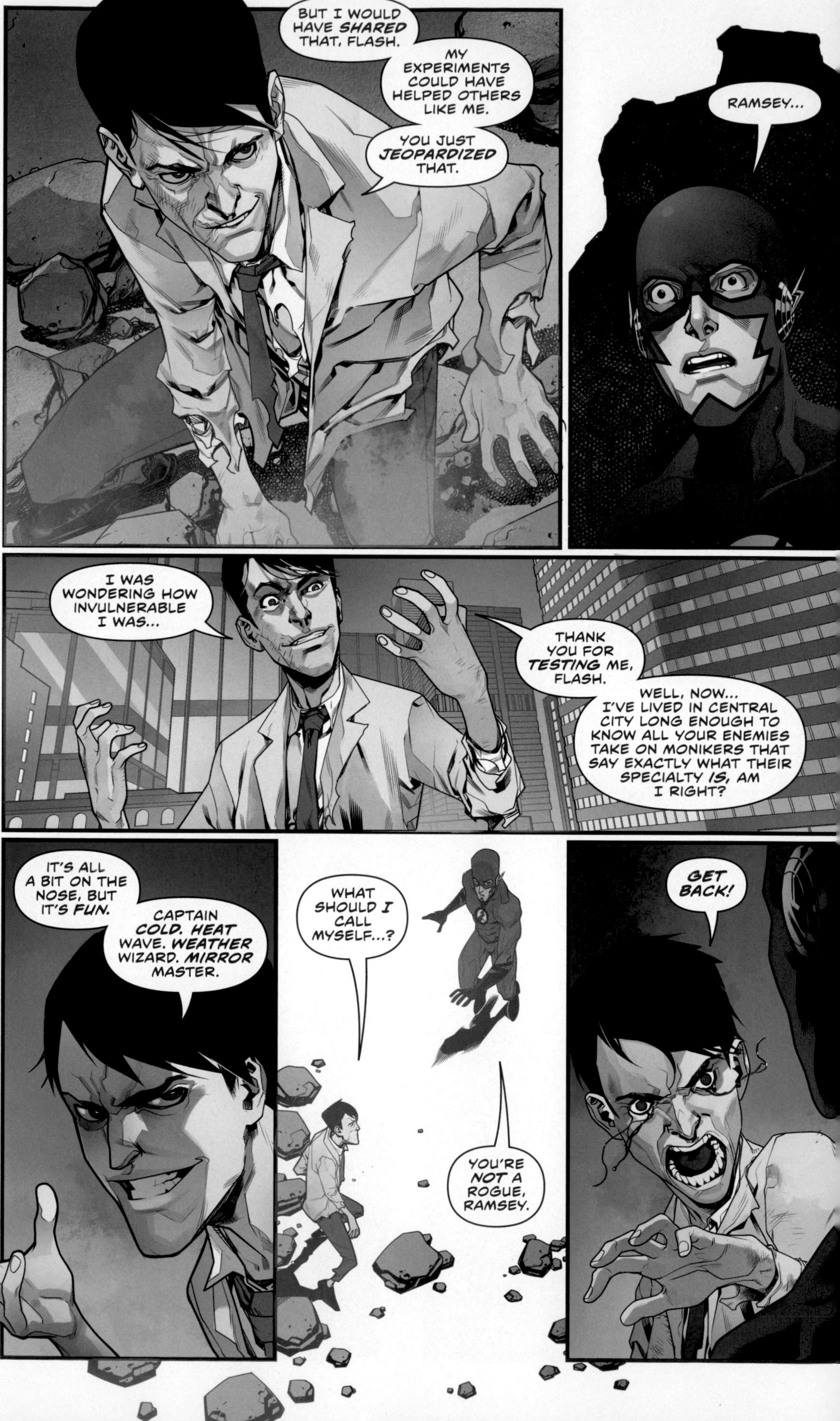
BUT I WOULD HAVE SHARED THAT, FLASH.
MY EXPERIMENTS COULD HAVE HELPED OTHERS LIKE ME.
YOU JUST JEOPARDIZED THAT.
RAMSEY...
I WAS WONDERING HOW INVULNERABLE I WAS...
THANK YOU FOR TESTING ME, FLASH.
WELL, NOW... I'VE LIVED IN CENTRAL CITY LONG ENOUGH TO KNOW ALL YOUR ENEMIES TAKE ON MONIKERS THAT SAY EXACTLY WHAT THEIR SPECIALTY IS, AM I RIGHT?
IT'S ALL A BIT ON THE NOSE, BUT IT'S FUN.
CAPTAIN COLD. HEAT WAVE. WEATHER WIZARD. MIRROR MASTER.
WHAT SHOULD I CALL MYSELF...?
YOU'RE NOT A ROGUE, RAMSEY.
GET BACK!

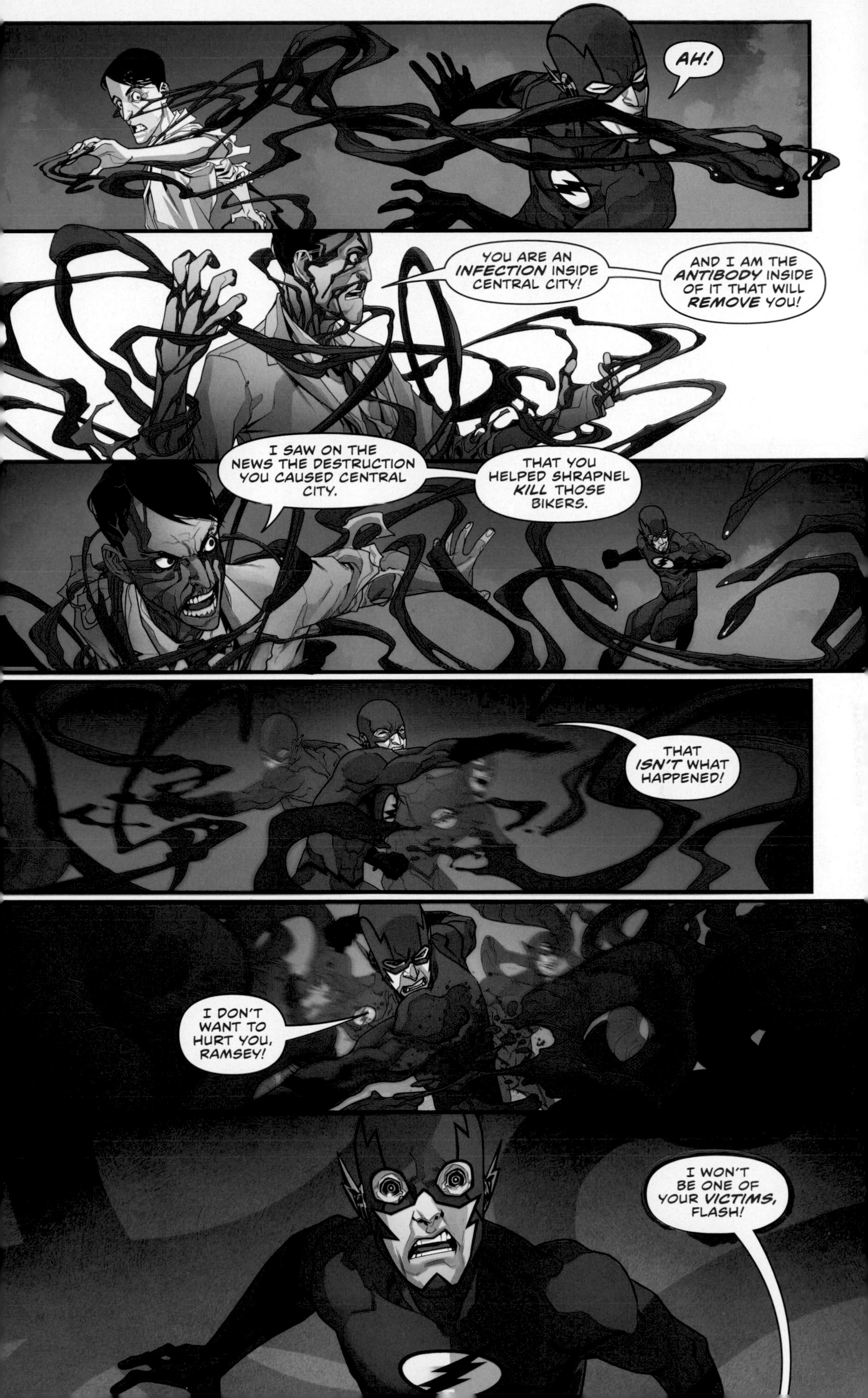
AH!
YOU ARE AN INFECTION INSIDE CENTRAL CITY!
AND I AM THE ANTIBODY INSIDE OF IT THAT WILL REMOVE YOU!
I SAW ON THE NEWS THE DESTRUCTION YOU CAUSED CENTRAL CITY.
THAT YOU HELPED SHRAPNEL KILL THOSE BIKERS.
THAT ISN'T WHAT HAPPENED!
I DON'T WANT TO HURT YOU, RAMSEY!
I WON'T BE ONE OF YOUR VICTIMS, FLASH!

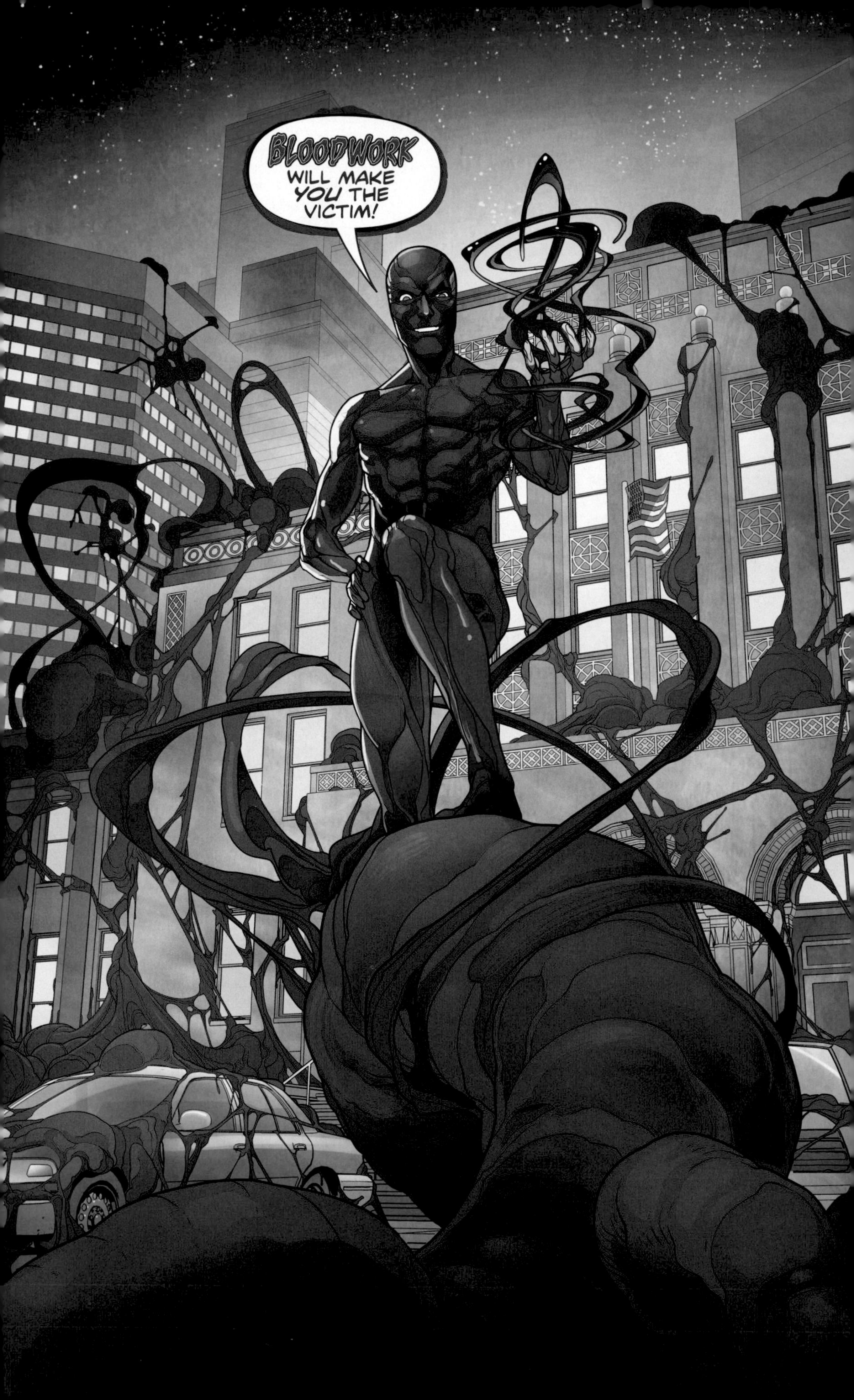
BLOODWORK WILL MAKE YOU THE VICTIM!

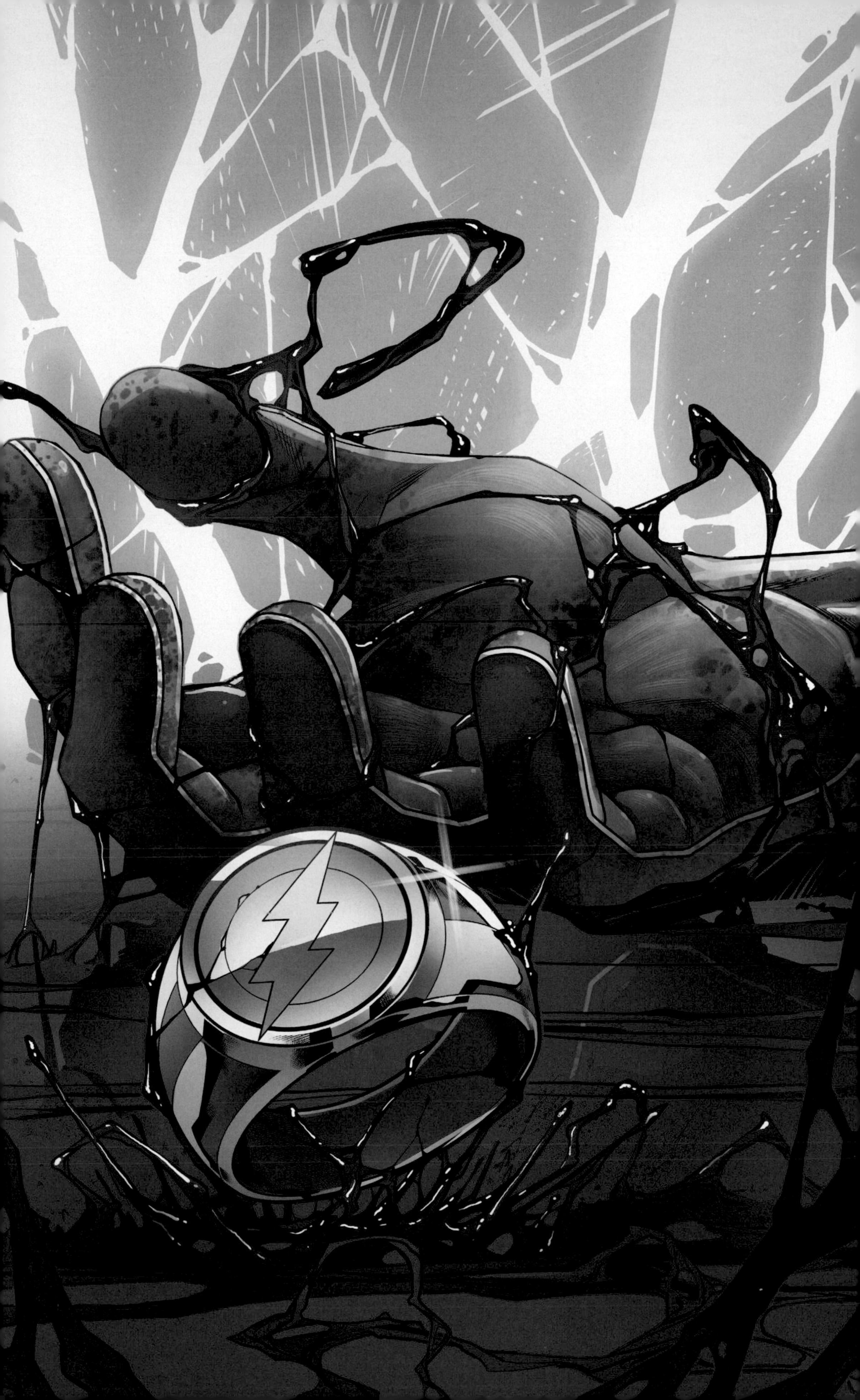

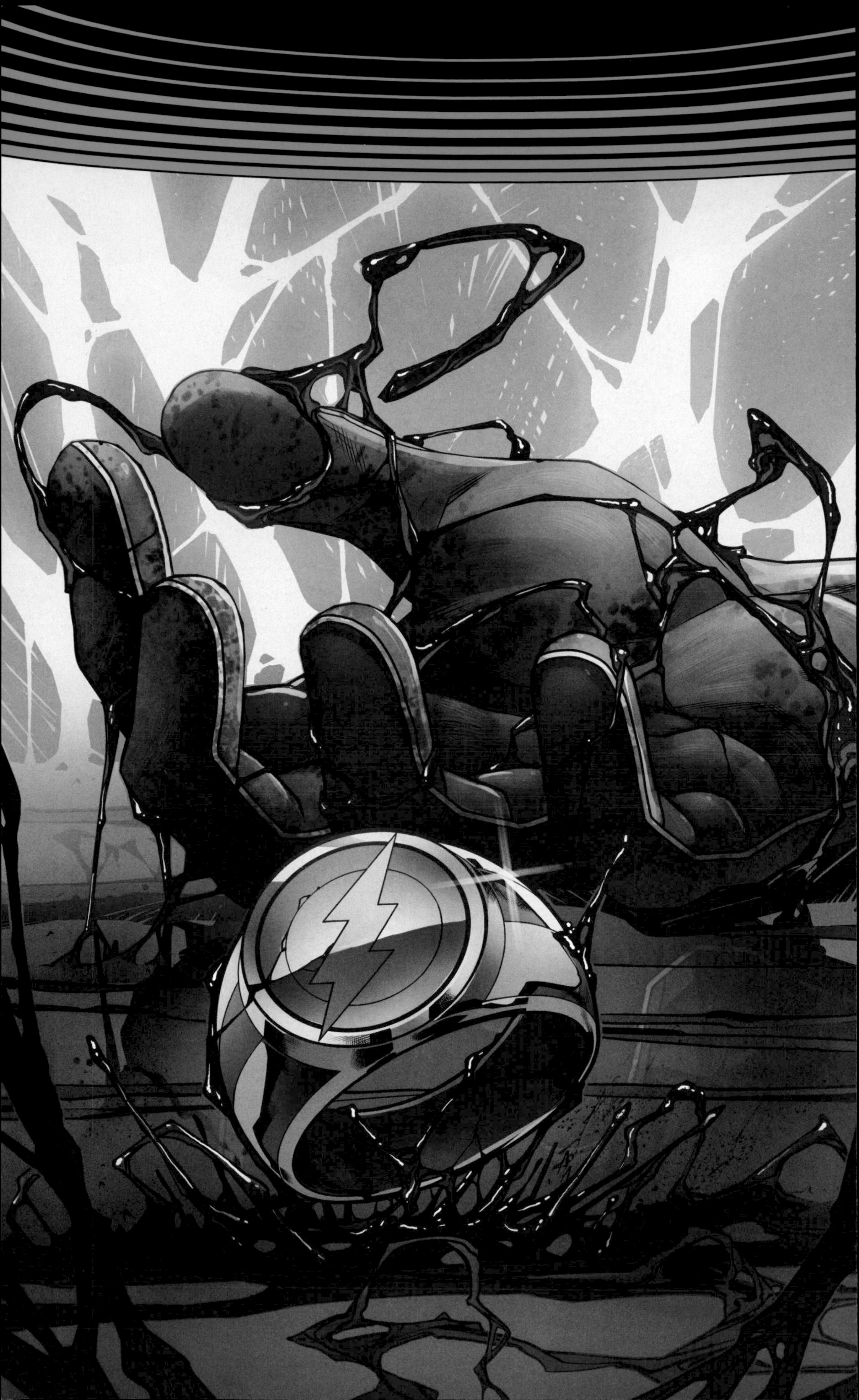

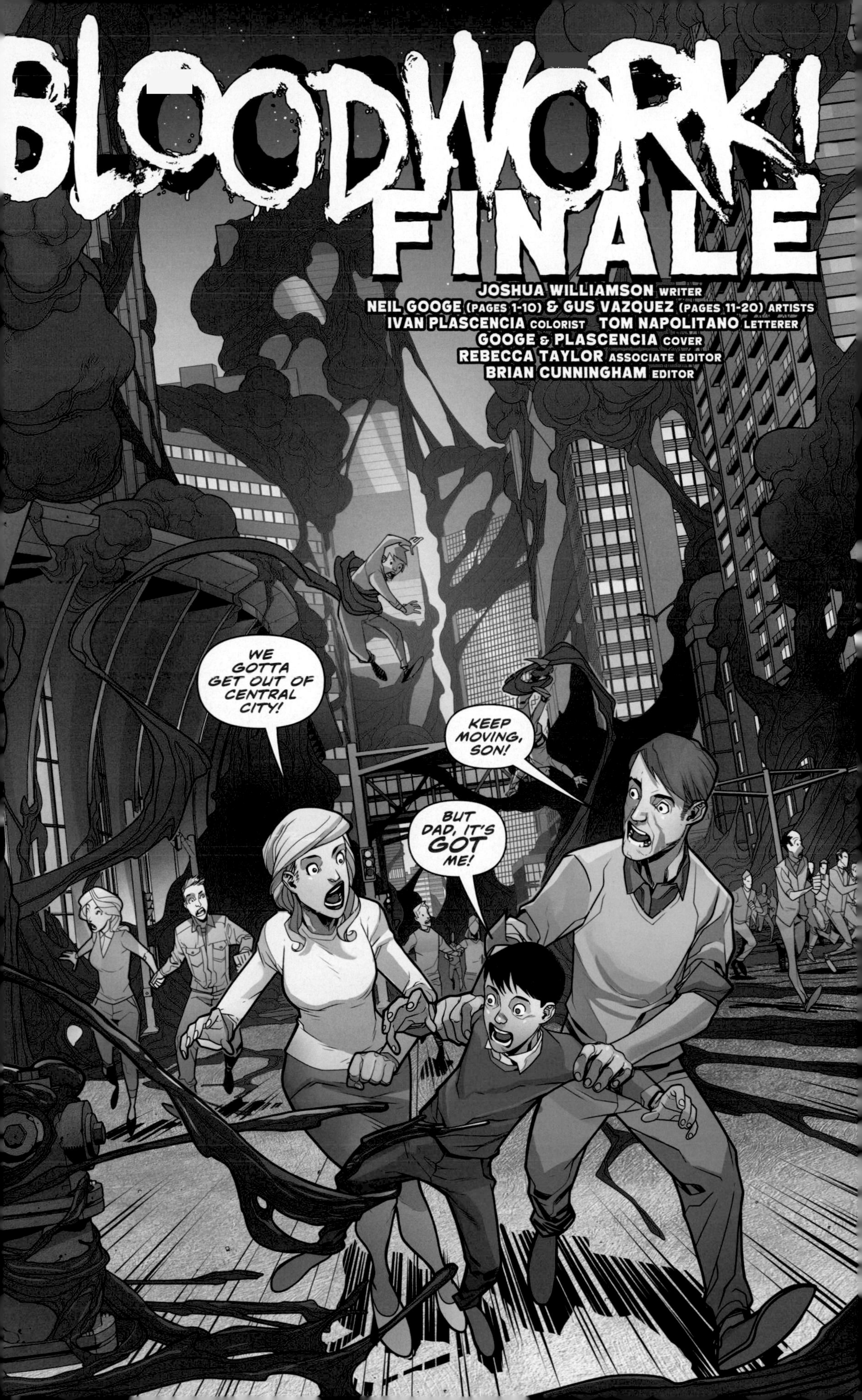
BLOODWORK! FINALE
JOSHUA WILLIAMSON WRITER
NEIL GOOGE (PAGES 1-10) & GUS VAZQUEZ (PAGES 11-20) ARTISTS
IVAN PLASCENCIA COLORIST TOM NAPOLITANO LETTERER
GOOGE & PLASCENCIA COVER
REBECCA TAYLOR ASSOCIATE EDITOR
BRIAN CUNNINGHAM EDITOR
WE GOTTA GET OUT OF CENTRAL CITY!
KEEP MOVING, SON!
BUT DAD, IT'S GOT ME!

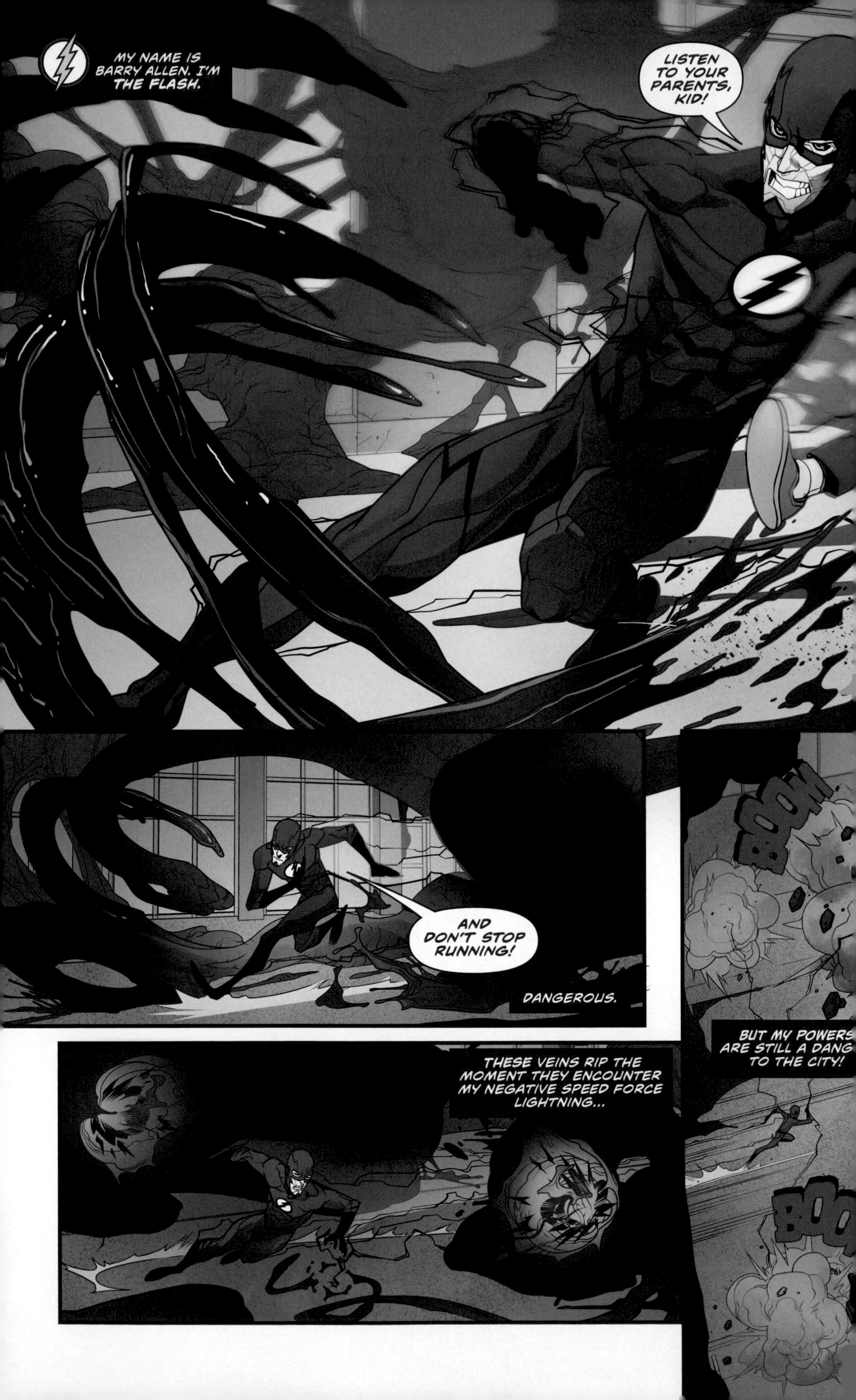
MY NAME IS BARRY ALLEN. I'M THE FLASH.
LISTEN TO YOUR PARENTS, KID!
AND DON'T STOP RUNNING!
DANGEROUS.
BOOM
BUT MY POWERS ARE STILL A DANG TO THE CITY!
BOO
THESE VEINS RIP THE MOMENT THEY ENCOUNTER MY NEGATIVE SPEED FORCE LIGHTNING...

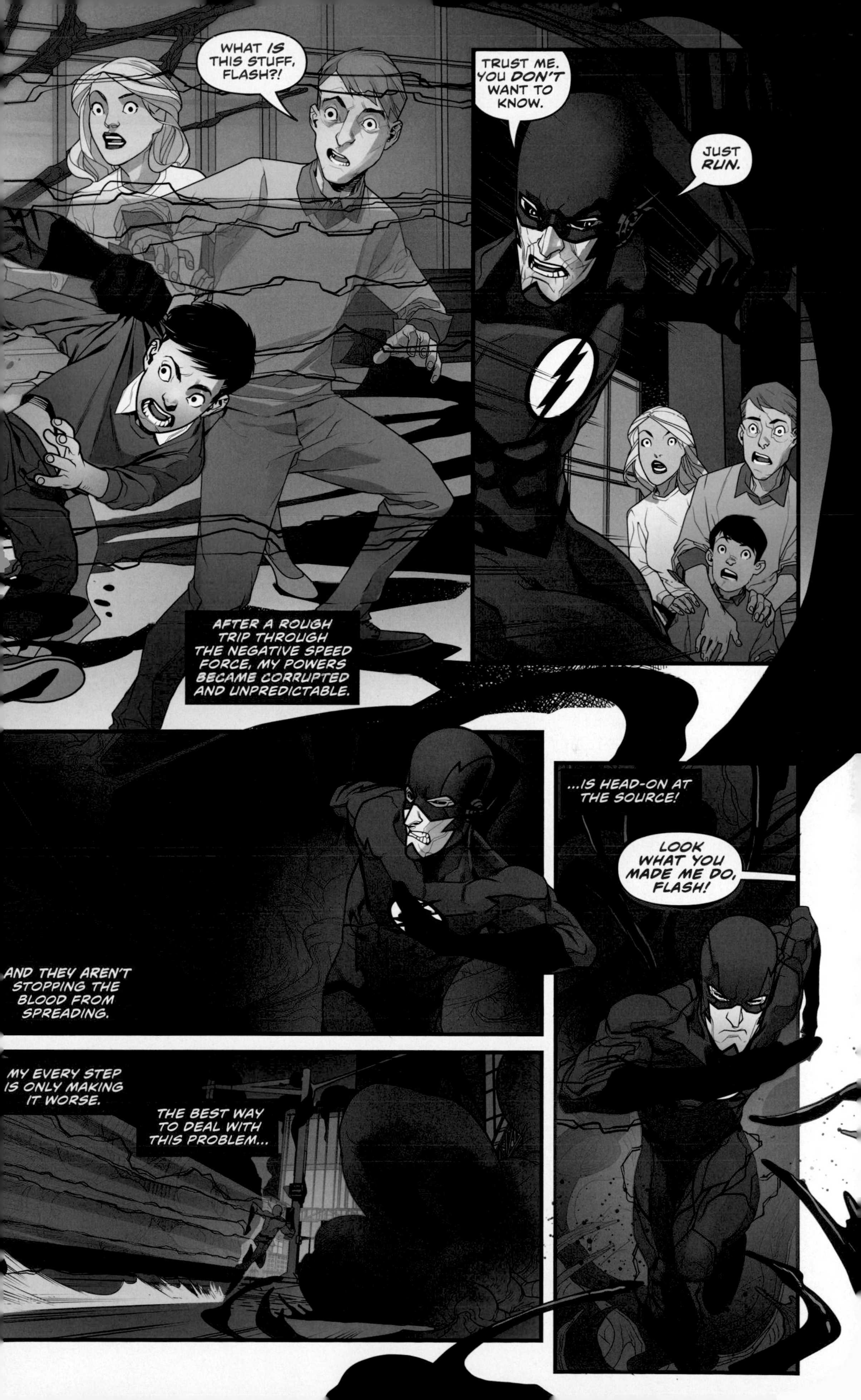
WHAT IS THIS STUFF, FLASH?!
TRUST ME. YOU DON'T WANT TO KNOW.
JUST RUN.
AFTER A ROUGH TRIP THROUGH THE NEGATIVE SPEED FORCE, MY POWERS BECAME CORRUPTED AND UNPREDICTABLE.
AND THEY AREN'T STOPPING THE BLOOD FROM SPREADING.
MY EVERY STEP IS ONLY MAKING IT WORSE.
THE BEST WAY TO DEAL WITH THIS PROBLEM...
...IS HEAD-ON AT THE SOURCE!
LOOK WHAT YOU MADE ME DO, FLASH!

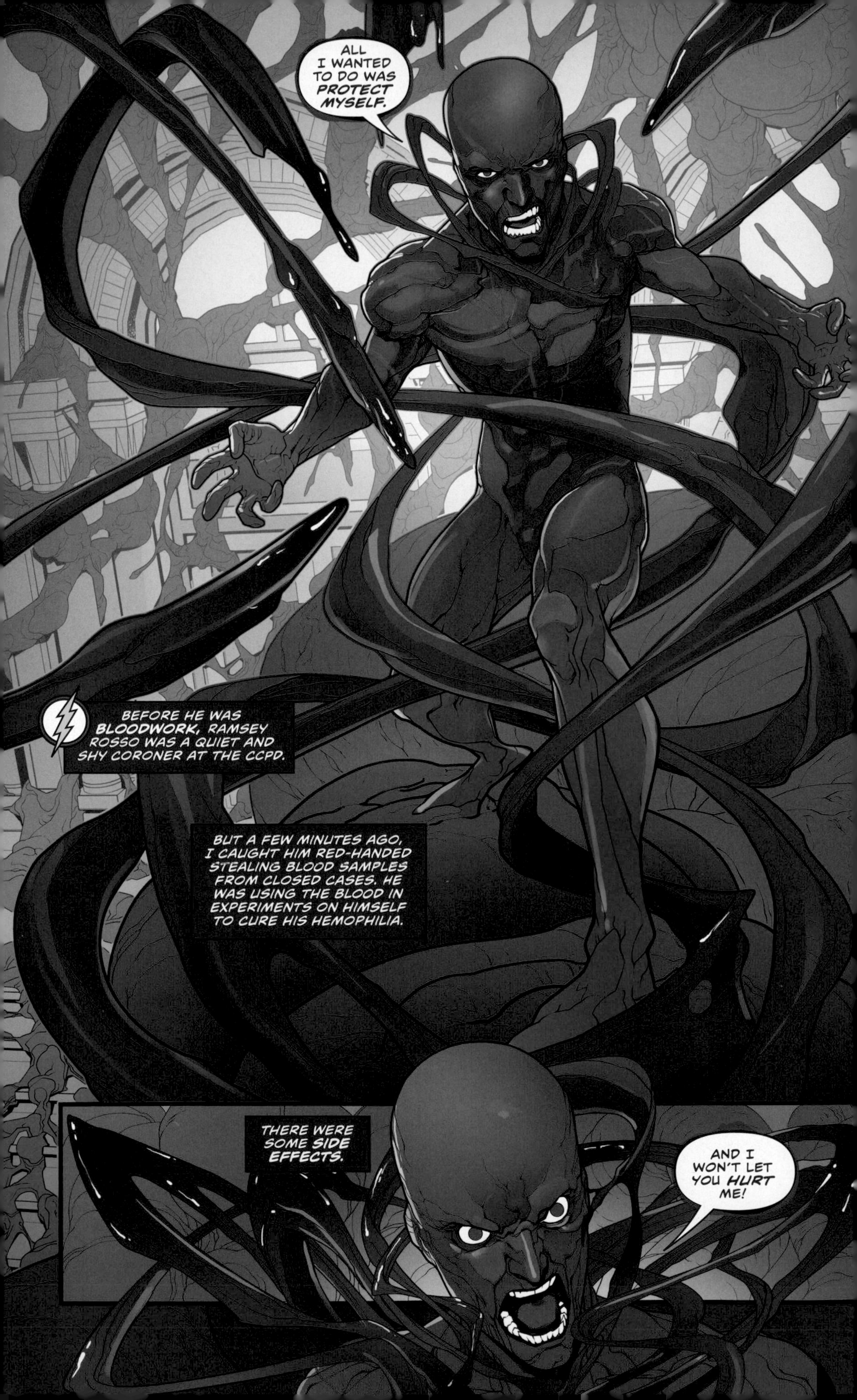
ALL I WANTED TO DO WAS PROTECT MYSELF.
BEFORE HE WAS BLOODWORK, RAMSEY ROSSO WAS A QUIET AND SHY CORONER AT THE CCPD.
BUT A FEW MINUTES AGO, I CAUGHT HIM RED-HANDED STEALING BLOOD SAMPLES FROM CLOSED CASES. HE WAS USING THE BLOOD IN EXPERIMENTS ON HIMSELF TO CURE HIS HEMOPHILIA.
THERE WERE SOME SIDE EFFECTS.
AND I WON'T LET YOU HURT ME!

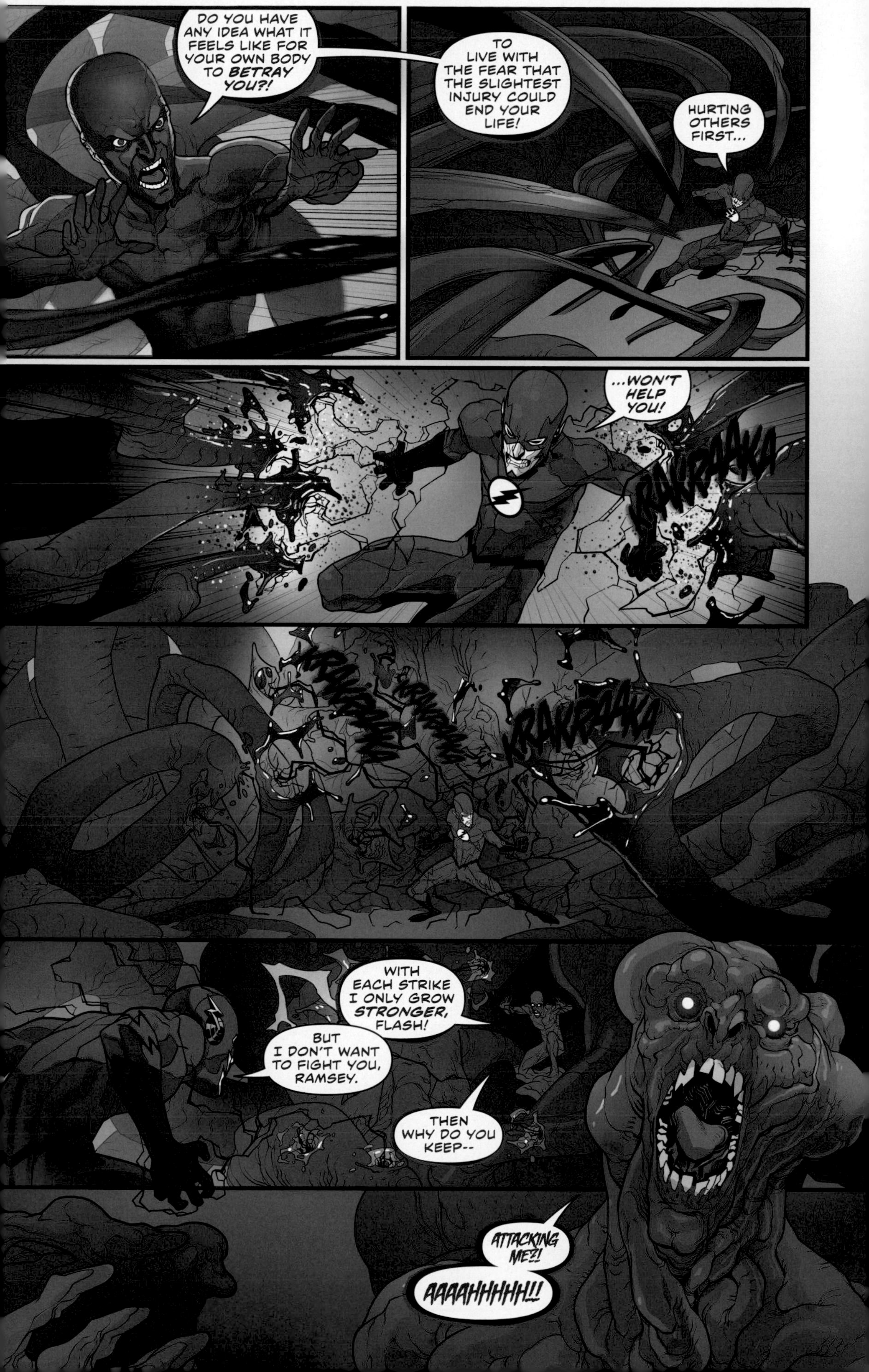

DO YOU HAVE ANY IDEA WHAT IT FEELS LIKE FOR YOUR OWN BODY TO BETRAY YOU?!
TO LIVE WITH THE FEAR THAT THE SLIGHTEST INJURY COULD END YOUR LIFE!
HURTING OTHERS FIRST...
...WON'T HELP YOU!
KRAKRAAKA
KRAKRAAKA
KRAKRAAKA
KRAKRAAKA
WITH EACH STRIKE I ONLY GROW STRONGER, FLASH!
BUT I DON'T WANT TO FIGHT YOU, RAMSEY.
THEN WHY DO YOU KEEP--
ATTACKING ME?!
AAAAHHHHH!!!

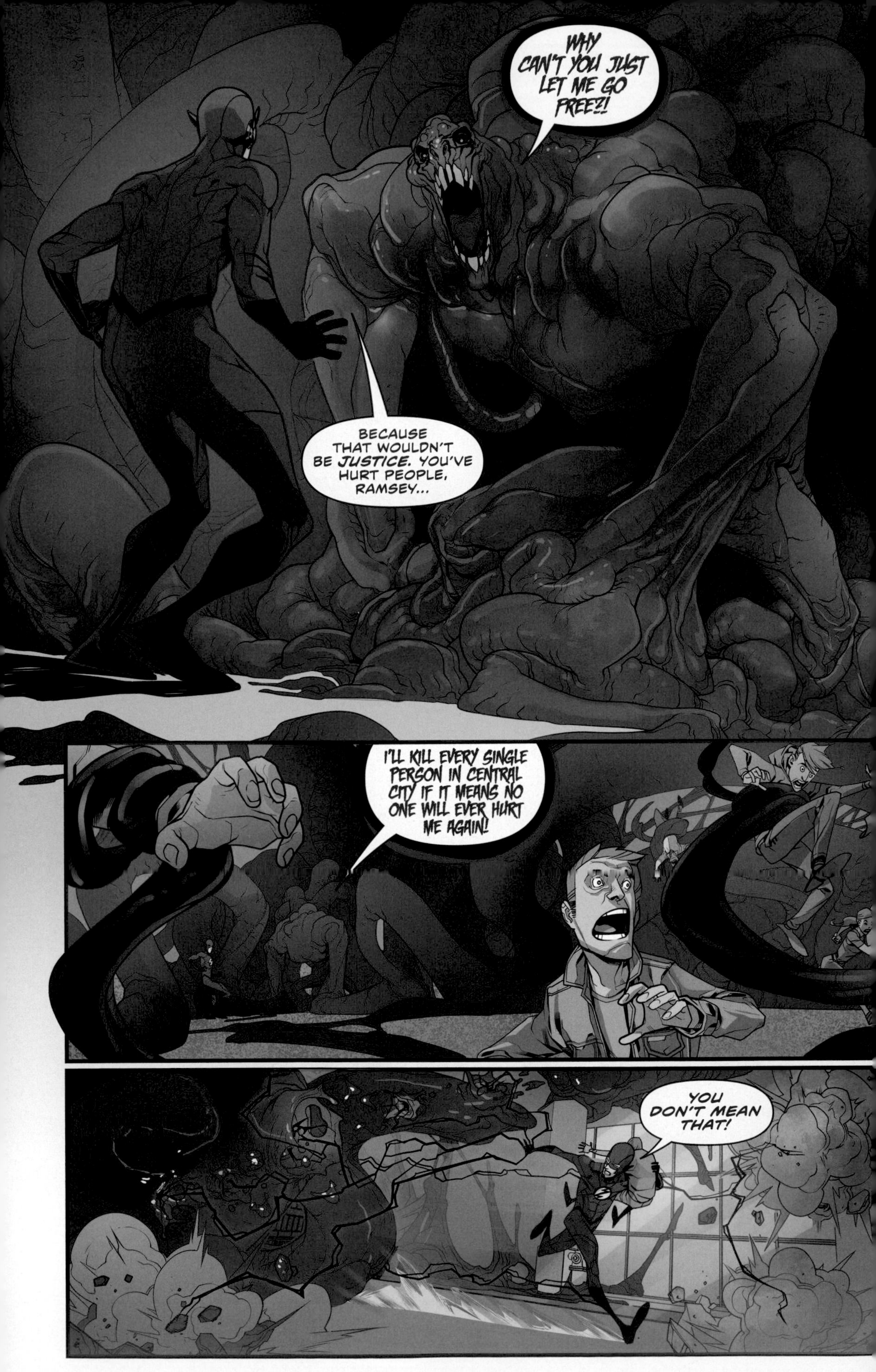
WHY CAN'T YOU JUST LET ME GO FREE?!
BECAUSE THAT WOULDN'T BE JUSTICE. YOU'VE HURT PEOPLE, RAMSEY...
I'LL KILL EVERY SINGLE PERSON IN CENTRAL CITY IF IT MEANS NO ONE WILL EVER HURT ME AGAIN!
YOU DON'T MEAN THAT!

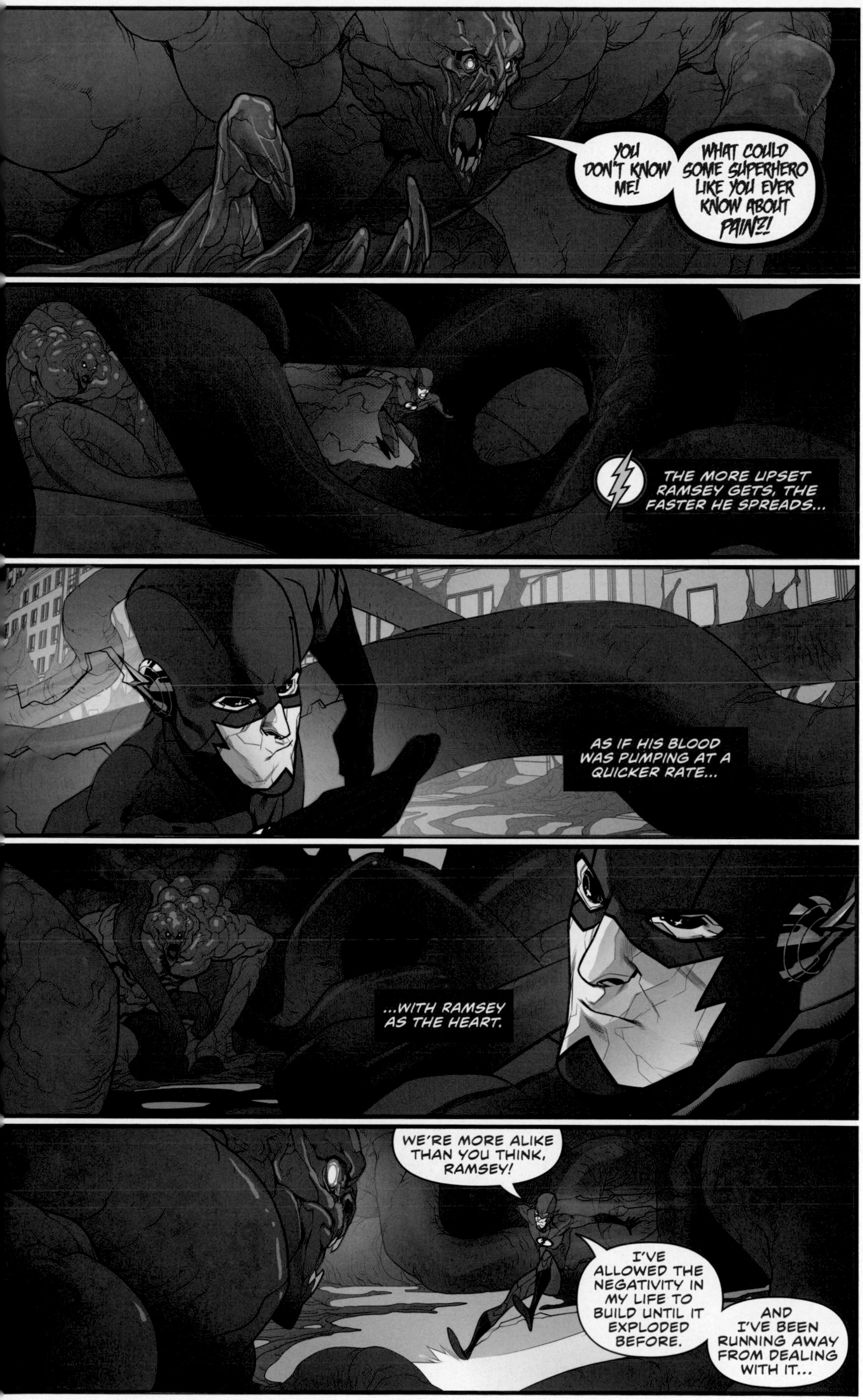
YOU DON'T KNOW ME!
WHAT COULD SOME SUPERHERO LIKE YOU EVER KNOW ABOUT PAIN?!
THE MORE UPSET RAMSEY GETS, THE FASTER HE SPREADS...
AS IF HIS BLOOD WAS PUMPING AT A QUICKER RATE...
...WITH RAMSEY AS THE HEART.
WE'RE MORE ALIKE THAN YOU THINK, RAMSEY!
I'VE ALLOWED THE NEGATIVITY IN MY LIFE TO BUILD UNTIL IT EXPLODED BEFORE.
AND I'VE BEEN RUNNING AWAY FROM DEALING WITH IT...

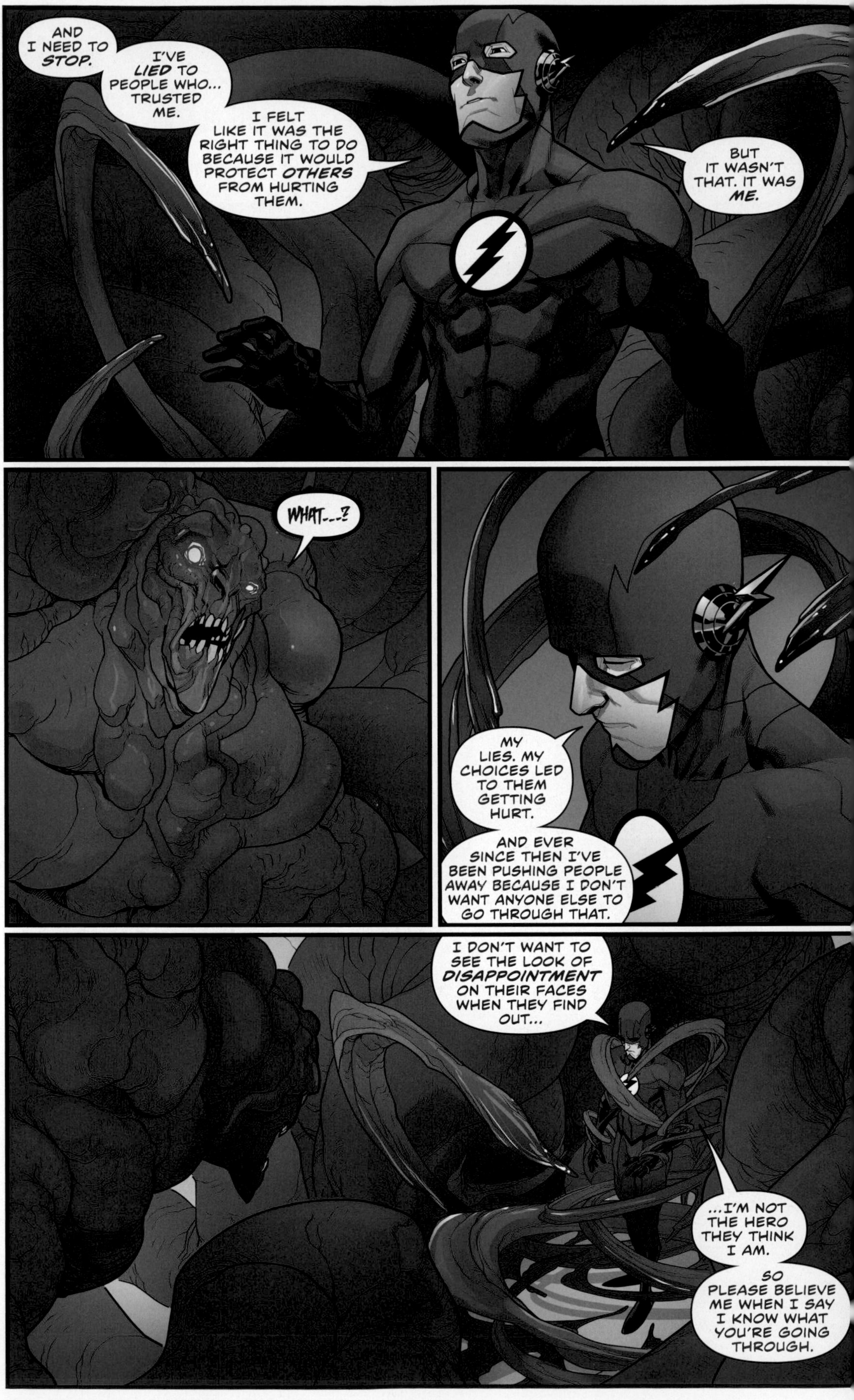
AND I NEED TO STOP.
I'VE LIED TO PEOPLE WHO... TRUSTED ME.
I FELT LIKE IT WAS THE RIGHT THING TO DO BECAUSE IT WOULD PROTECT OTHERS FROM HURTING THEM.
BUT IT WASN'T THAT. IT WAS ME.
WHAT...?
MY LIES. MY CHOICES LED TO THEM GETTING HURT.
AND EVER SINCE THEN I'VE BEEN PUSHING PEOPLE AWAY BECAUSE I DON'T WANT ANYONE ELSE TO GO THROUGH THAT.
I DON'T WANT TO SEE THE LOOK OF DISAPPOINTMENT ON THEIR FACES WHEN THEY FIND OUT...
...I'M NOT THE HERO THEY THINK I AM.
SO PLEASE BELIEVE ME WHEN I SAY I KNOW WHAT YOU'RE GOING THROUGH.

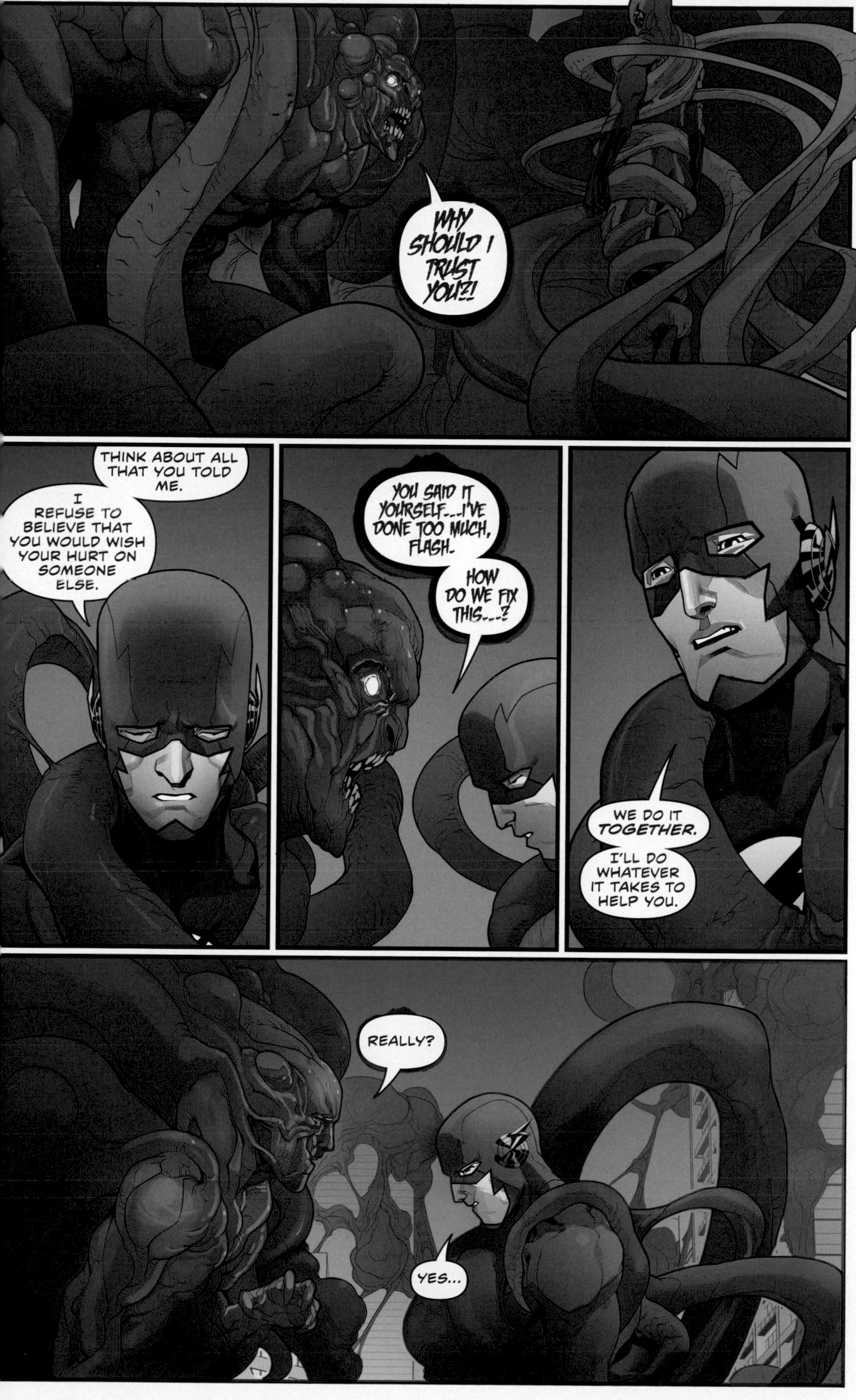
WHY SHOULD I TRUST YOU?!
THINK ABOUT ALL THAT YOU TOLD ME.
I REFUSE TO BELIEVE THAT YOU WOULD WISH YOUR HURT ON SOMEONE ELSE.
YOU SAID IT YOURSELF...I'VE DONE TOO MUCH, FLASH.
HOW DO WE FIX THIS...?
WE DO IT *TOGETHER.*
I'LL DO WHATEVER IT TAKES TO HELP YOU.
REALLY?
YES...

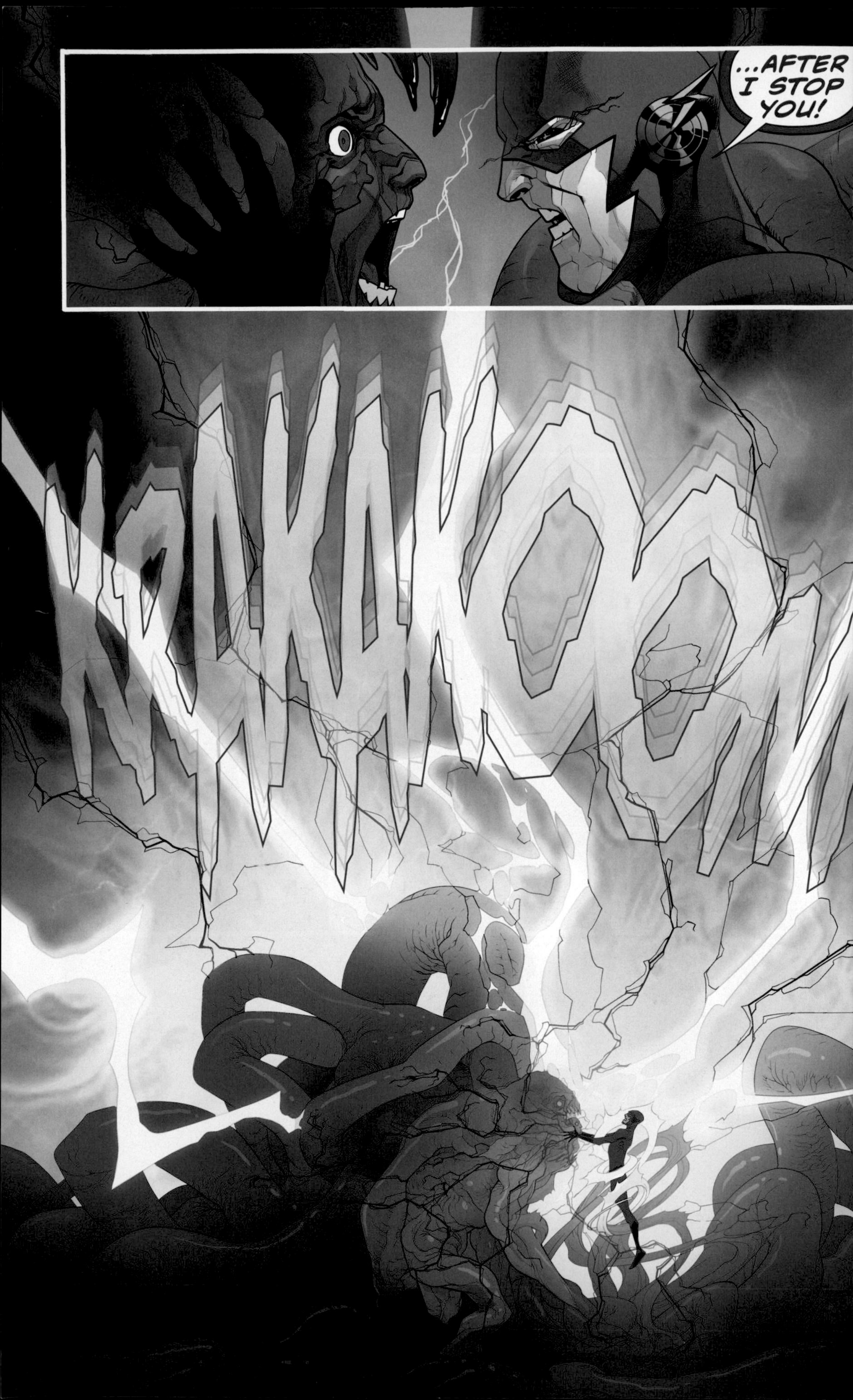
...AFTER I STOP YOU!

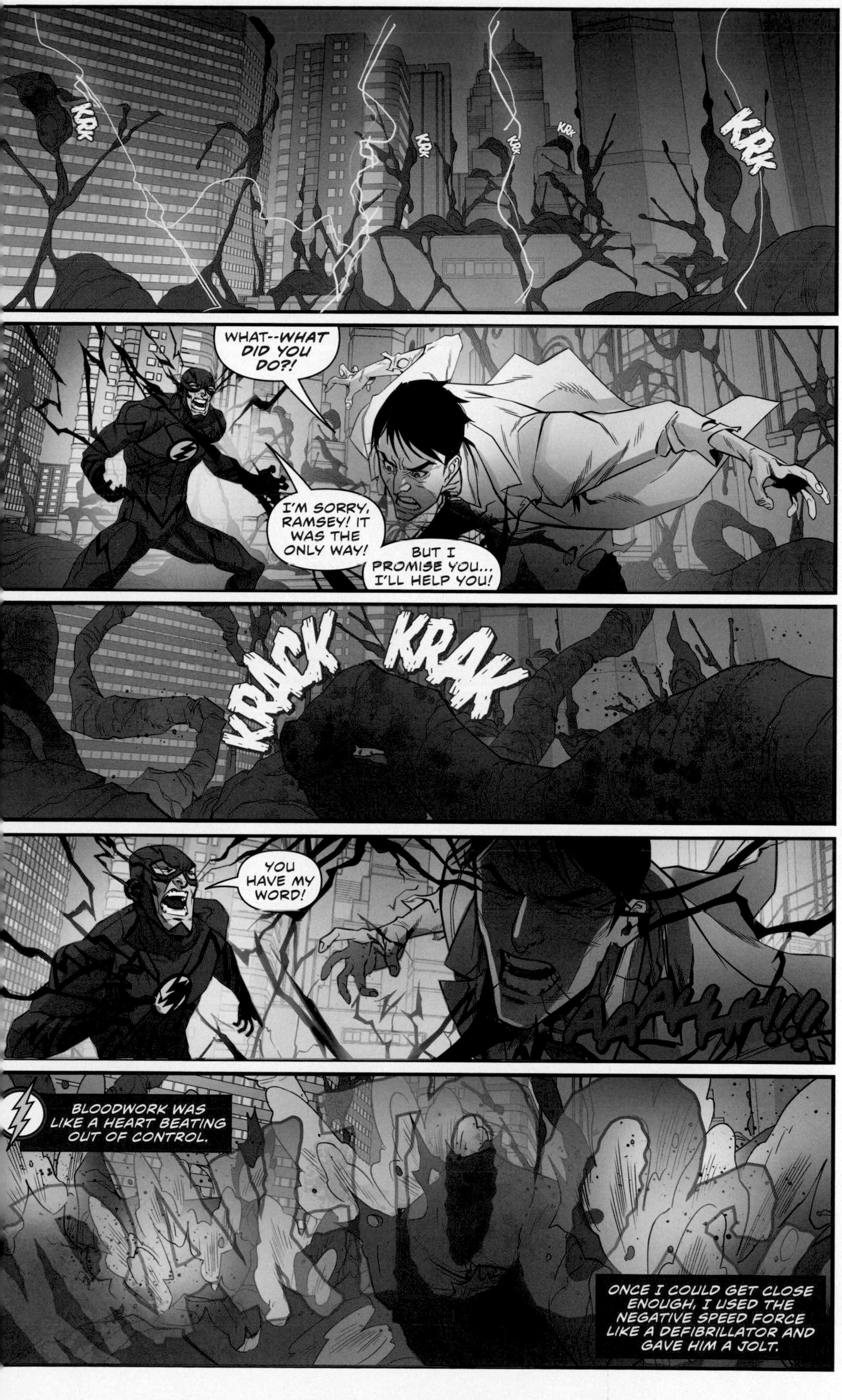
KRK
KRK
KRK
KRK
KRK
WHAT--WHAT DID YOU DO?!
I'M SORRY, RAMSEY! IT WAS THE ONLY WAY!
BUT I PROMISE YOU... I'LL HELP YOU!
KRACK
KRAK
YOU HAVE MY WORD!
AAAHHH!!!
BLOODWORK WAS LIKE A HEART BEATING OUT OF CONTROL.
ONCE I COULD GET CLOSE ENOUGH, I USED THE NEGATIVE SPEED FORCE LIKE A DEFIBRILLATOR AND GAVE HIM A JOLT.

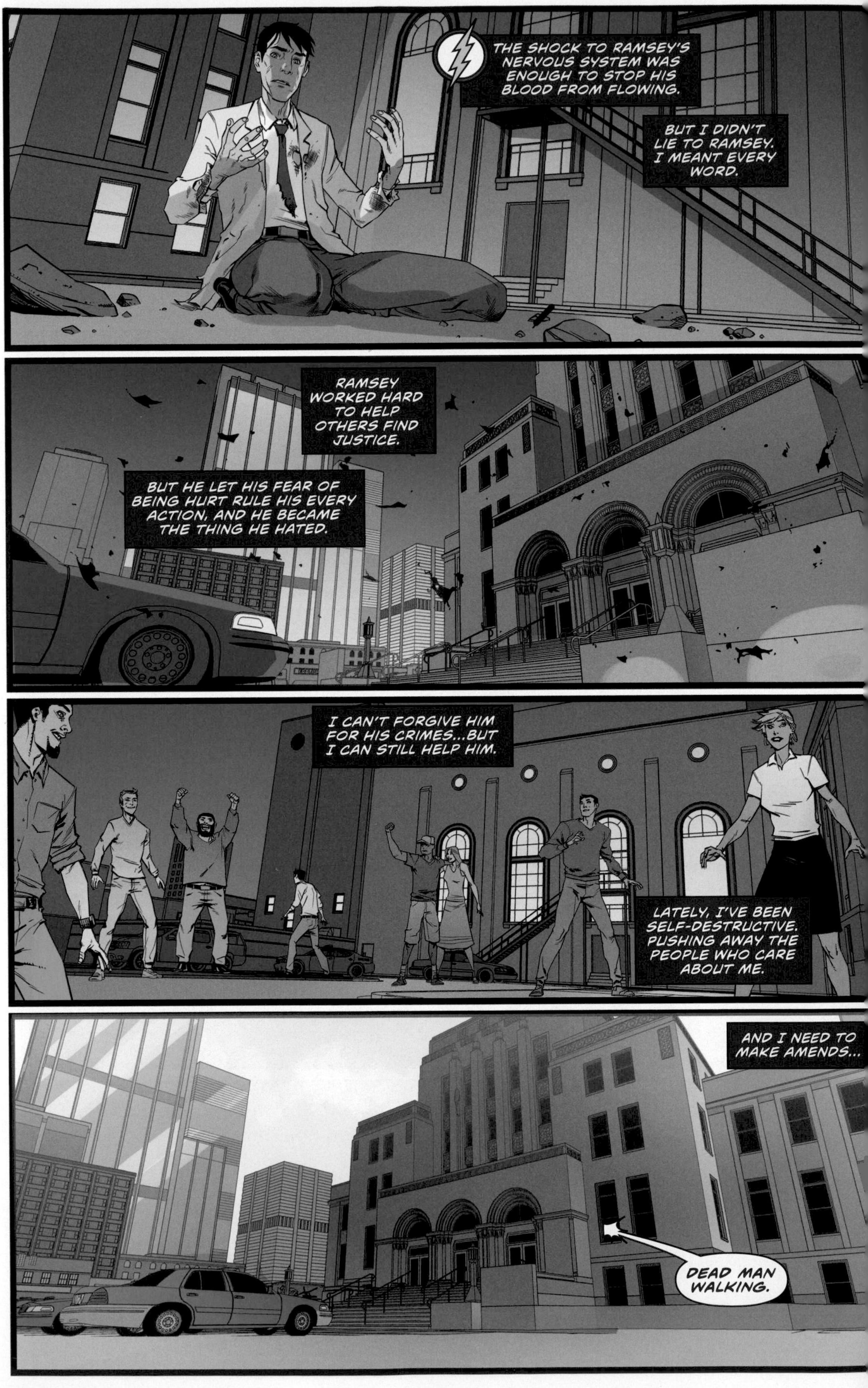
THE SHOCK TO RAMSEY'S NERVOUS SYSTEM WAS ENOUGH TO STOP HIS BLOOD FROM FLOWING.
BUT I DIDN'T LIE TO RAMSEY. I MEANT EVERY WORD.
RAMSEY WORKED HARD TO HELP OTHERS FIND JUSTICE.
BUT HE LET HIS FEAR OF BEING HURT RULE HIS EVERY ACTION, AND HE BECAME THE THING HE HATED.
I CAN'T FORGIVE HIM FOR HIS CRIMES...BUT I CAN STILL HELP HIM.
LATELY, I'VE BEEN SELF-DESTRUCTIVE. PUSHING AWAY THE PEOPLE WHO CARE ABOUT ME.
AND I NEED TO MAKE AMENDS...
DEAD MAN WALKING.

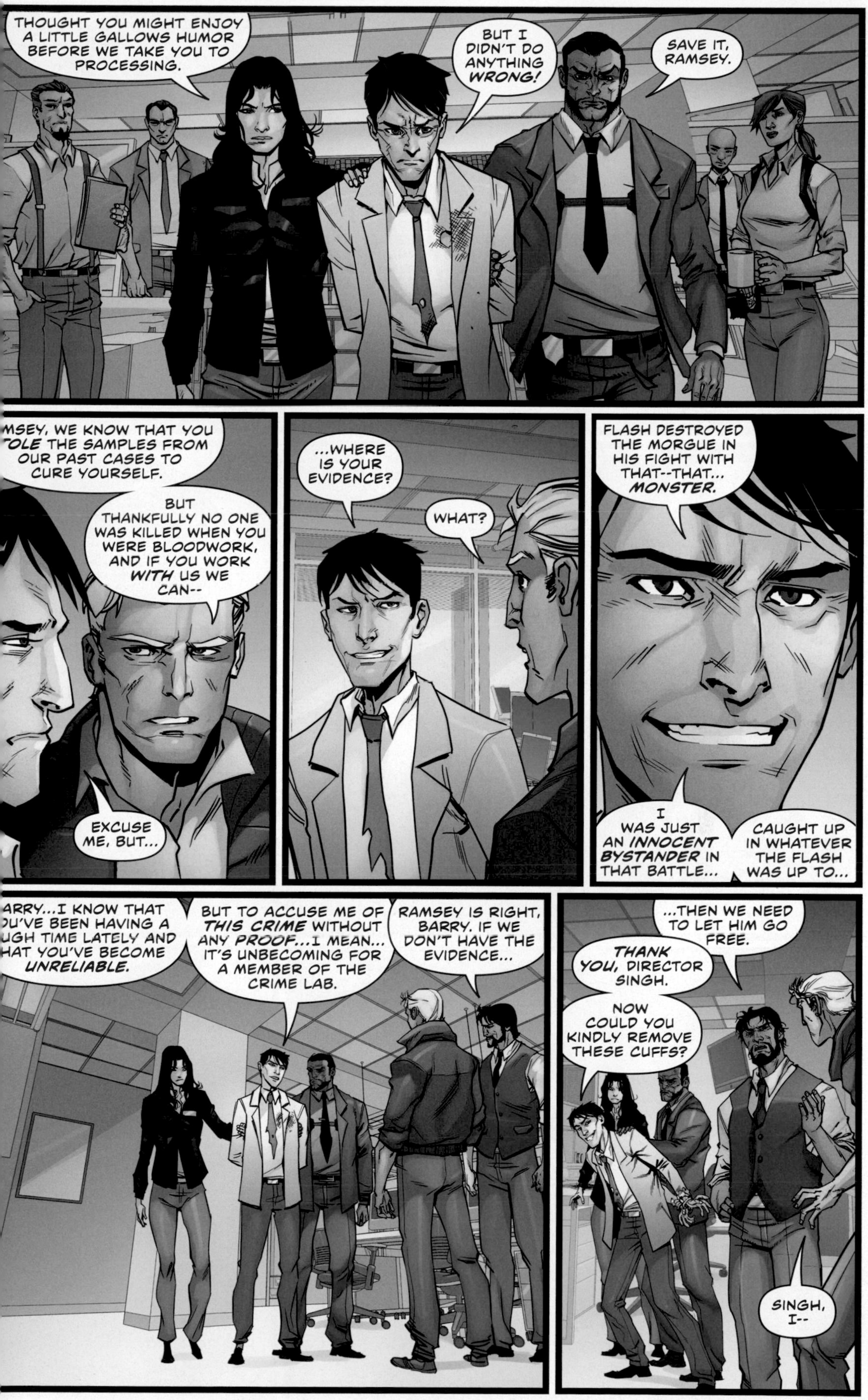

THOUGHT YOU MIGHT ENJOY A LITTLE GALLOWS HUMOR BEFORE WE TAKE YOU TO PROCESSING.
BUT I DIDN'T DO ANYTHING WRONG!
SAVE IT, RAMSEY.
MSEY, WE KNOW THAT YOU TOLE THE SAMPLES FROM OUR PAST CASES TO CURE YOURSELF.
BUT THANKFULLY NO ONE WAS KILLED WHEN YOU WERE BLOODWORK, AND IF YOU WORK WITH US WE CAN--
EXCUSE ME, BUT...
...WHERE IS YOUR EVIDENCE?
WHAT?
FLASH DESTROYED THE MORGUE IN HIS FIGHT WITH THAT--THAT... MONSTER.
I WAS JUST AN INNOCENT BYSTANDER IN THAT BATTLE...
CAUGHT UP IN WHATEVER THE FLASH WAS UP TO...
ARRY...I KNOW THAT OU'VE BEEN HAVING A UGH TIME LATELY AND HAT YOU'VE BECOME UNRELIABLE.
BUT TO ACCUSE ME OF THIS CRIME WITHOUT ANY PROOF...I MEAN... IT'S UNBECOMING FOR A MEMBER OF THE CRIME LAB.
RAMSEY IS RIGHT, BARRY. IF WE DON'T HAVE THE EVIDENCE...
...THEN WE NEED TO LET HIM GO FREE.
THANK YOU, DIRECTOR SINGH.
NOW COULD YOU KINDLY REMOVE THESE CUFFS?
SINGH, I--

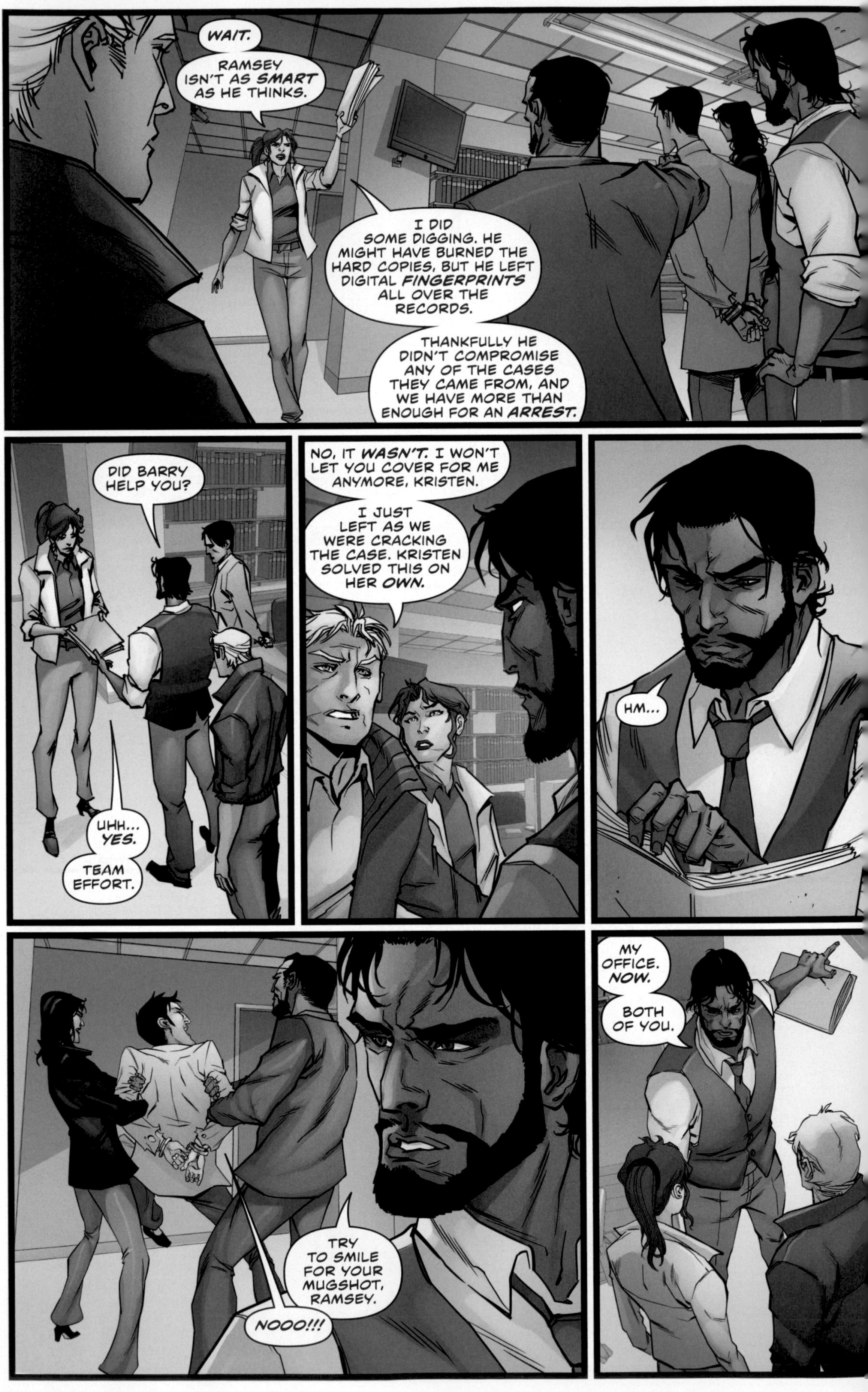
WAIT.
RAMSEY ISN'T AS SMART AS HE THINKS.
I DID SOME DIGGING. HE MIGHT HAVE BURNED THE HARD COPIES, BUT HE LEFT DIGITAL FINGERPRINTS ALL OVER THE RECORDS.
THANKFULLY HE DIDN'T COMPROMISE ANY OF THE CASES THEY CAME FROM, AND WE HAVE MORE THAN ENOUGH FOR AN ARREST.
DID BARRY HELP YOU?
UHH... YES.
TEAM EFFORT.
NO, IT WASN'T. I WON'T LET YOU COVER FOR ME ANYMORE, KRISTEN.
I JUST LEFT AS WE WERE CRACKING THE CASE. KRISTEN SOLVED THIS ON HER OWN.
HM...
TRY TO SMILE FOR YOUR MUGSHOT, RAMSEY.
NOOO!!!
MY OFFICE. NOW.
BOTH OF YOU.

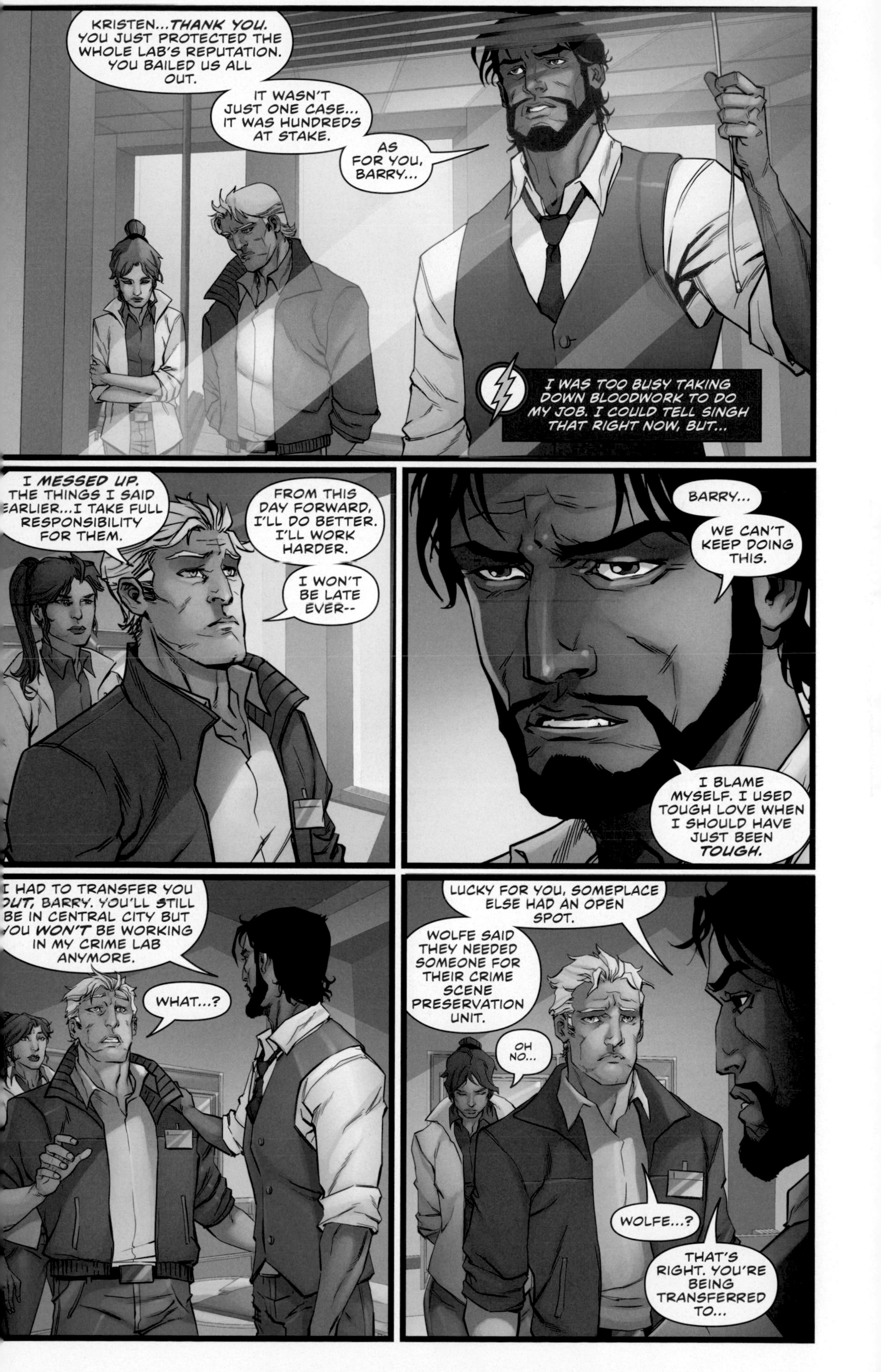
KRISTEN...THANK YOU. YOU JUST PROTECTED THE WHOLE LAB'S REPUTATION. YOU BAILED US ALL OUT.
IT WASN'T JUST ONE CASE... IT WAS HUNDREDS AT STAKE.
AS FOR YOU, BARRY...
I WAS TOO BUSY TAKING DOWN BLOODWORK TO DO MY JOB. I COULD TELL SINGH THAT RIGHT NOW, BUT...
I MESSED UP. THE THINGS I SAID EARLIER...I TAKE FULL RESPONSIBILITY FOR THEM.
FROM THIS DAY FORWARD, I'LL DO BETTER. I'LL WORK HARDER.
I WON'T BE LATE EVER--
BARRY...
WE CAN'T KEEP DOING THIS.
I BLAME MYSELF. I USED TOUGH LOVE WHEN I SHOULD HAVE JUST BEEN TOUGH.
I HAD TO TRANSFER YOU OUT, BARRY. YOU'LL STILL BE IN CENTRAL CITY BUT YOU WON'T BE WORKING IN MY CRIME LAB ANYMORE.
WHAT...?
LUCKY FOR YOU, SOMEPLACE ELSE HAD AN OPEN SPOT.
WOLFE SAID THEY NEEDED SOMEONE FOR THEIR CRIME SCENE PRESERVATION UNIT.
OH NO...
WOLFE...?
THAT'S RIGHT. YOU'RE BEING TRANSFERRED TO...

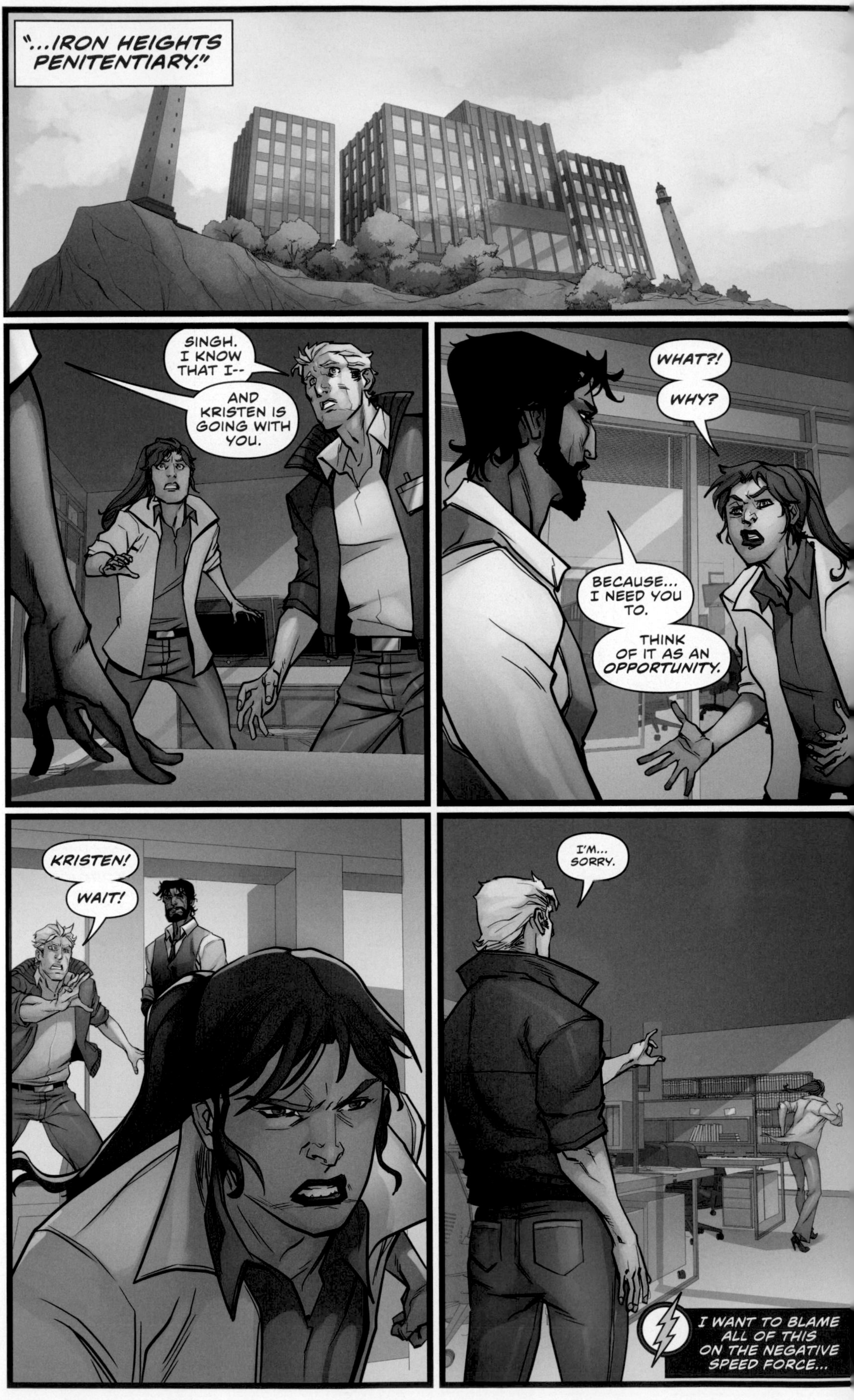
"...IRON HEIGHTS PENITENTIARY."
SINGH. I KNOW THAT I--
AND KRISTEN IS GOING WITH YOU.
WHAT?!
WHY?
BECAUSE... I NEED YOU TO.
THINK OF IT AS AN OPPORTUNITY.
KRISTEN!
WAIT!
I'M... SORRY.
I WANT TO BLAME ALL OF THIS ON THE NEGATIVE SPEED FORCE...

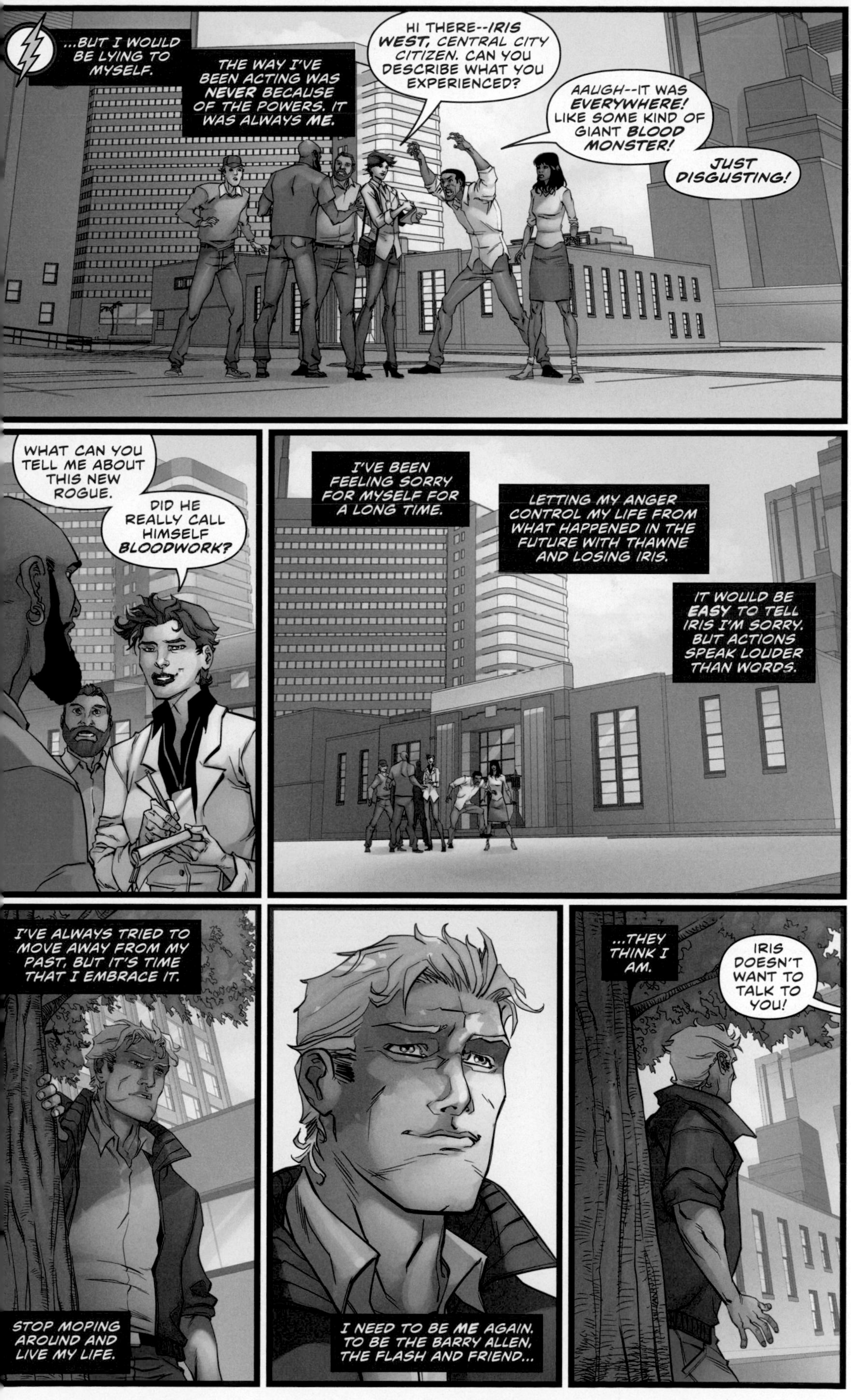

...BUT I WOULD BE LYING TO MYSELF.
THE WAY I'VE BEEN ACTING WAS NEVER BECAUSE OF THE POWERS. IT WAS ALWAYS ME.
HI THERE--IRIS WEST, CENTRAL CITY CITIZEN. CAN YOU DESCRIBE WHAT YOU EXPERIENCED?
AAUGH--IT WAS EVERYWHERE! LIKE SOME KIND OF GIANT BLOOD MONSTER!
JUST DISGUSTING!
WHAT CAN YOU TELL ME ABOUT THIS NEW ROGUE.
DID HE REALLY CALL HIMSELF BLOODWORK?
I'VE BEEN FEELING SORRY FOR MYSELF FOR A LONG TIME.
LETTING MY ANGER CONTROL MY LIFE FROM WHAT HAPPENED IN THE FUTURE WITH THAWNE AND LOSING IRIS.
IT WOULD BE EASY TO TELL IRIS I'M SORRY. BUT ACTIONS SPEAK LOUDER THAN WORDS.
I'VE ALWAYS TRIED TO MOVE AWAY FROM MY PAST, BUT IT'S TIME THAT I EMBRACE IT.
STOP MOPING AROUND AND LIVE MY LIFE.
I NEED TO BE ME AGAIN. TO BE THE BARRY ALLEN, THE FLASH AND FRIEND...
...THEY THINK I AM.
IRIS DOESN'T WANT TO TALK TO YOU!

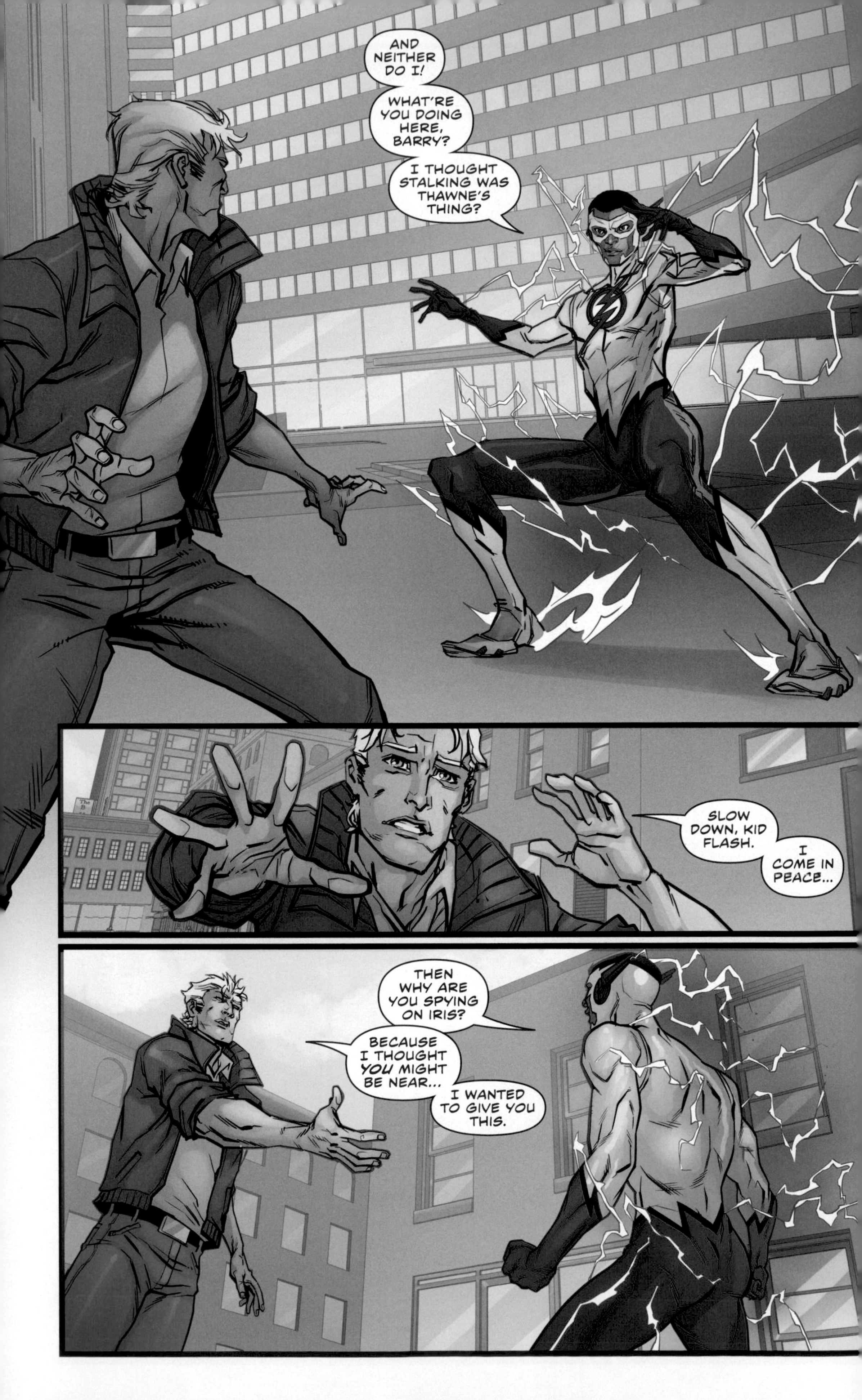
AND NEITHER DO I!
WHAT'RE YOU DOING HERE, BARRY?
I THOUGHT STALKING WAS THAWNE'S THING?
SLOW DOWN, KID FLASH.
I COME IN PEACE...
THEN WHY ARE YOU SPYING ON IRIS?
BECAUSE I THOUGHT *YOU* MIGHT BE NEAR...
I WANTED TO GIVE YOU THIS.

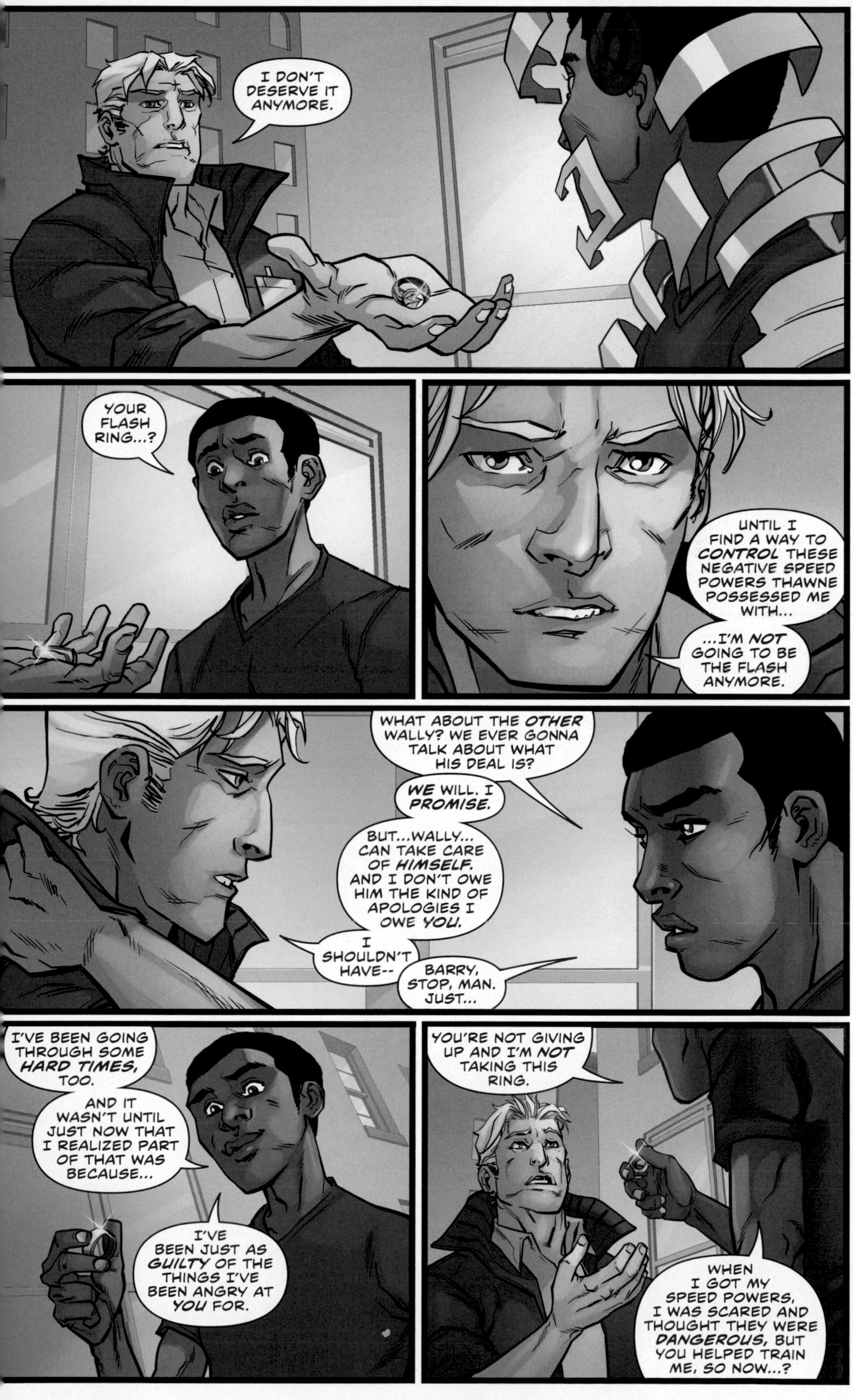
I DON'T DESERVE IT ANYMORE.
YOUR FLASH RING...?
UNTIL I FIND A WAY TO *CONTROL* THESE NEGATIVE SPEED POWERS THAWNE POSSESSED ME WITH...
...I'M *NOT* GOING TO BE THE FLASH ANYMORE.
WHAT ABOUT THE *OTHER* WALLY? WE EVER GONNA TALK ABOUT WHAT HIS DEAL IS?
WE WILL. I *PROMISE.*
BUT...WALLY... CAN TAKE CARE OF *HIMSELF.* AND I DON'T OWE HIM THE KIND OF APOLOGIES I OWE *YOU.*
I SHOULDN'T HAVE--
BARRY, STOP, MAN. JUST...
I'VE BEEN GOING THROUGH SOME *HARD TIMES,* TOO.
AND IT WASN'T UNTIL JUST NOW THAT I REALIZED PART OF THAT WAS BECAUSE...
I'VE BEEN JUST AS *GUILTY* OF THE THINGS I'VE BEEN ANGRY AT *YOU* FOR.
YOU'RE NOT GIVING UP AND I'M *NOT* TAKING THIS RING.
WHEN I GOT MY SPEED POWERS, I WAS SCARED AND THOUGHT THEY WERE *DANGEROUS,* BUT YOU HELPED TRAIN ME, SO NOW...?

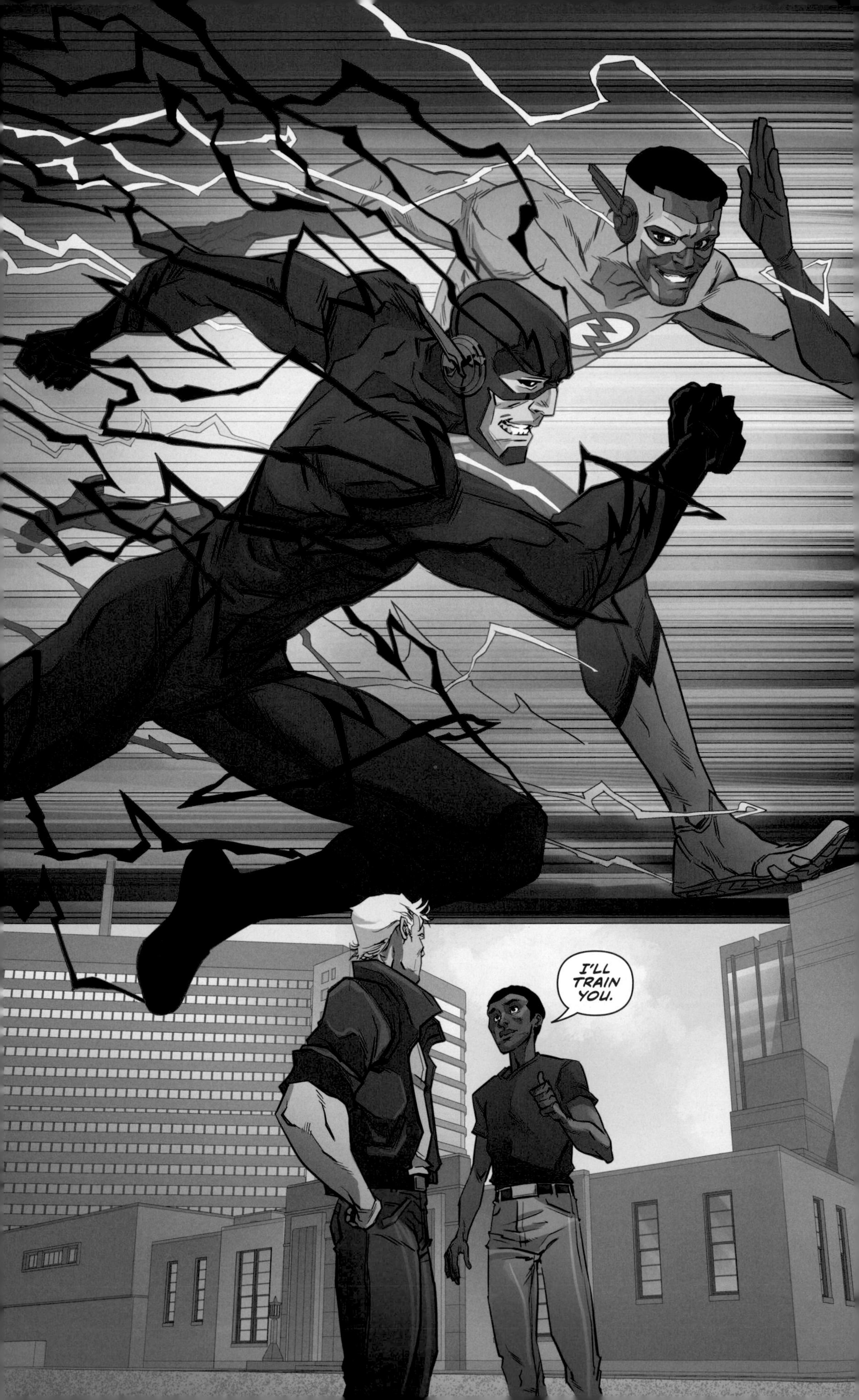
I'LL TRAIN YOU.

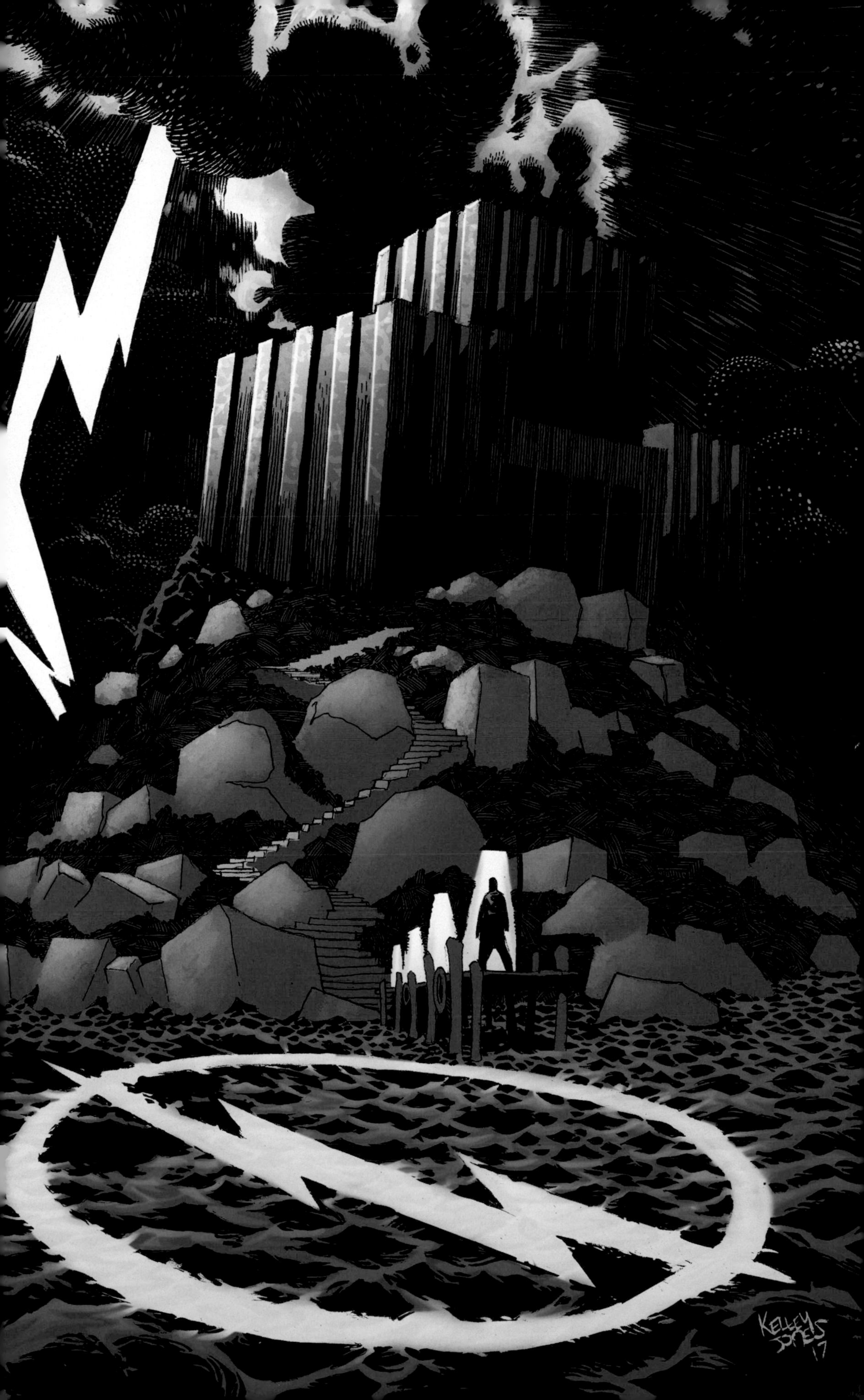
KELLEY JONES
17

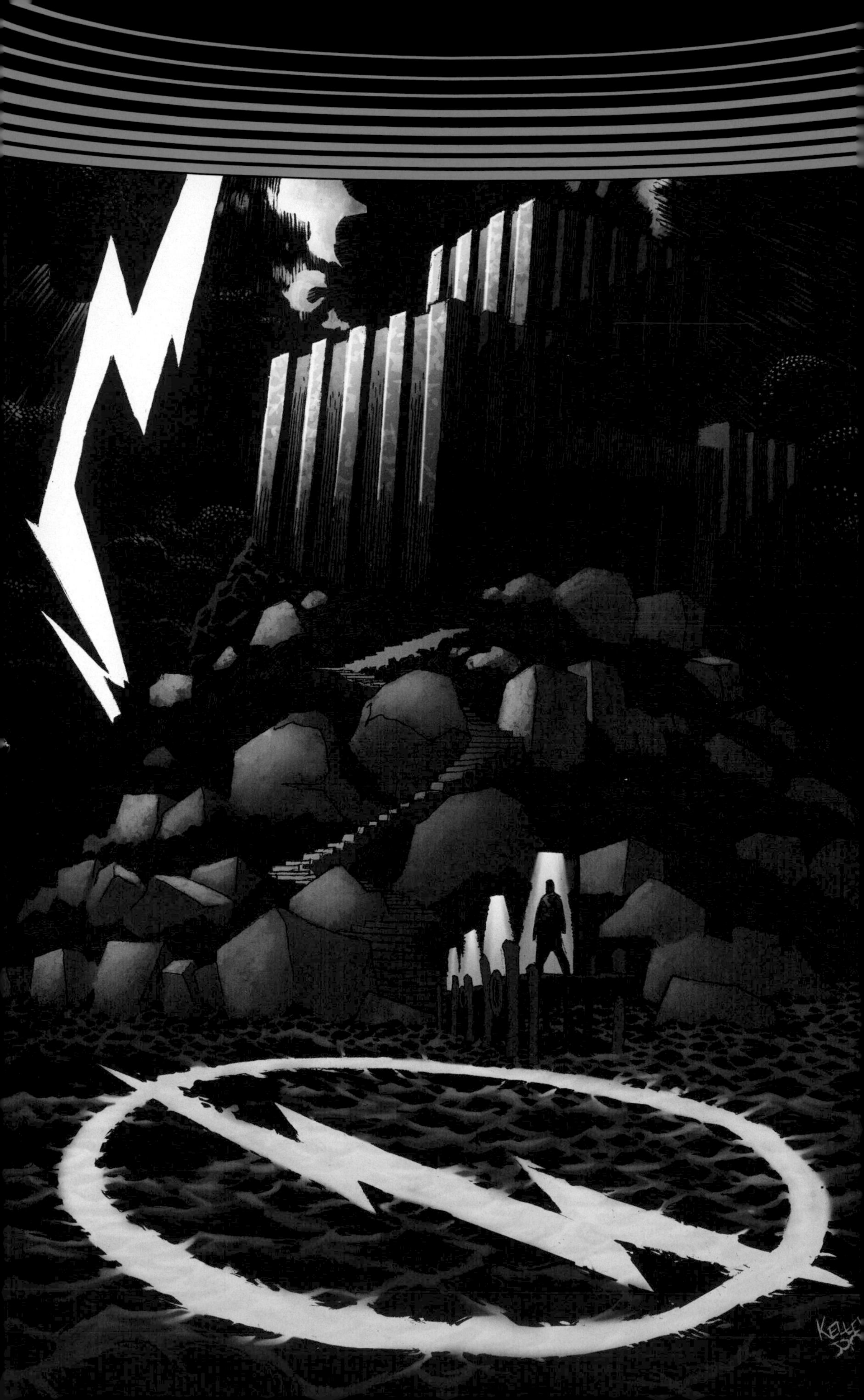

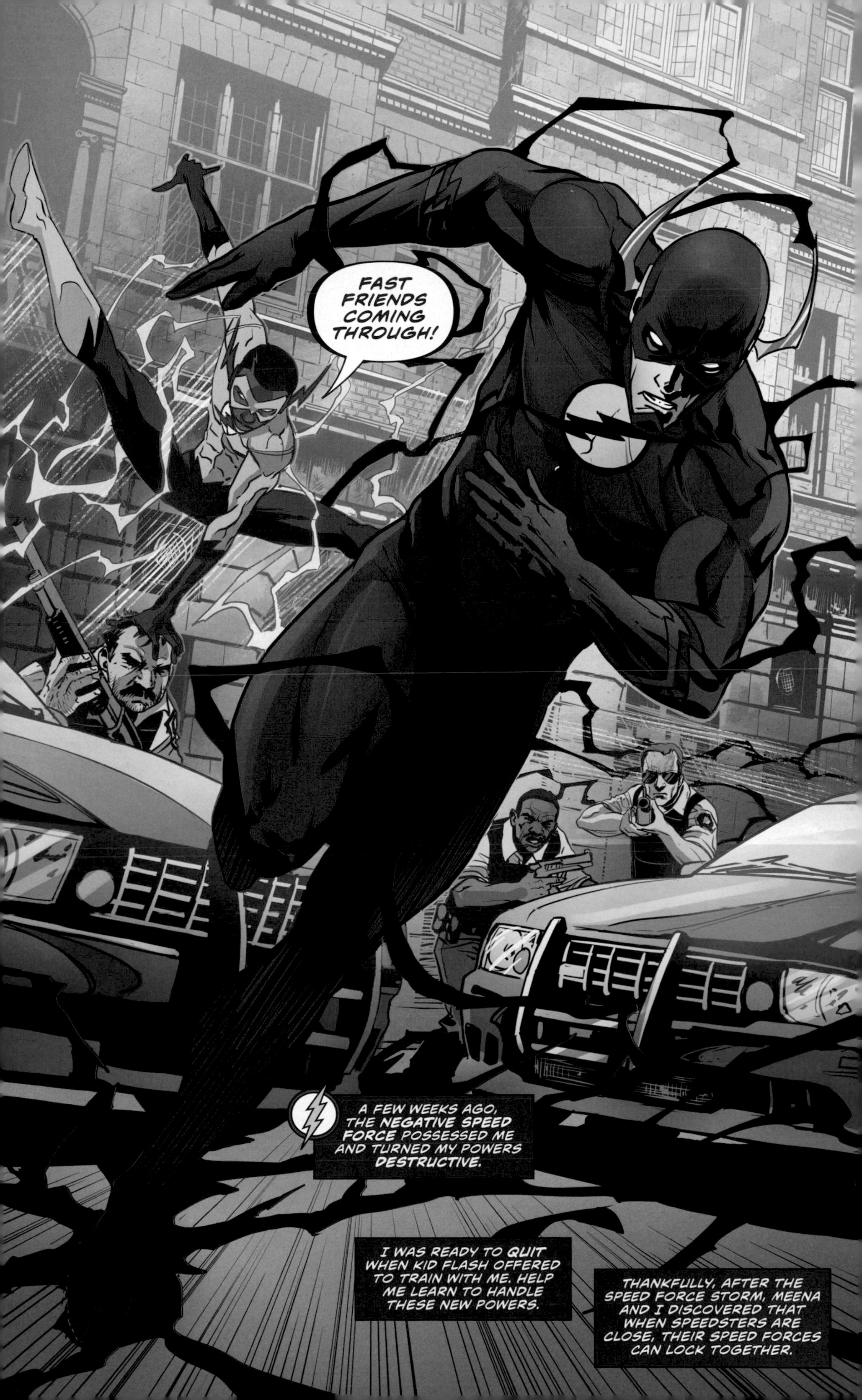
FAST FRIENDS COMING THROUGH!
A FEW WEEKS AGO, THE NEGATIVE SPEED FORCE POSSESSED ME AND TURNED MY POWERS DESTRUCTIVE.
I WAS READY TO QUIT WHEN KID FLASH OFFERED TO TRAIN WITH ME. HELP ME LEARN TO HANDLE THESE NEW POWERS.
THANKFULLY, AFTER THE SPEED FORCE STORM, MEENA AND I DISCOVERED THAT WHEN SPEEDSTERS ARE CLOSE, THEIR SPEED FORCES CAN LOCK TOGETHER.

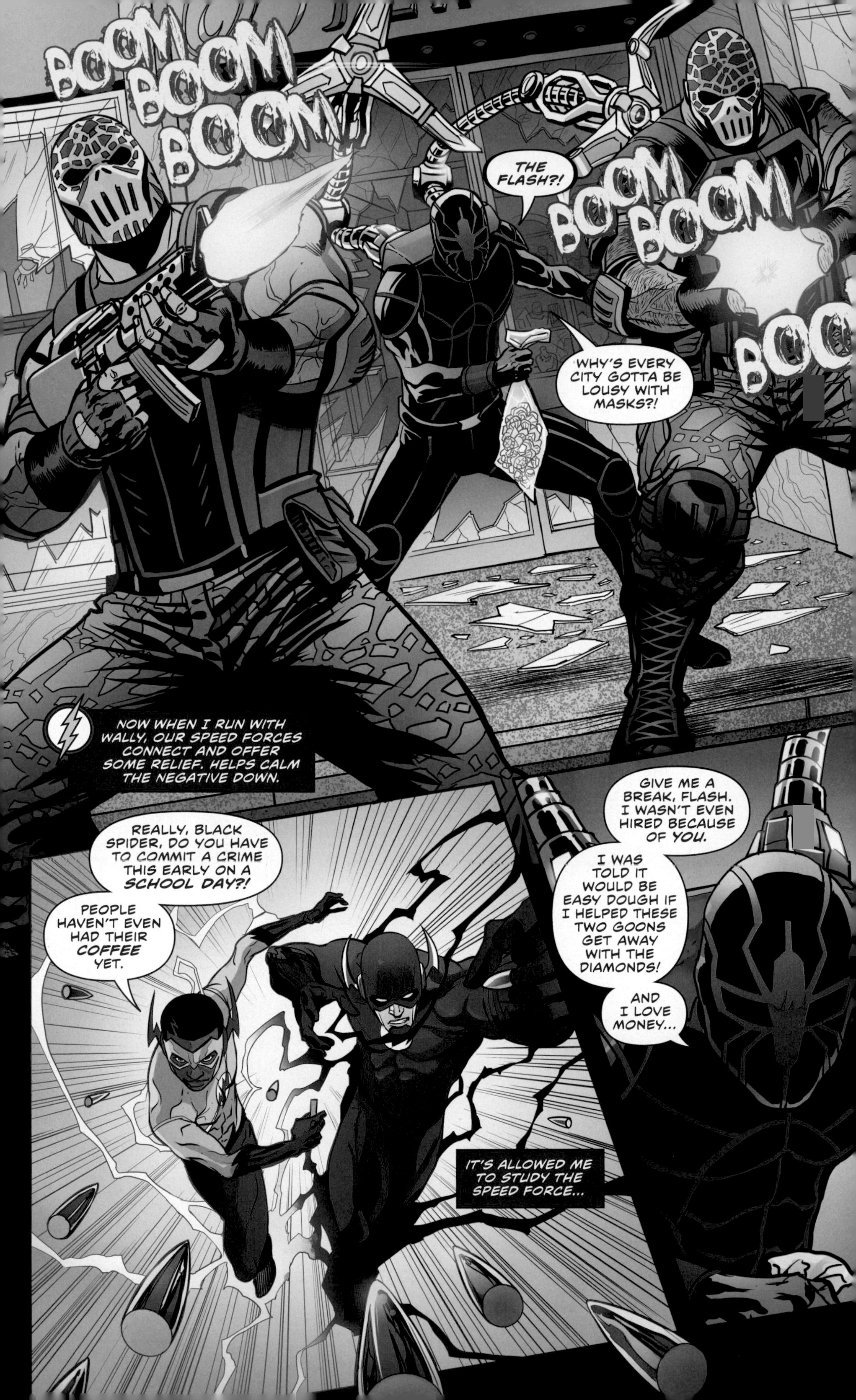

BOOM BOOM BOOM
THE FLASH?!
BOOM BOOM BOO
WHY'S EVERY CITY GOTTA BE LOUSY WITH MASKS?!
NOW WHEN I RUN WITH WALLY, OUR SPEED FORCES CONNECT AND OFFER SOME RELIEF. HELPS CALM THE NEGATIVE DOWN.
REALLY, BLACK SPIDER, DO YOU HAVE TO COMMIT A CRIME THIS EARLY ON A SCHOOL DAY?!
PEOPLE HAVEN'T EVEN HAD THEIR COFFEE YET.
GIVE ME A BREAK, FLASH. I WASN'T EVEN HIRED BECAUSE OF YOU.
I WAS TOLD IT WOULD BE EASY DOUGH IF I HELPED THESE TWO GOONS GET AWAY WITH THE DIAMONDS!
AND I LOVE MONEY...
IT'S ALLOWED ME TO STUDY THE SPEED FORCE...

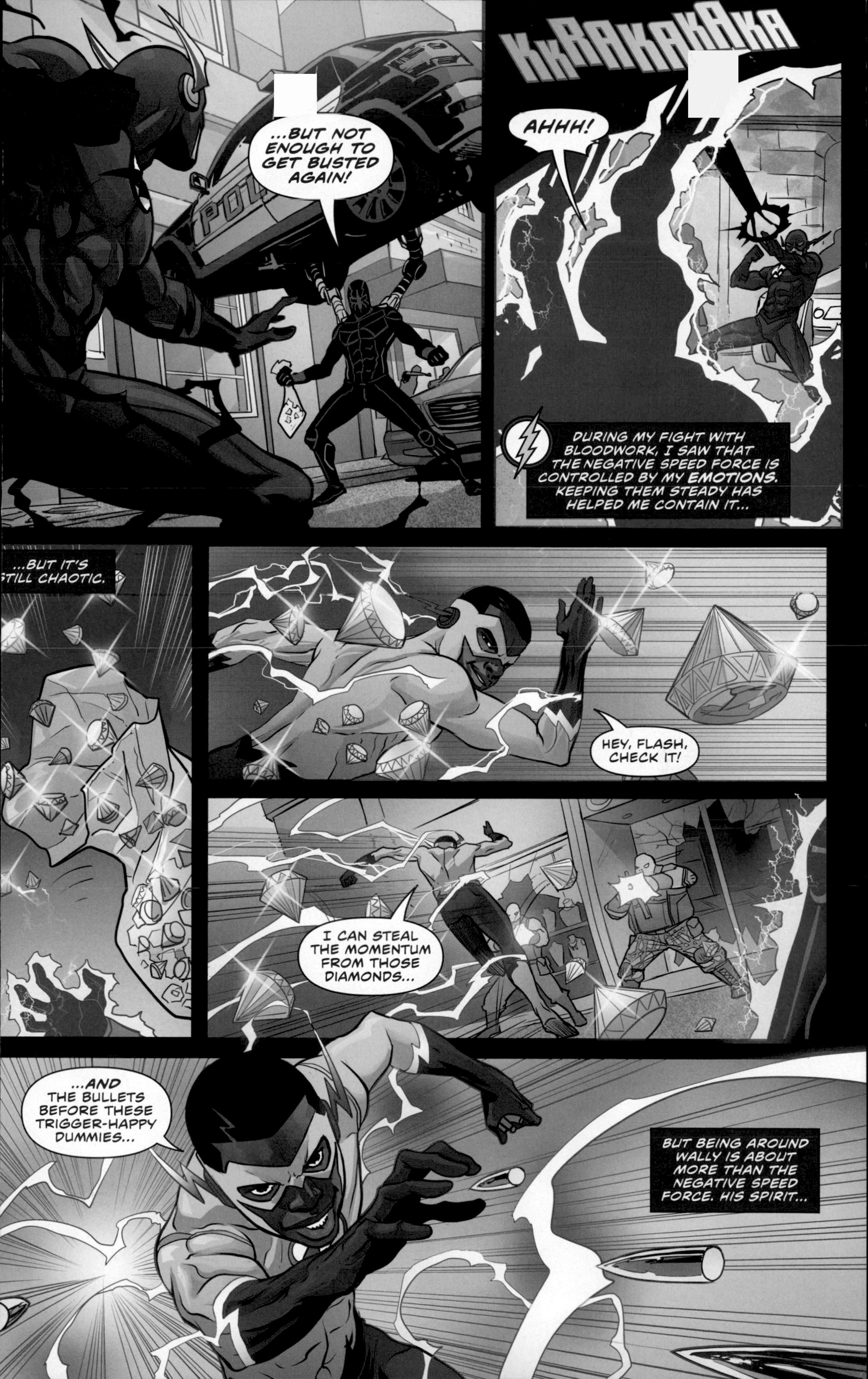
...BUT NOT ENOUGH TO GET BUSTED AGAIN!
KKRAKAKAKA
AHHH!
DURING MY FIGHT WITH BLOODWORK, I SAW THAT THE NEGATIVE SPEED FORCE IS CONTROLLED BY MY EMOTIONS. KEEPING THEM STEADY HAS HELPED ME CONTAIN IT...
...BUT IT'S STILL CHAOTIC.
HEY, FLASH, CHECK IT!
I CAN STEAL THE MOMENTUM FROM THOSE DIAMONDS...
...AND THE BULLETS BEFORE THESE TRIGGER-HAPPY DUMMIES...
BUT BEING AROUND WALLY IS ABOUT MORE THAN THE NEGATIVE SPEED FORCE. HIS SPIRIT...

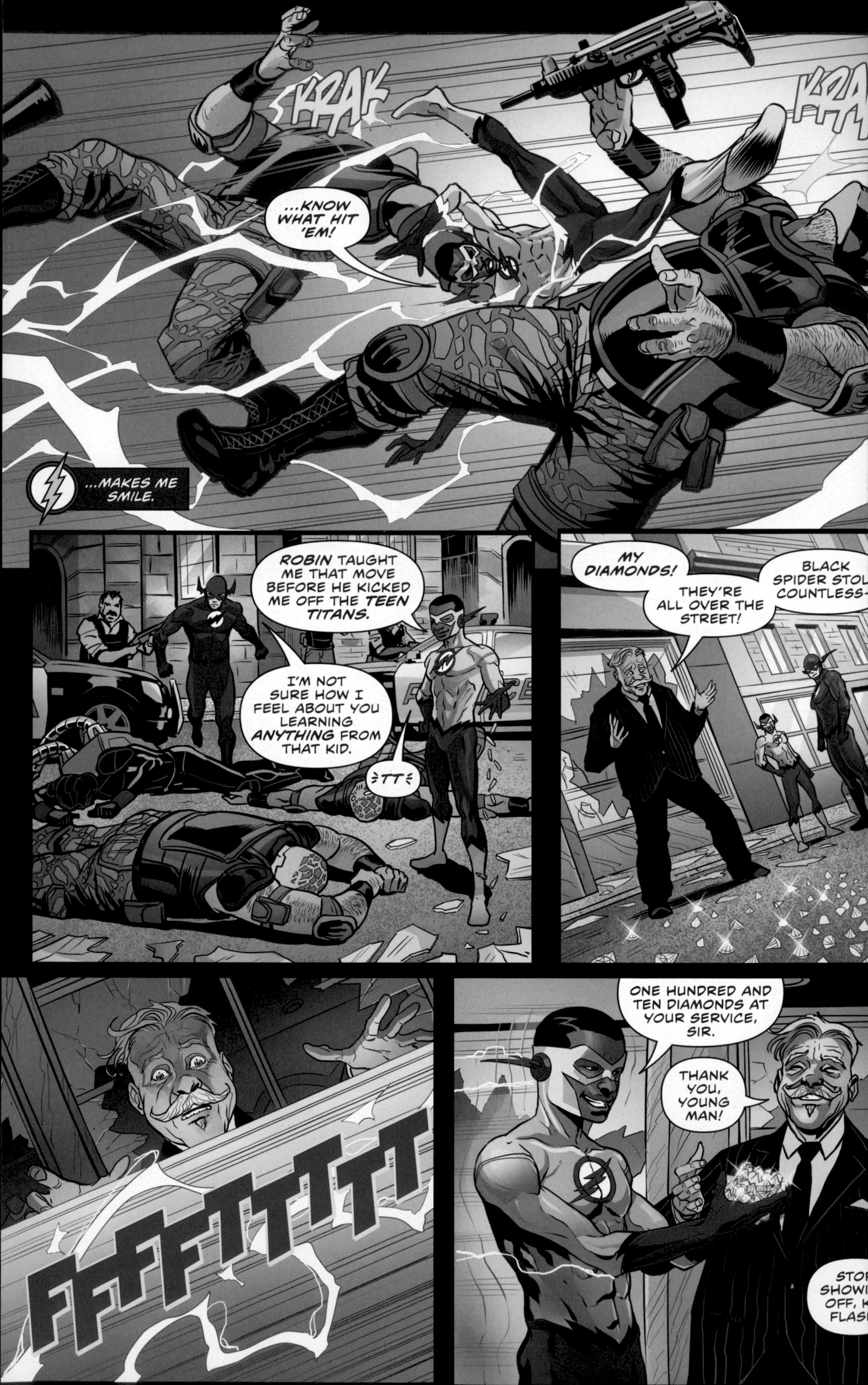
KRAK
KRAK
...KNOW WHAT HIT 'EM!
...MAKES ME SMILE.
ROBIN TAUGHT ME THAT MOVE BEFORE HE KICKED ME OFF THE TEEN TITANS.
I'M NOT SURE HOW I FEEL ABOUT YOU LEARNING ANYTHING FROM THAT KID.
TT
MY DIAMONDS!
THEY'RE ALL OVER THE STREET!
BLACK SPIDER STOL COUNTLESS-
FFFFTTTTTT
ONE HUNDRED AND TEN DIAMONDS AT YOUR SERVICE, SIR.
THANK YOU, YOUNG MAN!

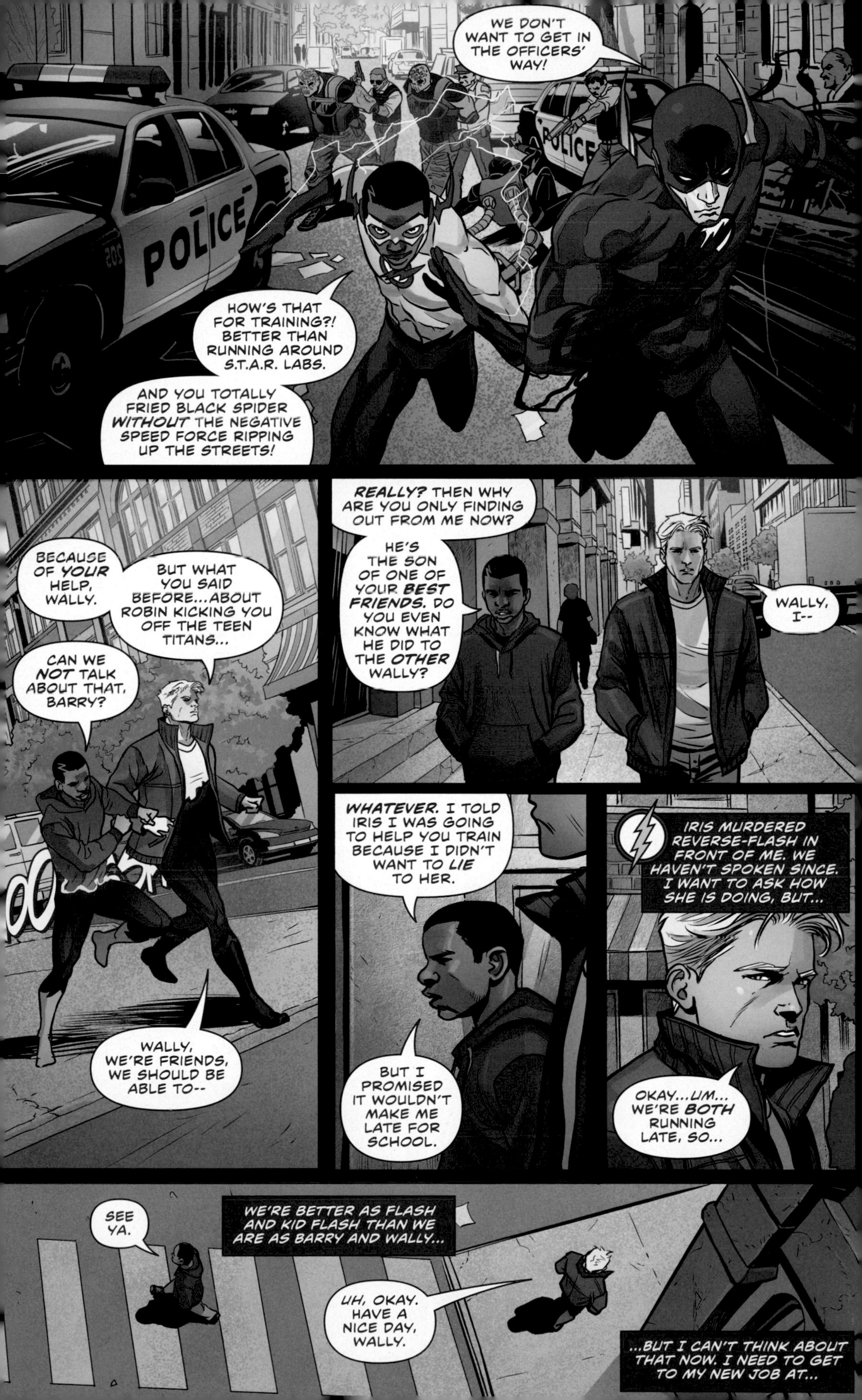
WE DON'T WANT TO GET IN THE OFFICERS' WAY!
POLICE
POLICE
HOW'S THAT FOR TRAINING?! BETTER THAN RUNNING AROUND S.T.A.R. LABS.
AND YOU TOTALLY FRIED BLACK SPIDER WITHOUT THE NEGATIVE SPEED FORCE RIPPING UP THE STREETS!
BECAUSE OF YOUR HELP, WALLY.
BUT WHAT YOU SAID BEFORE...ABOUT ROBIN KICKING YOU OFF THE TEEN TITANS...
CAN WE NOT TALK ABOUT THAT, BARRY?
WALLY, WE'RE FRIENDS, WE SHOULD BE ABLE TO--
REALLY? THEN WHY ARE YOU ONLY FINDING OUT FROM ME NOW?
HE'S THE SON OF ONE OF YOUR BEST FRIENDS. DO YOU EVEN KNOW WHAT HE DID TO THE OTHER WALLY?
WALLY, I--
WHATEVER. I TOLD IRIS I WAS GOING TO HELP YOU TRAIN BECAUSE I DIDN'T WANT TO LIE TO HER.
BUT I PROMISED IT WOULDN'T MAKE ME LATE FOR SCHOOL.
IRIS MURDERED REVERSE-FLASH IN FRONT OF ME. WE HAVEN'T SPOKEN SINCE. I WANT TO ASK HOW SHE IS DOING, BUT...
OKAY...UM... WE'RE BOTH RUNNING LATE, SO...
SEE YA.
WE'RE BETTER AS FLASH AND KID FLASH THAN WE ARE AS BARRY AND WALLY...
UH, OKAY. HAVE A NICE DAY, WALLY.
...BUT I CAN'T THINK ABOUT THAT NOW. I NEED TO GET TO MY NEW JOB AT...

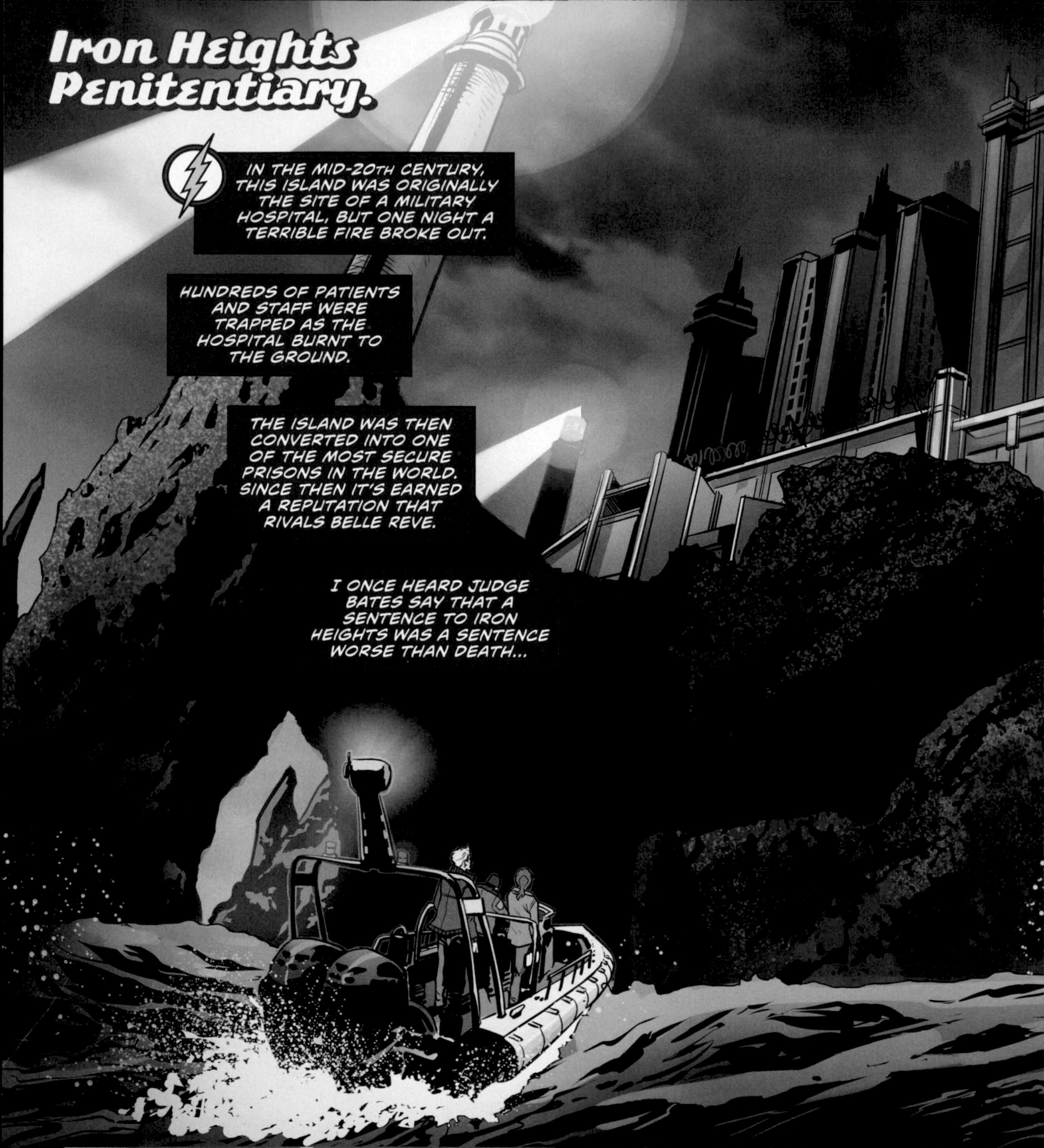
Iron Heights Penitentiary.
IN THE MID-20TH CENTURY, THIS ISLAND WAS ORIGINALLY THE SITE OF A MILITARY HOSPITAL, BUT ONE NIGHT A TERRIBLE FIRE BROKE OUT.
HUNDREDS OF PATIENTS AND STAFF WERE TRAPPED AS THE HOSPITAL BURNT TO THE GROUND.
THE ISLAND WAS THEN CONVERTED INTO ONE OF THE MOST SECURE PRISONS IN THE WORLD. SINCE THEN IT'S EARNED A REPUTATION THAT RIVALS BELLE REVE.
I ONCE HEARD JUDGE BATES SAY THAT A SENTENCE TO IRON HEIGHTS WAS A SENTENCE WORSE THAN DEATH...

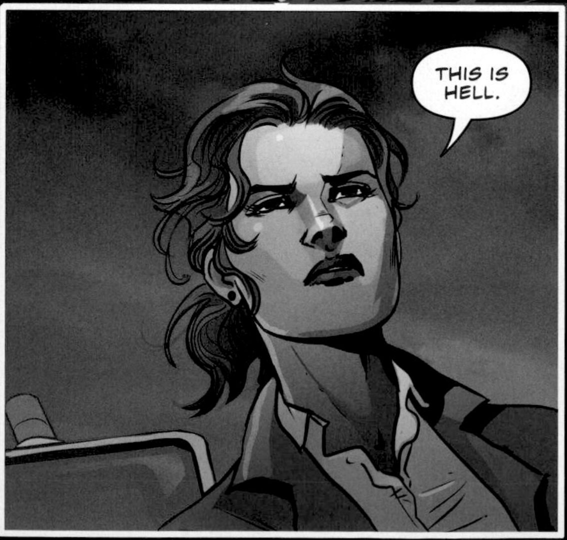
THIS IS HELL.

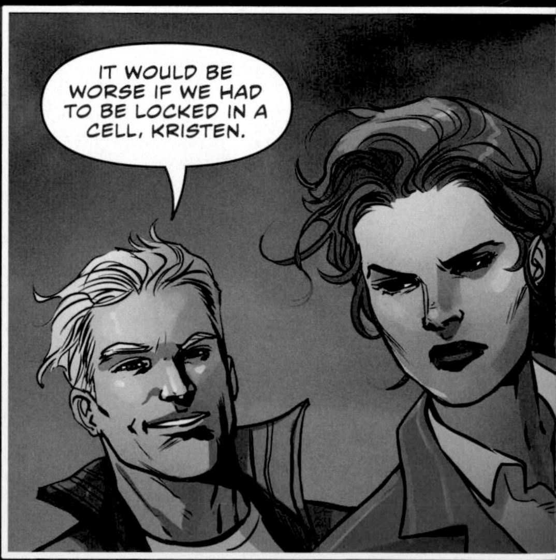
IT WOULD BE WORSE IF WE HAD TO BE LOCKED IN A CELL, KRISTEN.

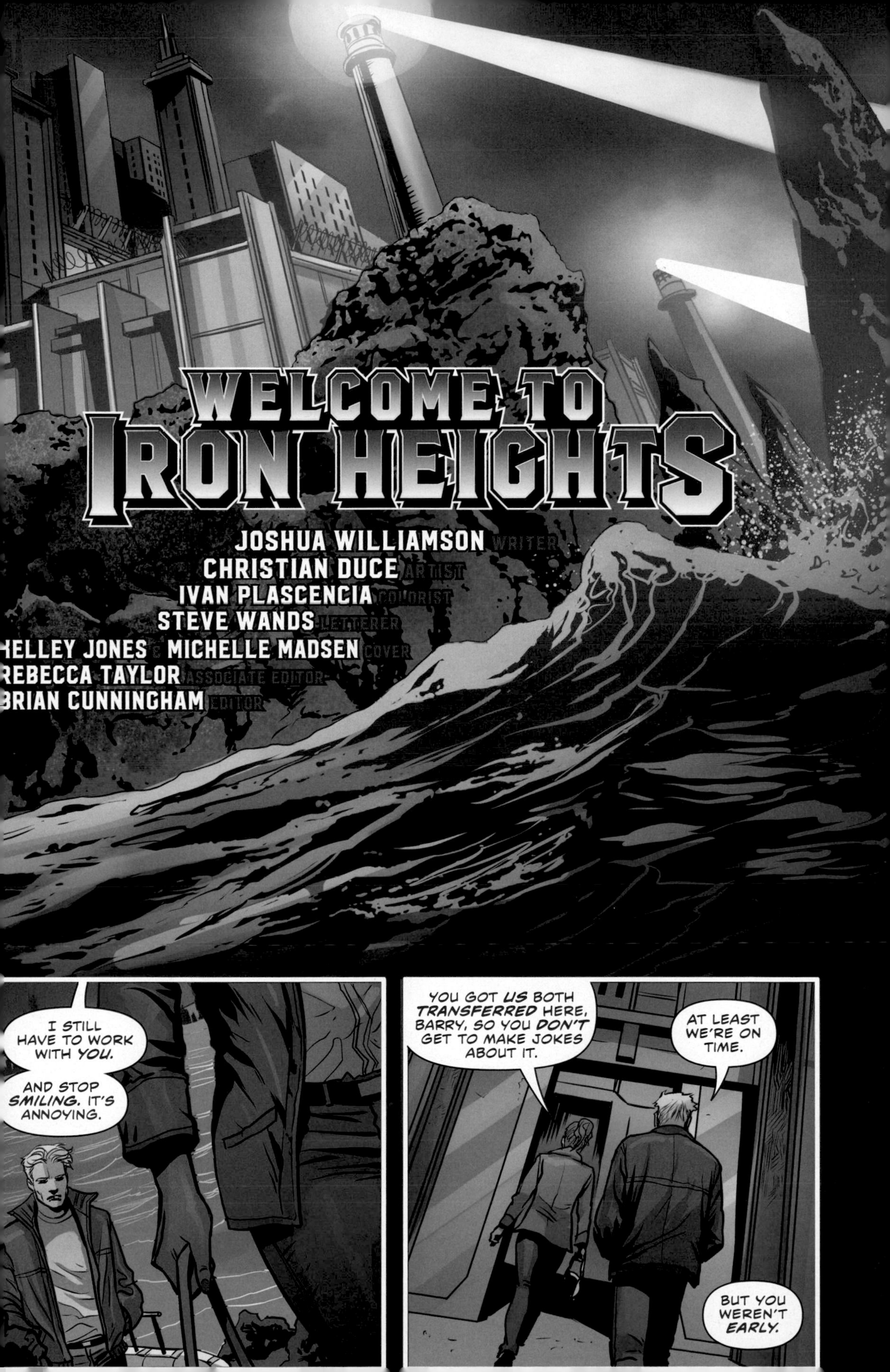
WELCOME TO
IRON HEIGHTS
JOSHUA WILLIAMSON WRITER
CHRISTIAN DUCE ARTIST
IVAN PLASCENCIA COLORIST
STEVE WANDS LETTERER
HELLEY JONES & MICHELLE MADSEN COVER
REBECCA TAYLOR ASSOCIATE EDITOR
BRIAN CUNNINGHAM EDITOR
I STILL HAVE TO WORK WITH YOU.
AND STOP SMILING. IT'S ANNOYING.
YOU GOT US BOTH TRANSFERRED HERE, BARRY, SO YOU DON'T GET TO MAKE JOKES ABOUT IT.
AT LEAST WE'RE ON TIME.
BUT YOU WEREN'T EARLY.

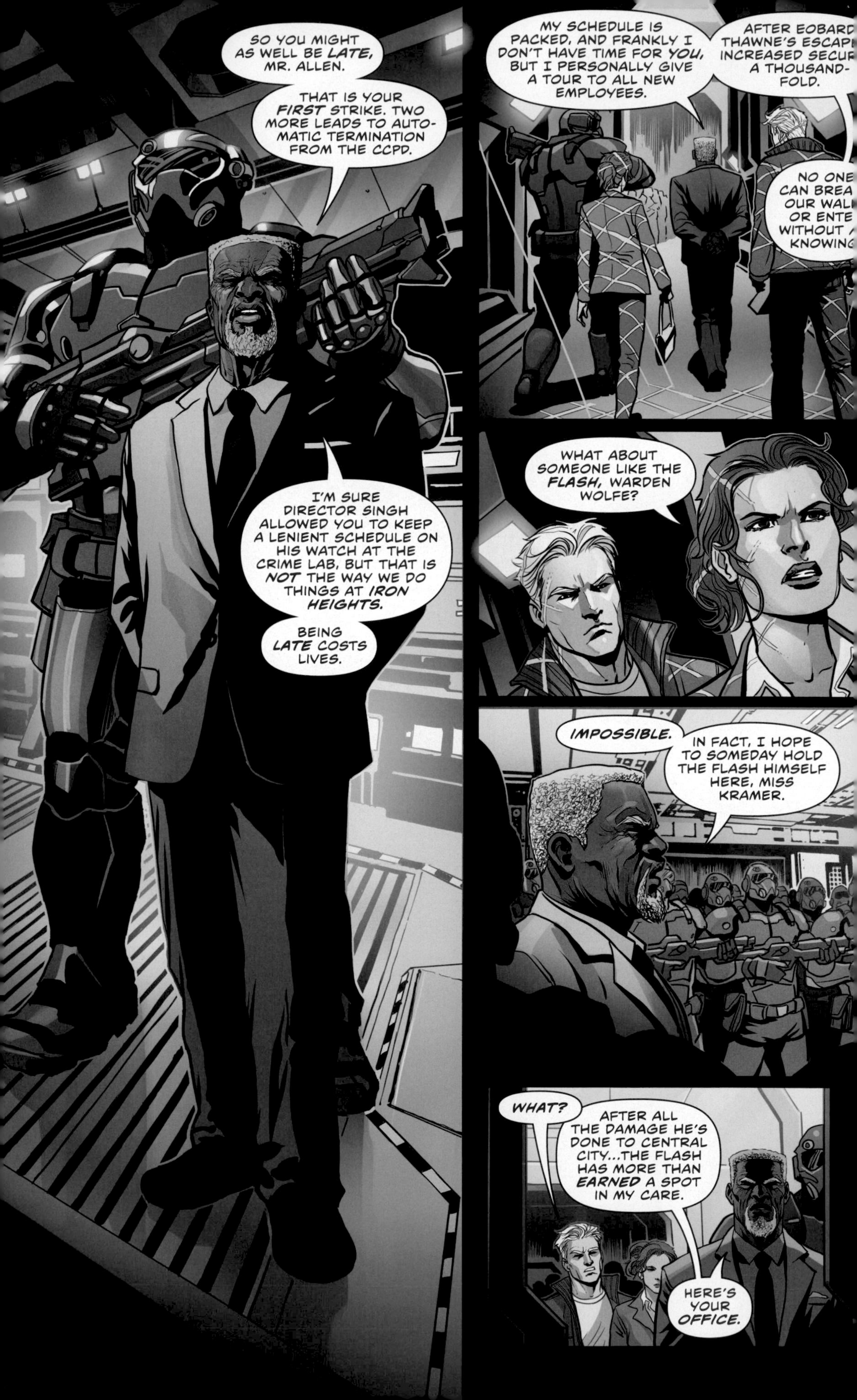

SO YOU MIGHT AS WELL BE LATE, MR. ALLEN.
THAT IS YOUR FIRST STRIKE. TWO MORE LEADS TO AUTOMATIC TERMINATION FROM THE CCPD.
I'M SURE DIRECTOR SINGH ALLOWED YOU TO KEEP A LENIENT SCHEDULE ON HIS WATCH AT THE CRIME LAB, BUT THAT IS NOT THE WAY WE DO THINGS AT IRON HEIGHTS.
BEING LATE COSTS LIVES.
MY SCHEDULE IS PACKED, AND FRANKLY I DON'T HAVE TIME FOR YOU, BUT I PERSONALLY GIVE A TOUR TO ALL NEW EMPLOYEES.
AFTER EOBARD THAWNE'S ESCAP INCREASED SECUR A THOUSAND-FOLD.
NO ONE CAN BREA OUR WAL OR ENTE WITHOUT KNOWING
WHAT ABOUT SOMEONE LIKE THE FLASH, WARDEN WOLFE?
IMPOSSIBLE.
IN FACT, I HOPE TO SOMEDAY HOLD THE FLASH HIMSELF HERE, MISS KRAMER.
WHAT?
AFTER ALL THE DAMAGE HE'S DONE TO CENTRAL CITY...THE FLASH HAS MORE THAN EARNED A SPOT IN MY CARE.
HERE'S YOUR OFFICE.

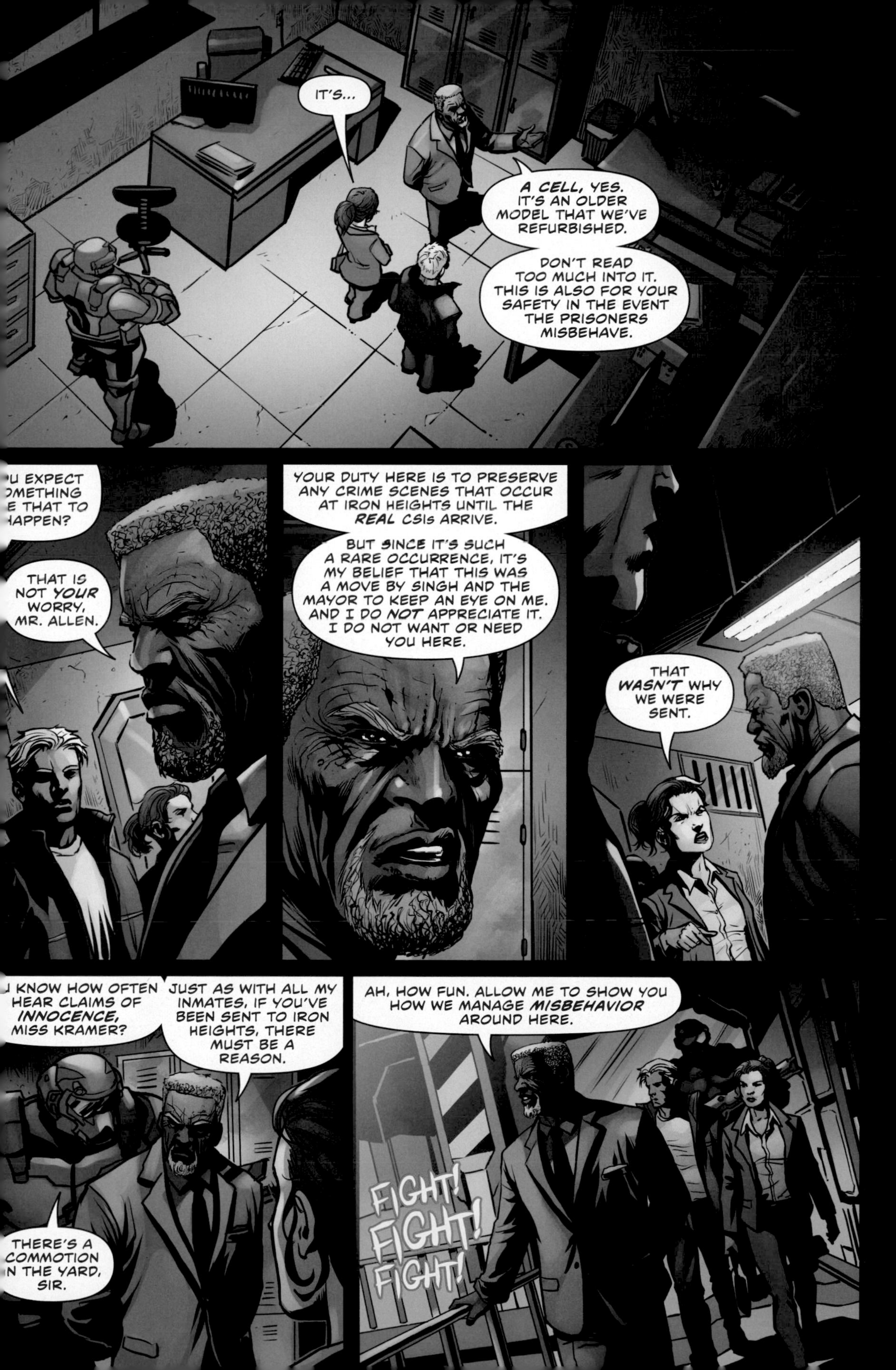

IT'S...
A CELL, YES. IT'S AN OLDER MODEL THAT WE'VE REFURBISHED.
DON'T READ TOO MUCH INTO IT. THIS IS ALSO FOR YOUR SAFETY IN THE EVENT THE PRISONERS MISBEHAVE.
U EXPECT OMETHING E THAT TO APPEN?
THAT IS NOT YOUR WORRY, MR. ALLEN.
YOUR DUTY HERE IS TO PRESERVE ANY CRIME SCENES THAT OCCUR AT IRON HEIGHTS UNTIL THE REAL CSIs ARRIVE.
BUT SINCE IT'S SUCH A RARE OCCURRENCE, IT'S MY BELIEF THAT THIS WAS A MOVE BY SINGH AND THE MAYOR TO KEEP AN EYE ON ME. AND I DO NOT APPRECIATE IT. I DO NOT WANT OR NEED YOU HERE.
THAT WASN'T WHY WE WERE SENT.
KNOW HOW OFTEN HEAR CLAIMS OF INNOCENCE, MISS KRAMER?
JUST AS WITH ALL MY INMATES, IF YOU'VE BEEN SENT TO IRON HEIGHTS, THERE MUST BE A REASON.
THERE'S A COMMOTION N THE YARD, SIR.
AH, HOW FUN. ALLOW ME TO SHOW YOU HOW WE MANAGE MISBEHAVIOR AROUND HERE.
FIGHT! FIGHT! FIGHT!

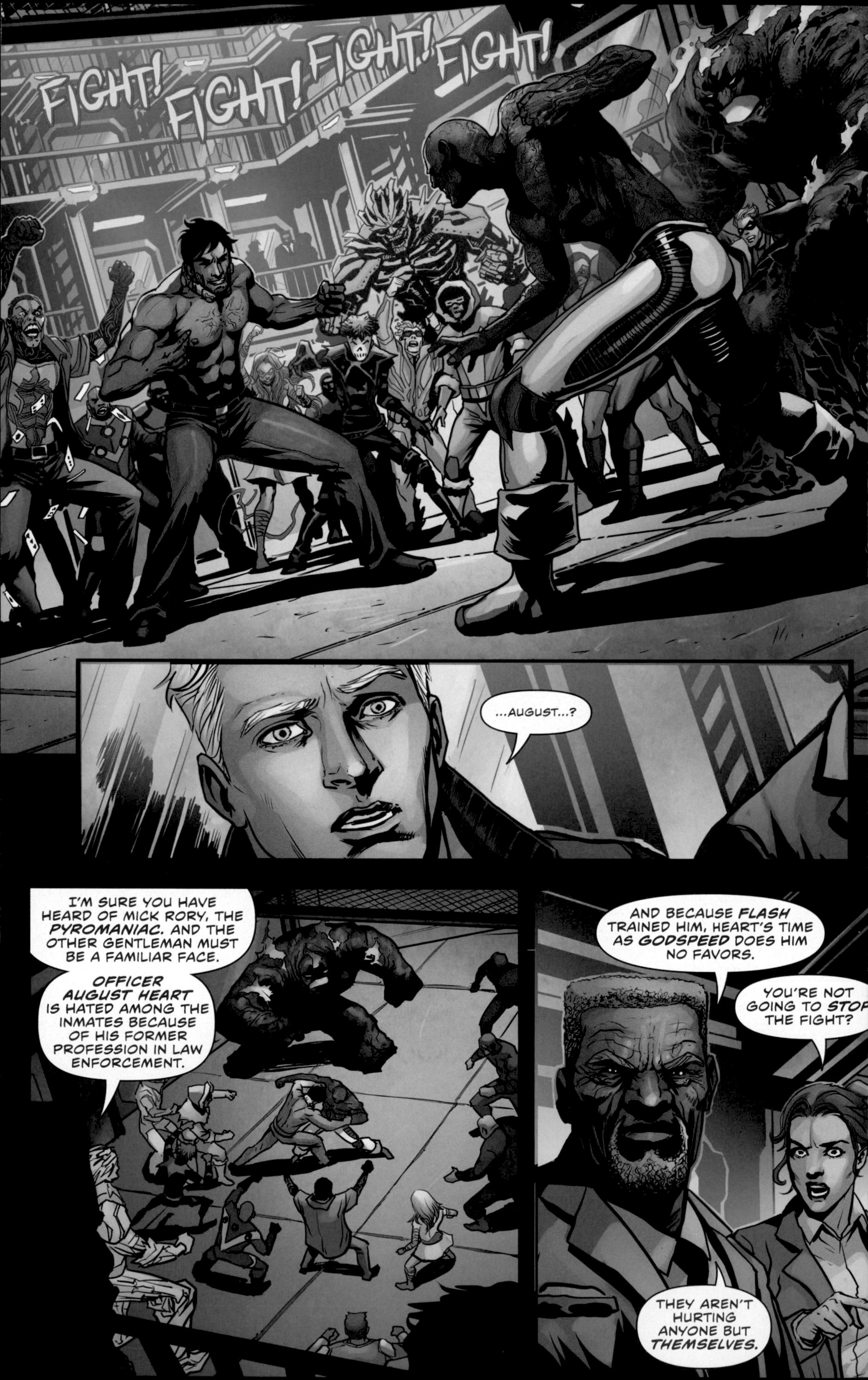
FIGHT! FIGHT! FIGHT! FIGHT!
...AUGUST...?
I'M SURE YOU HAVE HEARD OF MICK RORY, THE PYROMANIAC. AND THE OTHER GENTLEMAN MUST BE A FAMILIAR FACE.
OFFICER AUGUST HEART IS HATED AMONG THE INMATES BECAUSE OF HIS FORMER PROFESSION IN LAW ENFORCEMENT.
AND BECAUSE FLASH TRAINED HIM, HEART'S TIME AS GODSPEED DOES HIM NO FAVORS.
YOU'RE NOT GOING TO STOP THE FIGHT?
THEY AREN'T HURTING ANYONE BUT THEMSELVES.

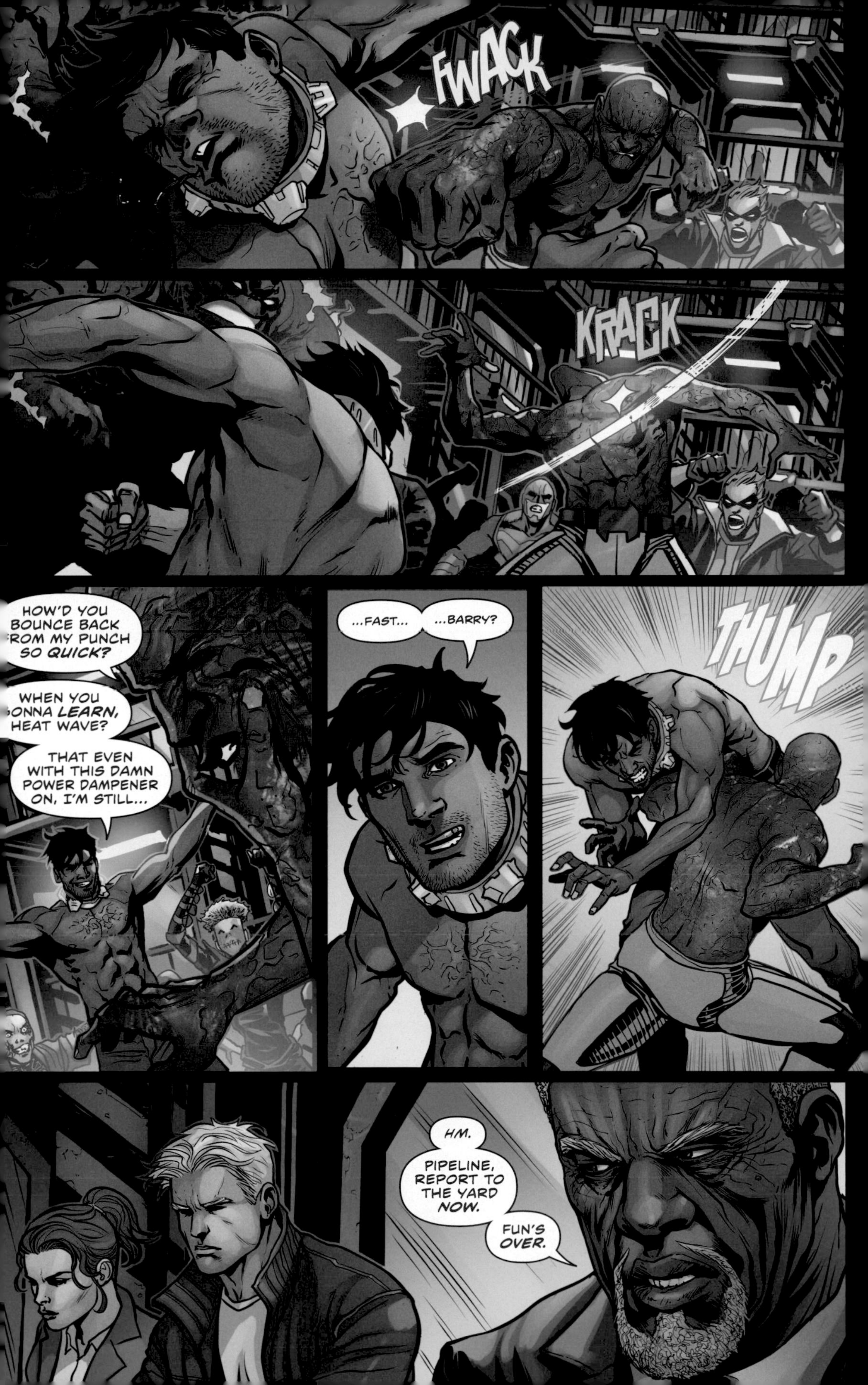
FWACK
KRACK
HOW'D YOU BOUNCE BACK FROM MY PUNCH SO QUICK?
WHEN YOU GONNA LEARN, HEAT WAVE?
THAT EVEN WITH THIS DAMN POWER DAMPENER ON, I'M STILL...
...FAST...
...BARRY?
THUMP
HM.
PIPELINE, REPORT TO THE YARD NOW.
FUN'S OVER.

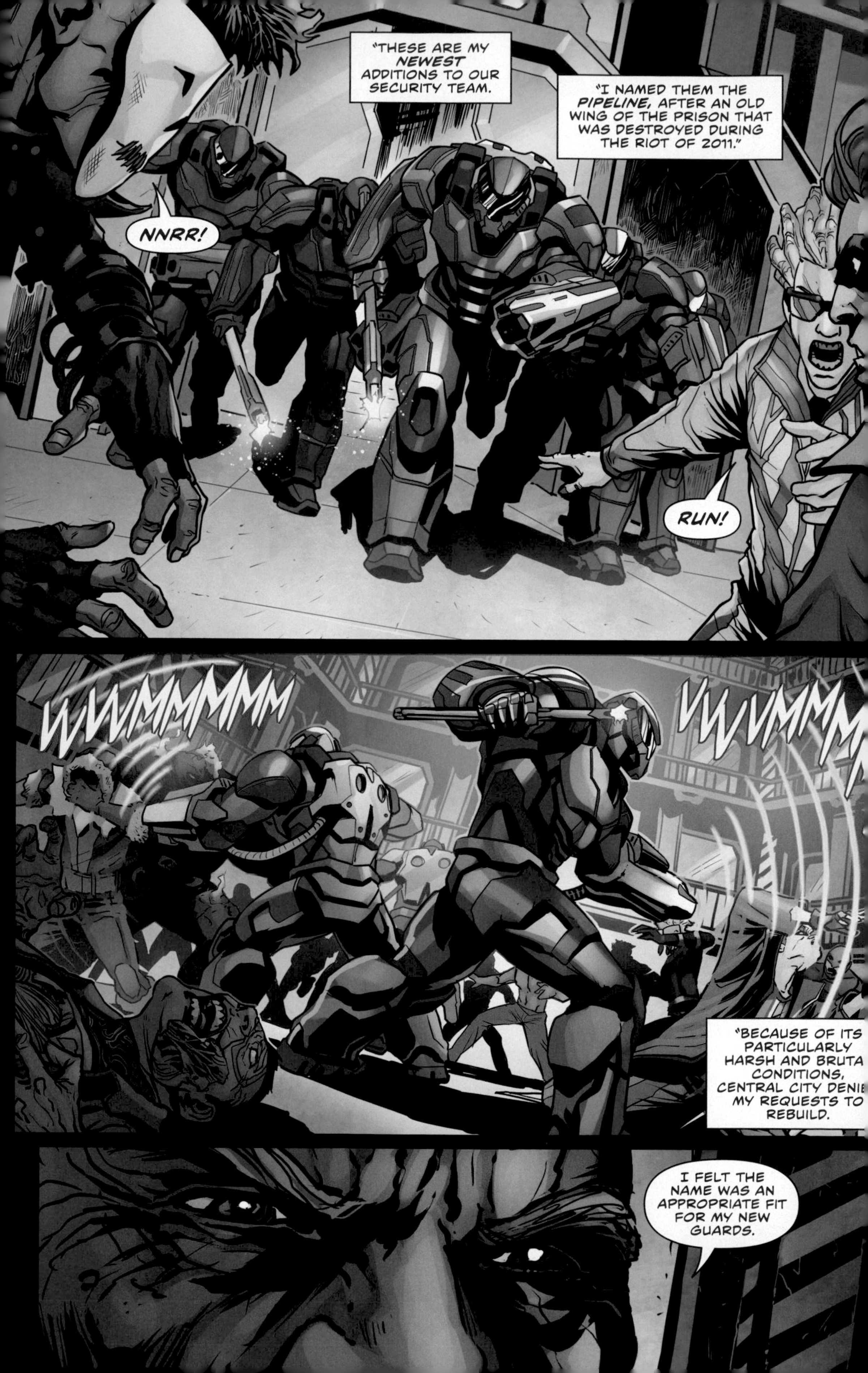

"THESE ARE MY *NEWEST* ADDITIONS TO OUR SECURITY TEAM.
"I NAMED THEM THE *PIPELINE,* AFTER AN OLD WING OF THE PRISON THAT WAS DESTROYED DURING THE RIOT OF 2011."
NNRR!
RUN!
VVVMMMMM
VVVMMM
"BECAUSE OF ITS PARTICULARLY HARSH AND BRUTA CONDITIONS, CENTRAL CITY DENIE MY REQUESTS TO REBUILD.
I FELT THE NAME WAS AN APPROPRIATE FIT FOR MY NEW GUARDS.

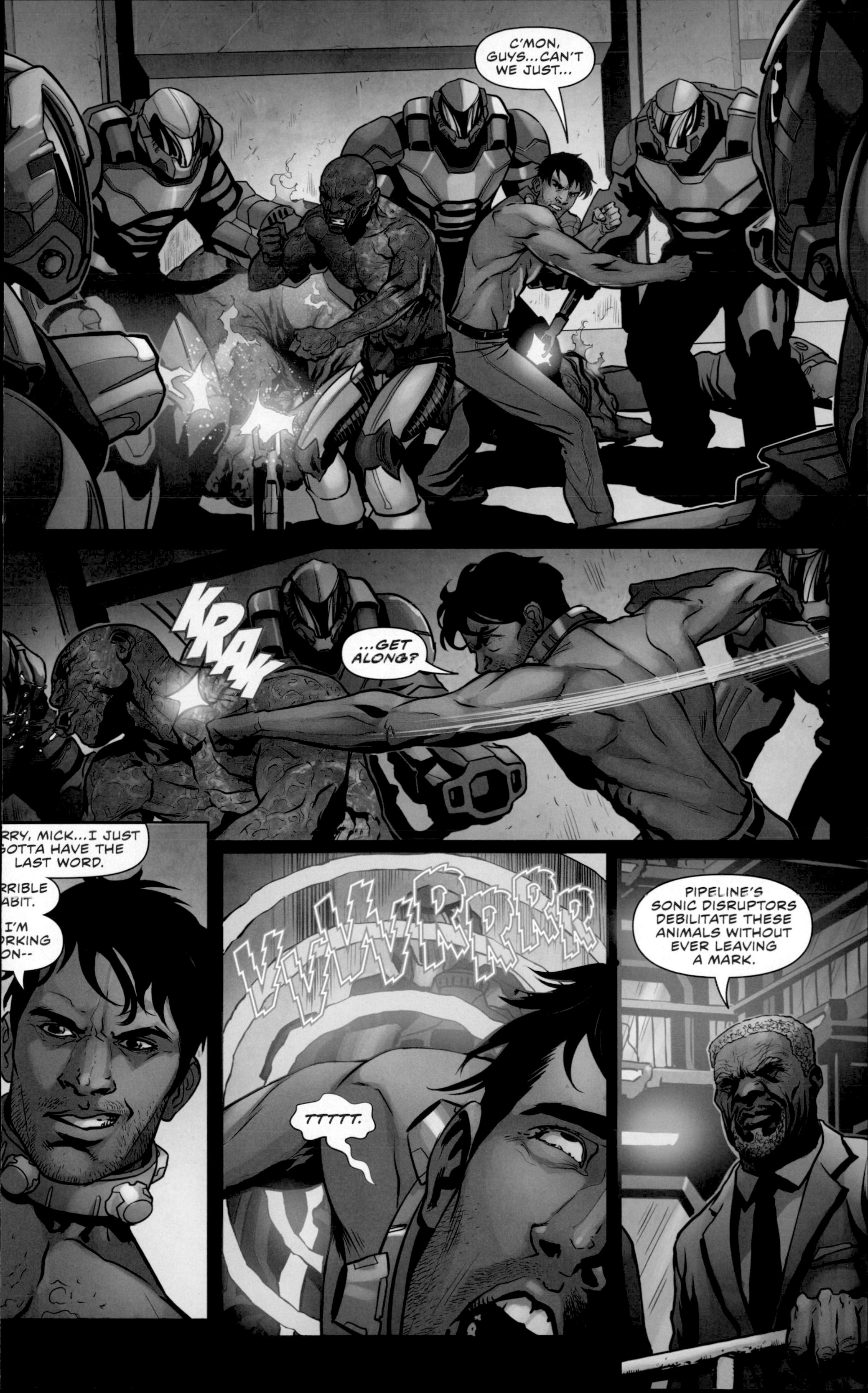
C'MON, GUYS...CAN'T WE JUST...
KRAK
...GET ALONG?
RRY, MICK...I JUST GOTTA HAVE THE LAST WORD.
RRIBLE ABIT.
I'M RKING ON--
VVVVRRRRR
TTTTT.
PIPELINE'S SONIC DISRUPTORS DEBILITATE THESE ANIMALS WITHOUT EVER LEAVING A MARK.

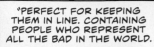

"PERFECT FOR KEEPING THEM IN LINE. CONTAINING PEOPLE WHO REPRESENT ALL THE BAD IN THE WORLD.

"IF I HAD MY WAY, THEY'D NEVER SEE THE LIGHT OF DAY *AGAIN*."

PSST, SIS, USE YOUR CONNECTIONS TO DIG UP WHY *ALLEN* IS HERE.

AND HOW HE KNOWS *HEART*.

SURE THING.

ISN'T THAT *FIGHT A CRIME SCENE?*

AUGUST HEART AND MICK RORY WERE ENGAGED IN AN ALTERCATION. *CASE CLOSED.*

WHY ARE THE *ROGUES* STILL DRESSED IN THEIR COSTU--

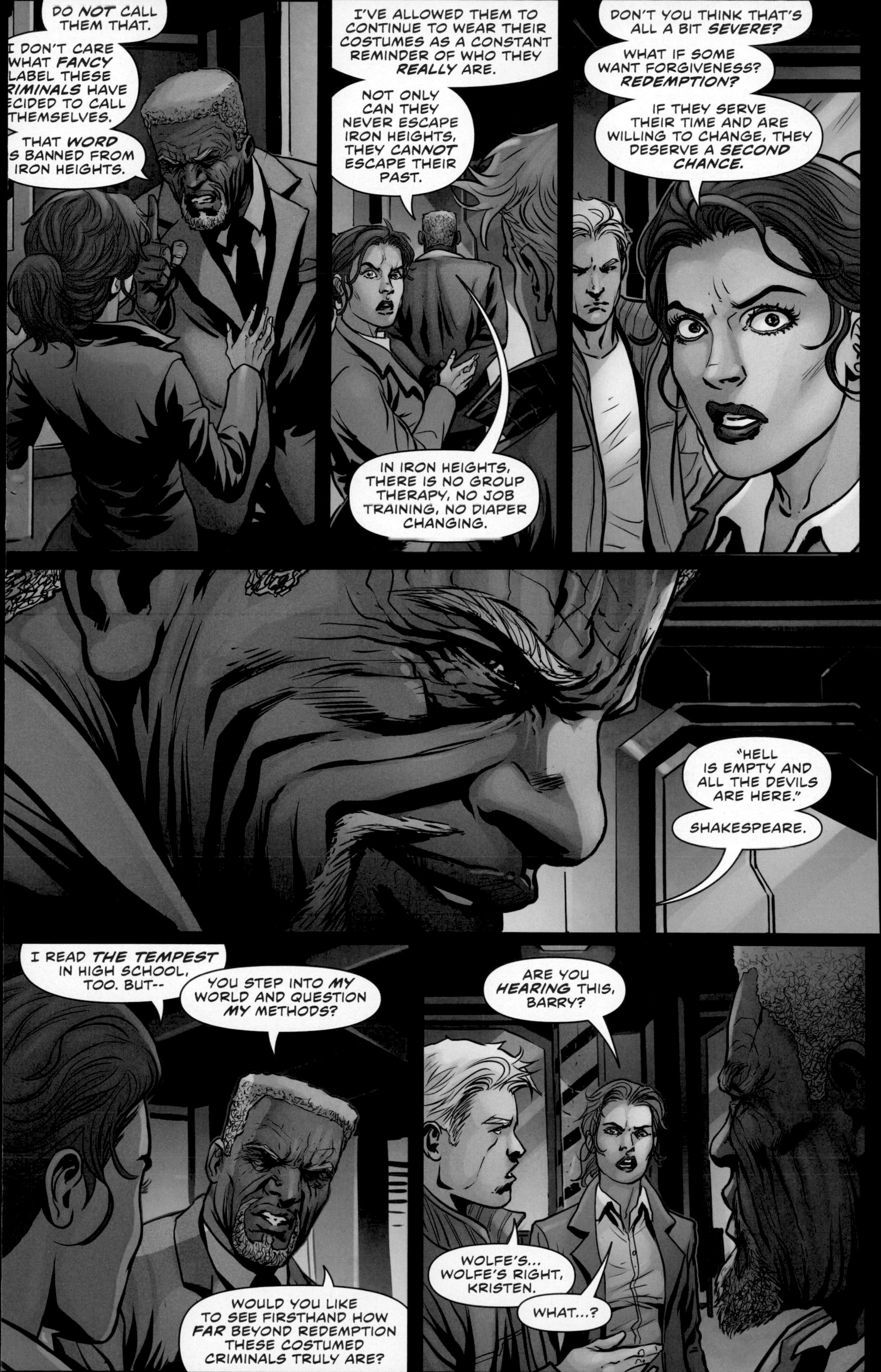
DO NOT CALL THEM THAT.
I DON'T CARE WHAT FANCY LABEL THESE CRIMINALS HAVE DECIDED TO CALL THEMSELVES.
THAT WORD IS BANNED FROM IRON HEIGHTS.
I'VE ALLOWED THEM TO CONTINUE TO WEAR THEIR COSTUMES AS A CONSTANT REMINDER OF WHO THEY REALLY ARE.
NOT ONLY CAN THEY NEVER ESCAPE IRON HEIGHTS, THEY CANNOT ESCAPE THEIR PAST.
IN IRON HEIGHTS, THERE IS NO GROUP THERAPY, NO JOB TRAINING, NO DIAPER CHANGING.
DON'T YOU THINK THAT'S ALL A BIT SEVERE?
WHAT IF SOME WANT FORGIVENESS? REDEMPTION?
IF THEY SERVE THEIR TIME AND ARE WILLING TO CHANGE, THEY DESERVE A SECOND CHANCE.
"HELL IS EMPTY AND ALL THE DEVILS ARE HERE."
SHAKESPEARE.
I READ THE TEMPEST IN HIGH SCHOOL, TOO. BUT--
YOU STEP INTO MY WORLD AND QUESTION MY METHODS?
WOULD YOU LIKE TO SEE FIRSTHAND HOW FAR BEYOND REDEMPTION THESE COSTUMED CRIMINALS TRULY ARE?
ARE YOU HEARING THIS, BARRY?
WOLFE'S... WOLFE'S RIGHT, KRISTEN.
WHAT...?

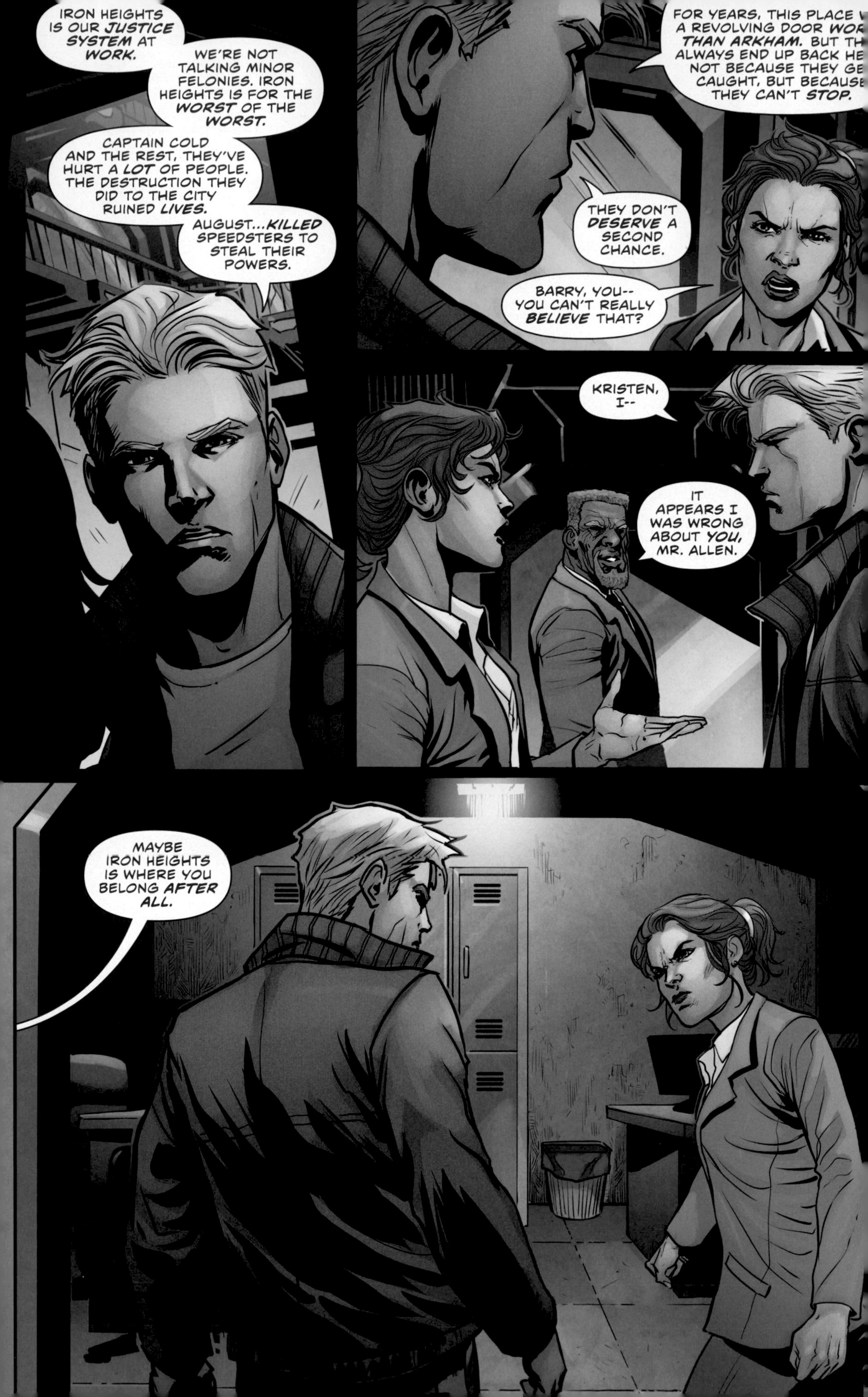
IRON HEIGHTS IS OUR JUSTICE SYSTEM AT WORK.
WE'RE NOT TALKING MINOR FELONIES. IRON HEIGHTS IS FOR THE WORST OF THE WORST.
CAPTAIN COLD AND THE REST, THEY'VE HURT A LOT OF PEOPLE. THE DESTRUCTION THEY DID TO THE CITY RUINED LIVES.
AUGUST...KILLED SPEEDSTERS TO STEAL THEIR POWERS.
FOR YEARS, THIS PLACE A REVOLVING DOOR THAN ARKHAM. BUT TH ALWAYS END UP BACK HE NOT BECAUSE THEY GE CAUGHT, BUT BECAUSE THEY CAN'T STOP.
THEY DON'T DESERVE A SECOND CHANCE.
BARRY, YOU-- YOU CAN'T REALLY BELIEVE THAT?
KRISTEN, I--
IT APPEARS I WAS WRONG ABOUT YOU, MR. ALLEN.
MAYBE IRON HEIGHTS IS WHERE YOU BELONG AFTER ALL.

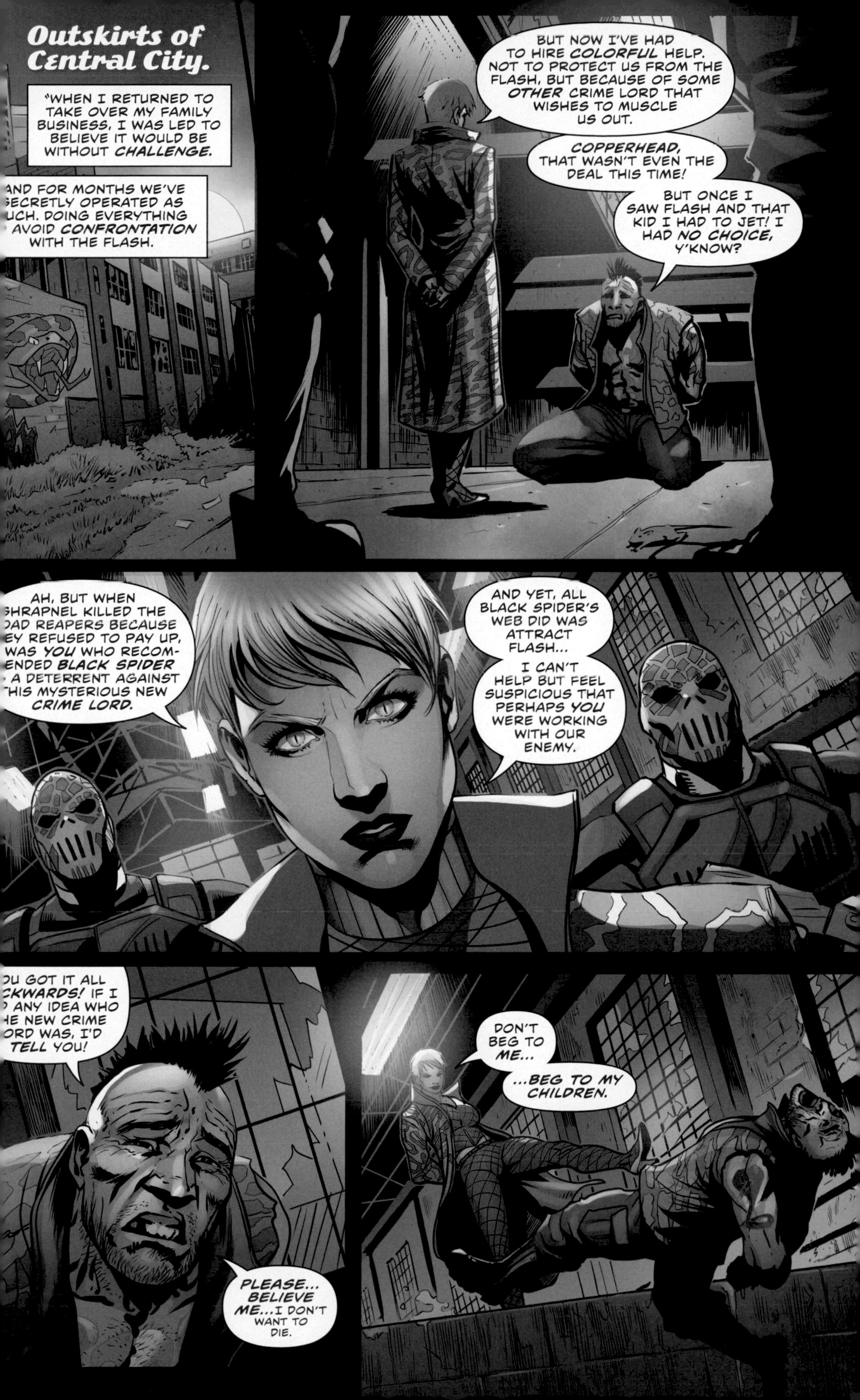
Outskirts of Central City.
"WHEN I RETURNED TO TAKE OVER MY FAMILY BUSINESS, I WAS LED TO BELIEVE IT WOULD BE WITHOUT CHALLENGE.
AND FOR MONTHS WE'VE SECRETLY OPERATED AS SUCH. DOING EVERYTHING AVOID CONFRONTATION WITH THE FLASH.
BUT NOW I'VE HAD TO HIRE COLORFUL HELP. NOT TO PROTECT US FROM THE FLASH, BUT BECAUSE OF SOME OTHER CRIME LORD THAT WISHES TO MUSCLE US OUT.
COPPERHEAD, THAT WASN'T EVEN THE DEAL THIS TIME!
BUT ONCE I SAW FLASH AND THAT KID I HAD TO JET! I HAD NO CHOICE, Y'KNOW?
AH, BUT WHEN SHRAPNEL KILLED THE ROAD REAPERS BECAUSE THEY REFUSED TO PAY UP, IT WAS YOU WHO RECOM-MENDED BLACK SPIDER AS A DETERRENT AGAINST THIS MYSTERIOUS NEW CRIME LORD.
AND YET, ALL BLACK SPIDER'S WEB DID WAS ATTRACT FLASH...
I CAN'T HELP BUT FEEL SUSPICIOUS THAT PERHAPS YOU WERE WORKING WITH OUR ENEMY.
YOU GOT IT ALL BACKWARDS! IF I HAD ANY IDEA WHO THE NEW CRIME LORD WAS, I'D TELL YOU!
PLEASE... BELIEVE ME...I DON'T WANT TO DIE.
DON'T BEG TO ME...
...BEG TO MY CHILDREN.

AGGHHH!

BEFORE COMING TO CENTRAL CITY, I WAS AN ASSASSIN FOR HIRE.

I WOULD SAVE MY TARGETS THE PAIN OF A BITE AND INJECT THEM WITH A PERSONAL CONCOCTION OF THE DEADLIEST SNAKE VENOMS IN THE WORLD.

DEATH'S VISIT WAS SO SLOW I'D NEVER STAY TO WITNESS THE TOXIN SETTING IN.

NOW SOMEONE ELSE HAS POISONED THE ORDER OF THINGS IN CENTRAL CITY.

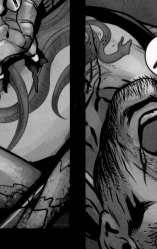

AHHH!

AND NO MATTER WHO WE TORTURE, NO ONE WILL GIVE ME A NAME.

BUT I WILL FIND THIS PERSON...AND WHEN I POISON THEM?

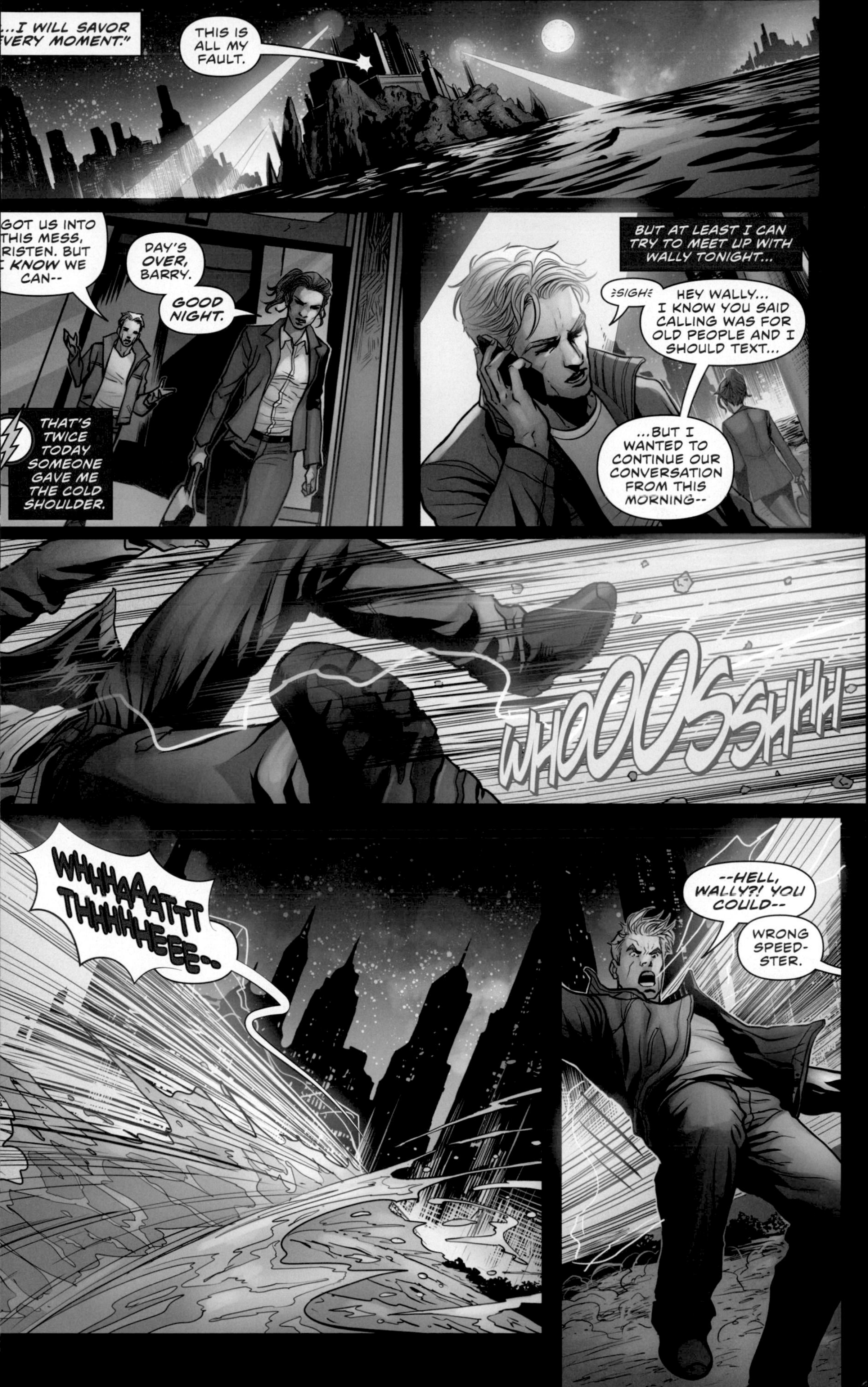
...I WILL SAVOR
EVERY MOMENT."
THIS IS ALL MY FAULT.
GOT US INTO THIS MESS, KRISTEN. BUT I KNOW WE CAN--
DAY'S OVER, BARRY.
GOOD NIGHT.
THAT'S TWICE TODAY SOMEONE GAVE ME THE COLD SHOULDER.
BUT AT LEAST I CAN TRY TO MEET UP WITH WALLY TONIGHT...
SIGH
HEY WALLY... I KNOW YOU SAID CALLING WAS FOR OLD PEOPLE AND I SHOULD TEXT...
...BUT I WANTED TO CONTINUE OUR CONVERSATION FROM THIS MORNING--
WHOOOOSSHHH
WHHHAAATTT THHHHHEEE--
--HELL, WALLY?! YOU COULD--
WRONG SPEEDSTER.

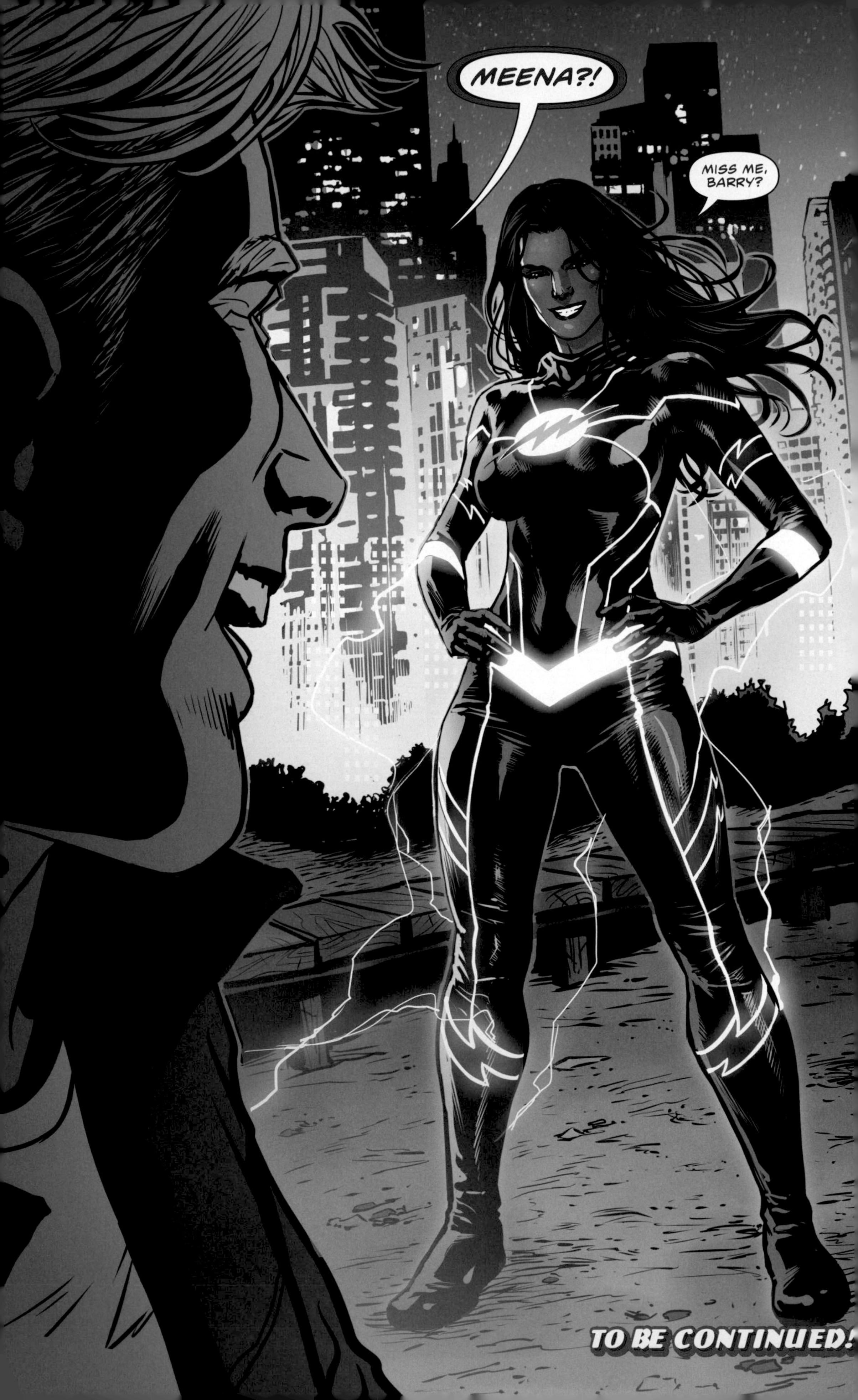
MEENA?!
MISS ME, BARRY?
TO BE CONTINUED!

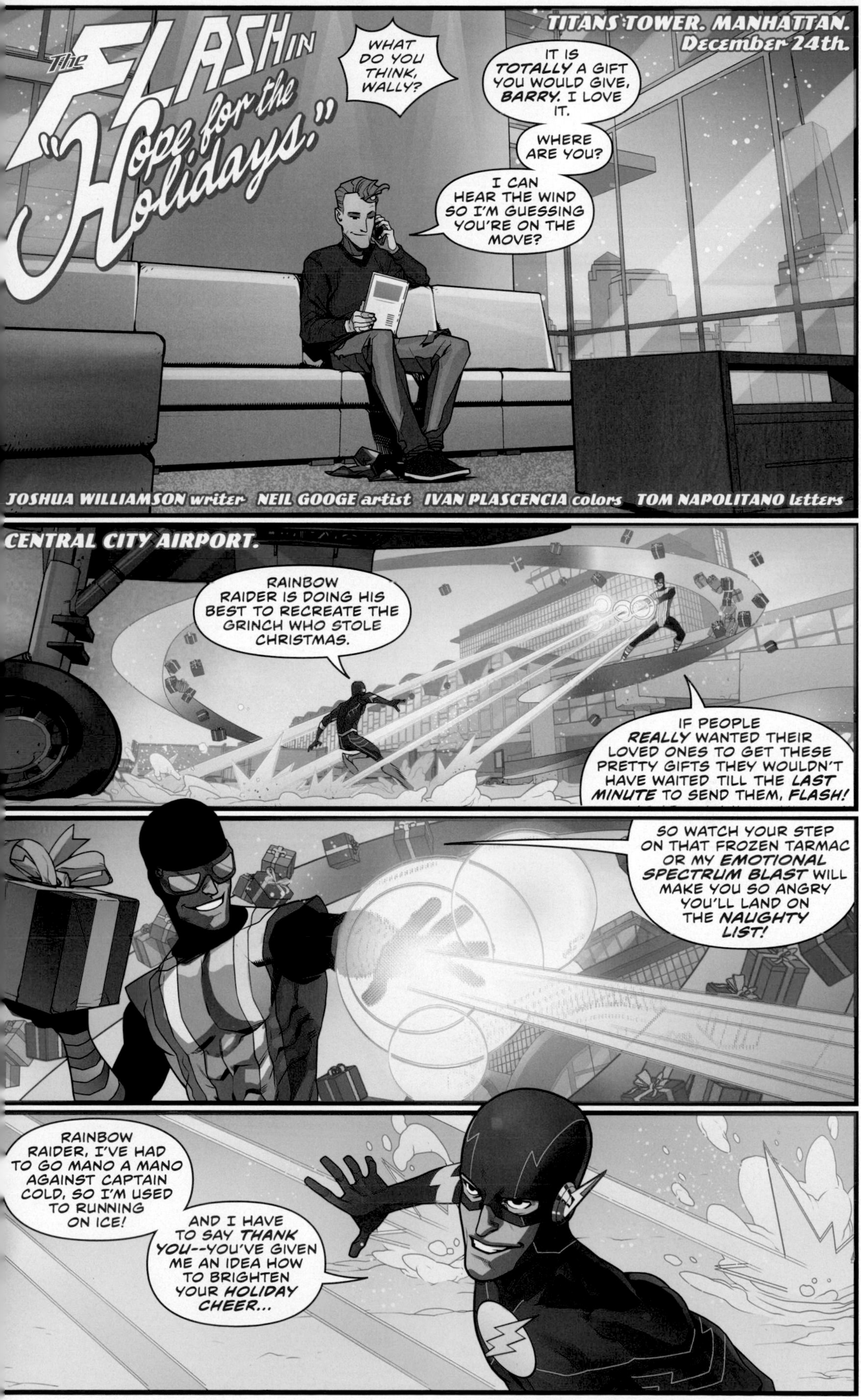
The FLASH in "Hope for the Holidays."
TITANS TOWER. MANHATTAN. December 24th.
WHAT DO YOU THINK, WALLY?
IT IS TOTALLY A GIFT YOU WOULD GIVE, BARRY. I LOVE IT.
WHERE ARE YOU?
I CAN HEAR THE WIND SO I'M GUESSING YOU'RE ON THE MOVE?
JOSHUA WILLIAMSON writer NEIL GOOGE artist IVAN PLASCENCIA colors TOM NAPOLITANO letters
CENTRAL CITY AIRPORT.
RAINBOW RAIDER IS DOING HIS BEST TO RECREATE THE GRINCH WHO STOLE CHRISTMAS.
IF PEOPLE REALLY WANTED THEIR LOVED ONES TO GET THESE PRETTY GIFTS THEY WOULDN'T HAVE WAITED TILL THE LAST MINUTE TO SEND THEM, FLASH!
SO WATCH YOUR STEP ON THAT FROZEN TARMAC OR MY EMOTIONAL SPECTRUM BLAST WILL MAKE YOU SO ANGRY YOU'LL LAND ON THE NAUGHTY LIST!
RAINBOW RAIDER, I'VE HAD TO GO MANO A MANO AGAINST CAPTAIN COLD, SO I'M USED TO RUNNING ON ICE!
AND I HAVE TO SAY THANK YOU--YOU'VE GIVEN ME AN IDEA HOW TO BRIGHTEN YOUR HOLIDAY CHEER...

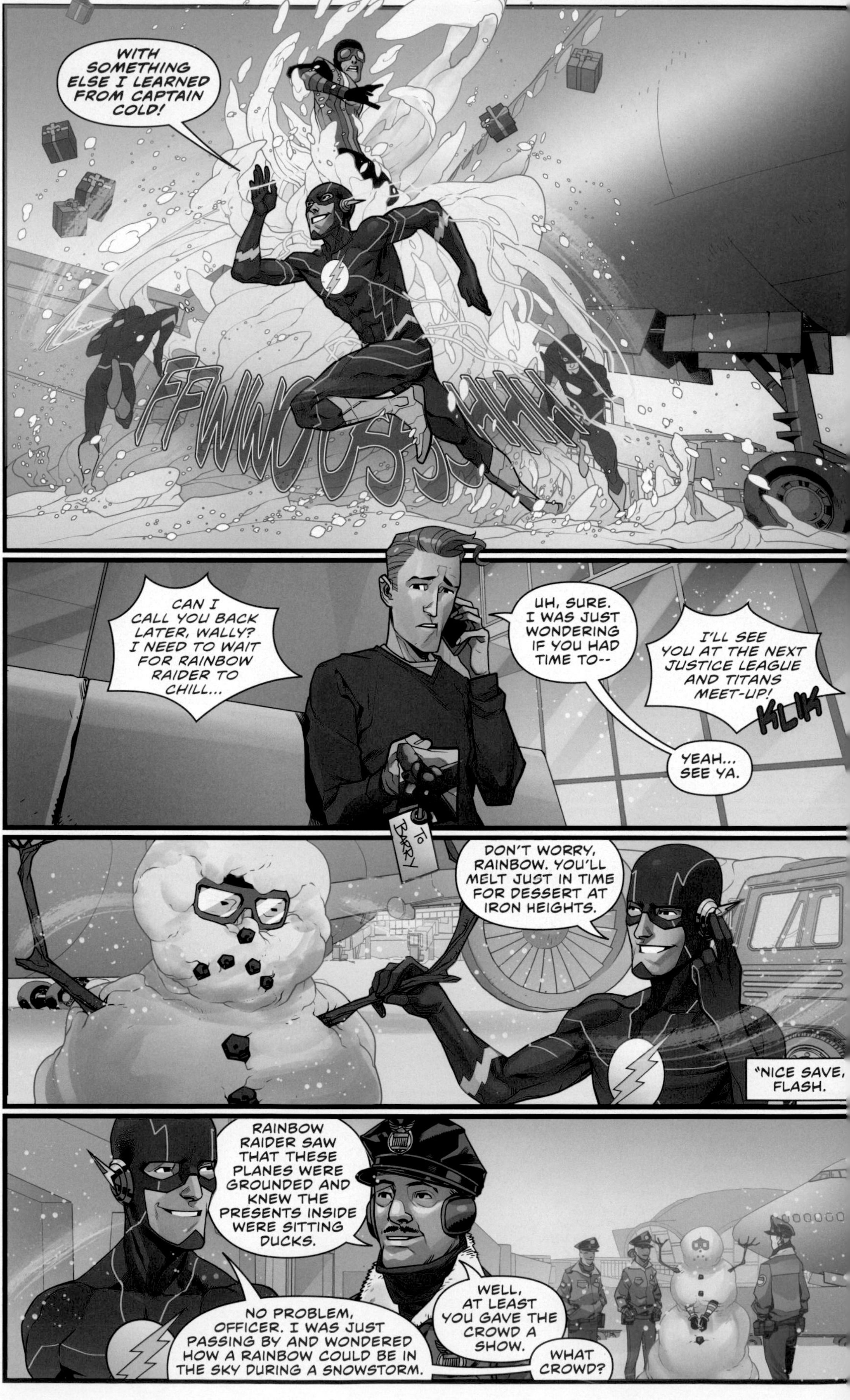
WITH SOMETHING ELSE I LEARNED FROM CAPTAIN COLD!
FFWWOOSSHHH
CAN I CALL YOU BACK LATER, WALLY? I NEED TO WAIT FOR RAINBOW RAIDER TO CHILL...
UH, SURE. I WAS JUST WONDERING IF YOU HAD TIME TO--
I'LL SEE YOU AT THE NEXT JUSTICE LEAGUE AND TITANS MEET-UP!
KLIK
YEAH... SEE YA.
TO BARRY
DON'T WORRY, RAINBOW. YOU'LL MELT JUST IN TIME FOR DESSERT AT IRON HEIGHTS.
"NICE SAVE, FLASH.
RAINBOW RAIDER SAW THAT THESE PLANES WERE GROUNDED AND KNEW THE PRESENTS INSIDE WERE SITTING DUCKS.
NO PROBLEM, OFFICER. I WAS JUST PASSING BY AND WONDERED HOW A RAINBOW COULD BE IN THE SKY DURING A SNOWSTORM.
WELL, AT LEAST YOU GAVE THE CROWD A SHOW.
WHAT CROWD?

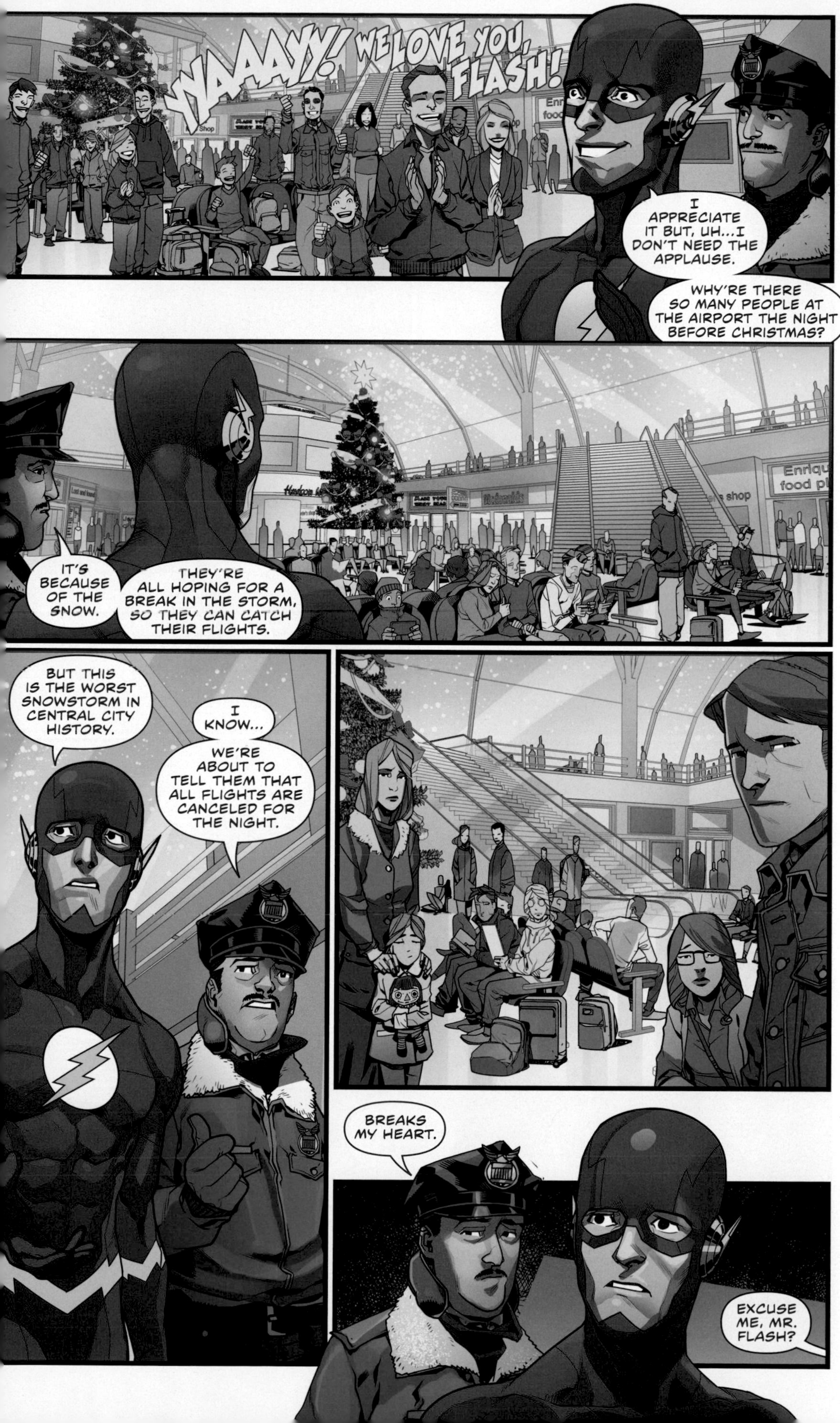
YAAAYY! WE LOVE YOU, FLASH!
I APPRECIATE IT BUT, UH...I DON'T NEED THE APPLAUSE.
WHY'RE THERE SO MANY PEOPLE AT THE AIRPORT THE NIGHT BEFORE CHRISTMAS?
Enriq food pl
IT'S BECAUSE OF THE SNOW.
THEY'RE ALL HOPING FOR A BREAK IN THE STORM, SO THEY CAN CATCH THEIR FLIGHTS.
BUT THIS IS THE WORST SNOWSTORM IN CENTRAL CITY HISTORY.
I KNOW...
WE'RE ABOUT TO TELL THEM THAT ALL FLIGHTS ARE CANCELED FOR THE NIGHT.
BREAKS MY HEART.
EXCUSE ME, MR. FLASH?

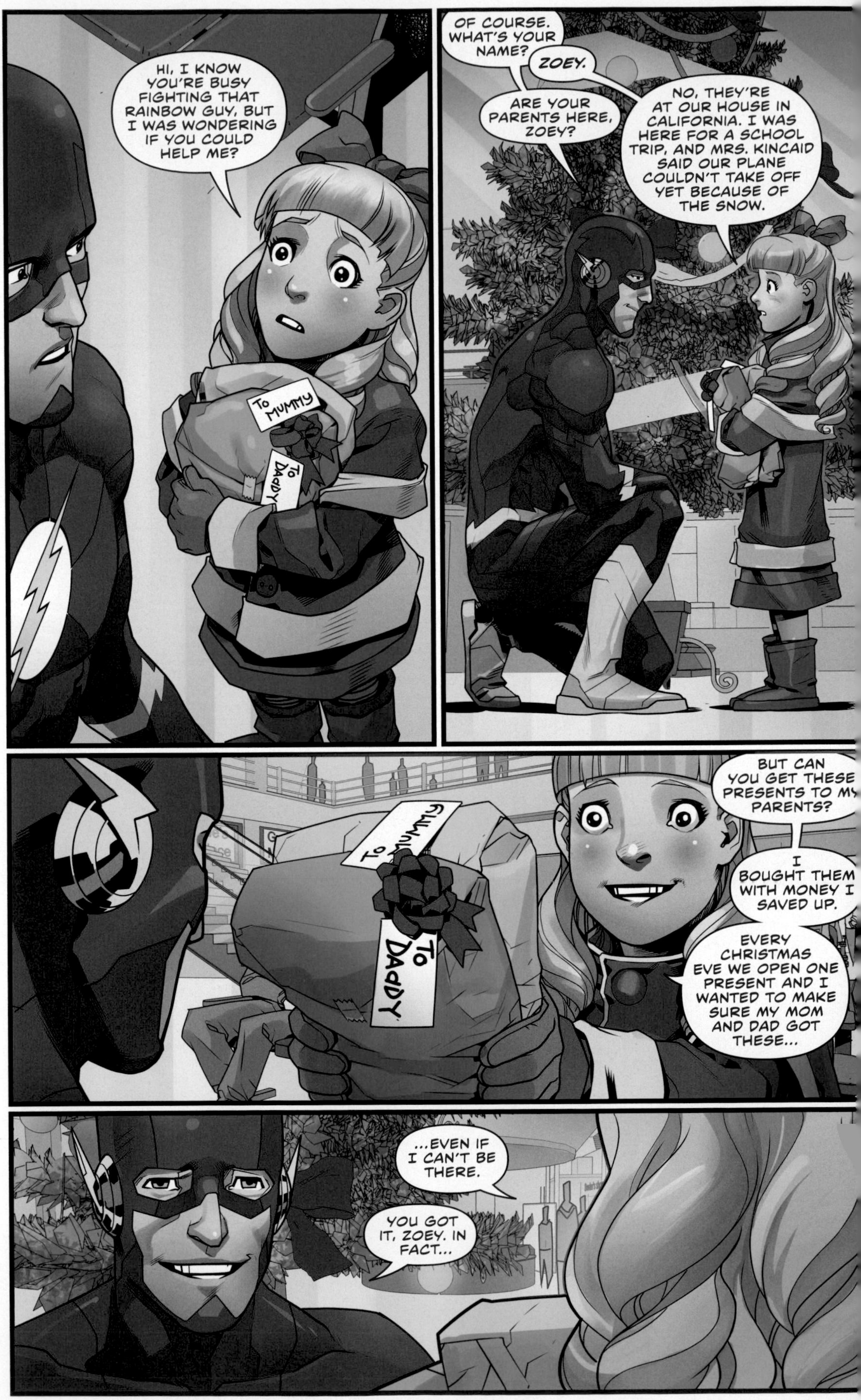
HI, I KNOW YOU'RE BUSY FIGHTING THAT RAINBOW GUY, BUT I WAS WONDERING IF YOU COULD HELP ME?
TO MUMMY
TO DADDY
OF COURSE. WHAT'S YOUR NAME?
ZOEY.
ARE YOUR PARENTS HERE, ZOEY?
NO, THEY'RE AT OUR HOUSE IN CALIFORNIA. I WAS HERE FOR A SCHOOL TRIP, AND MRS. KINCAID SAID OUR PLANE COULDN'T TAKE OFF YET BECAUSE OF THE SNOW.
BUT CAN YOU GET THESE PRESENTS TO MY PARENTS?
I BOUGHT THEM WITH MONEY I SAVED UP.
EVERY CHRISTMAS EVE WE OPEN ONE PRESENT AND I WANTED TO MAKE SURE MY MOM AND DAD GOT THESE...
TO DADDY
...EVEN IF I CAN'T BE THERE.
YOU GOT IT, ZOEY. IN FACT...

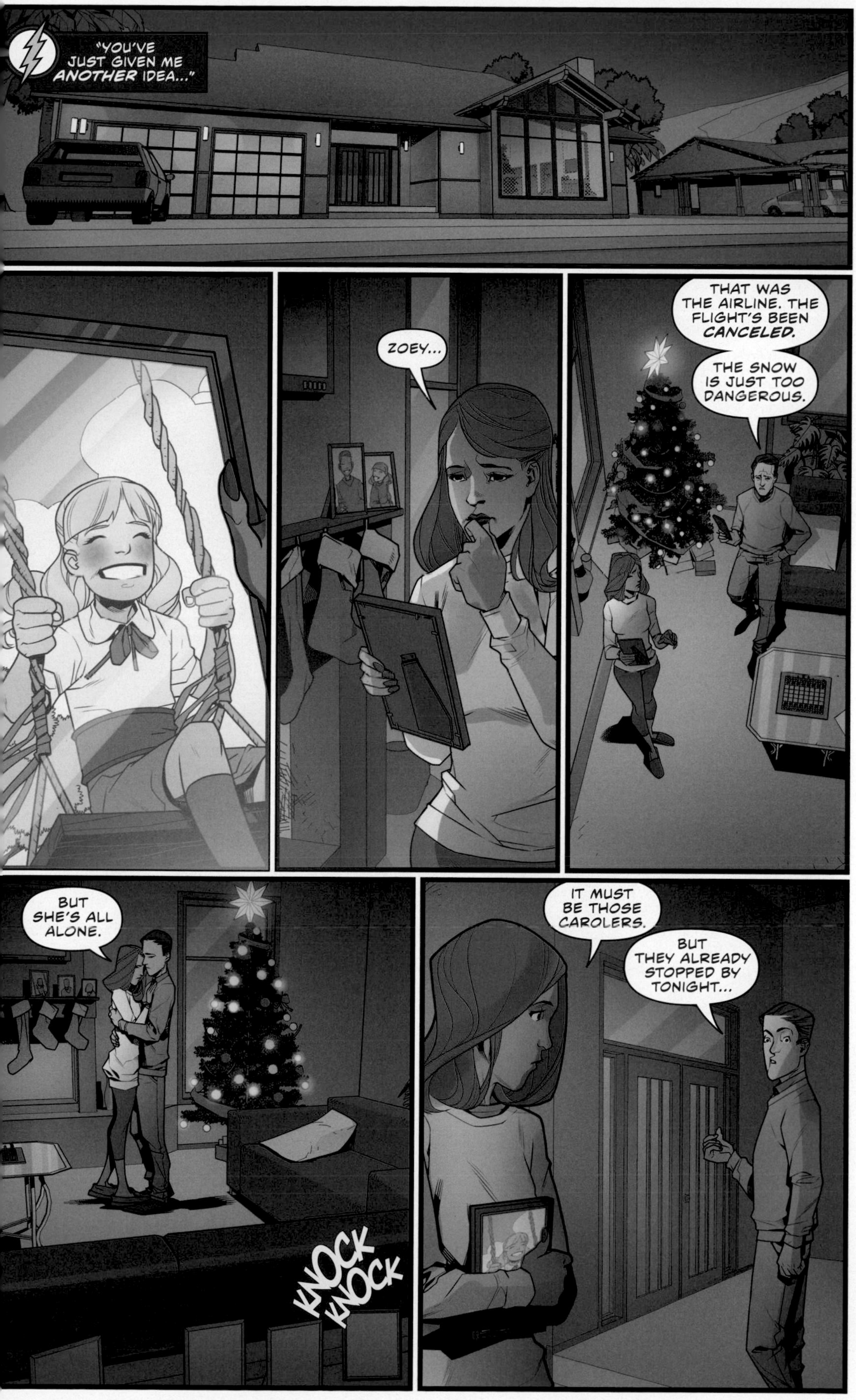
"YOU'VE JUST GIVEN ME ANOTHER IDEA..."
ZOEY...
THAT WAS THE AIRLINE. THE FLIGHT'S BEEN CANCELED.
THE SNOW IS JUST TOO DANGEROUS.
BUT SHE'S ALL ALONE.
KNOCK KNOCK
IT MUST BE THOSE CAROLERS.
BUT THEY ALREADY STOPPED BY TONIGHT...

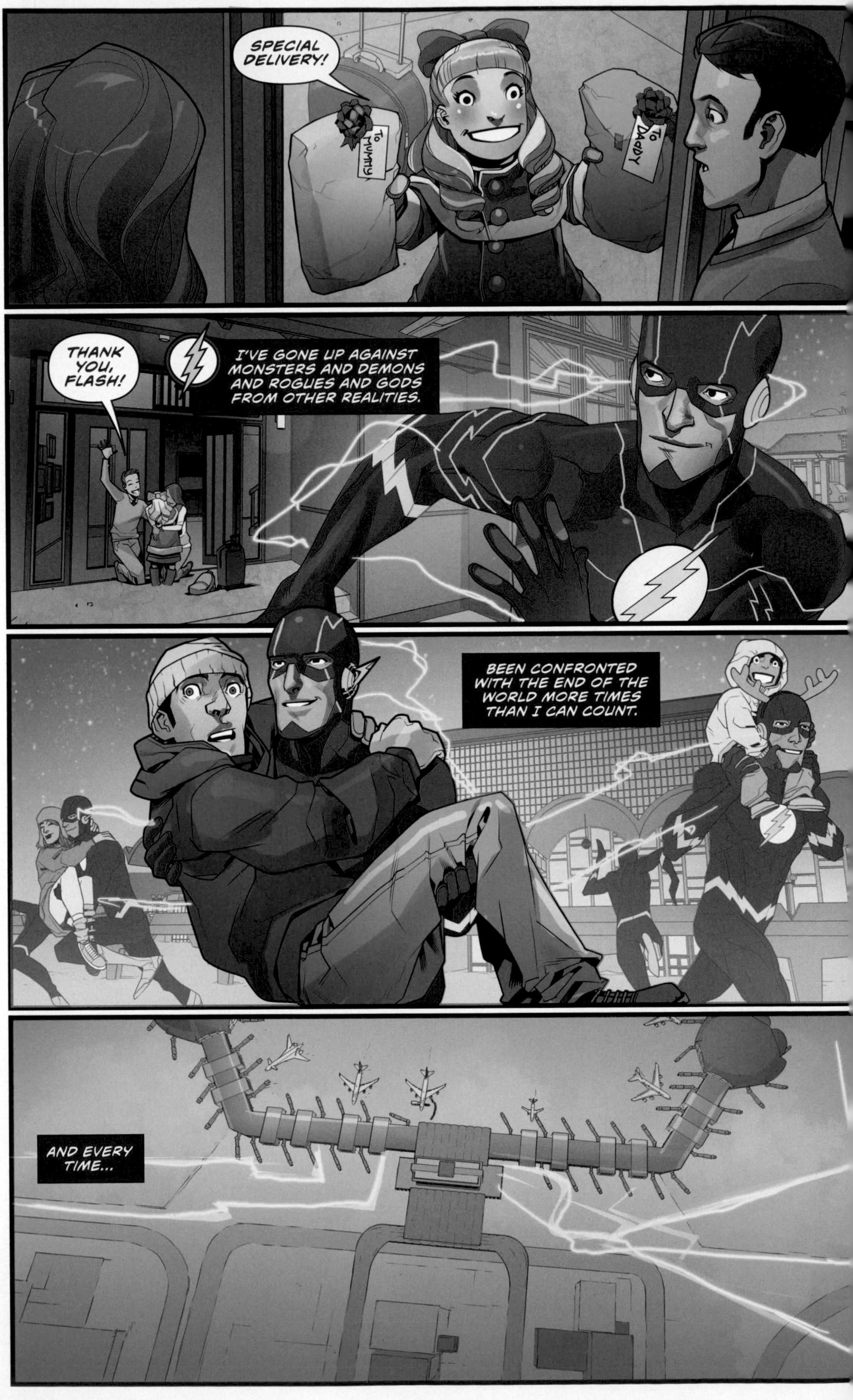
SPECIAL DELIVERY!
TO MUMMY
TO DADDY
THANK YOU, FLASH!
I'VE GONE UP AGAINST MONSTERS AND DEMONS AND ROGUES AND GODS FROM OTHER REALITIES.
BEEN CONFRONTED WITH THE END OF THE WORLD MORE TIMES THAN I CAN COUNT.
AND EVERY TIME...

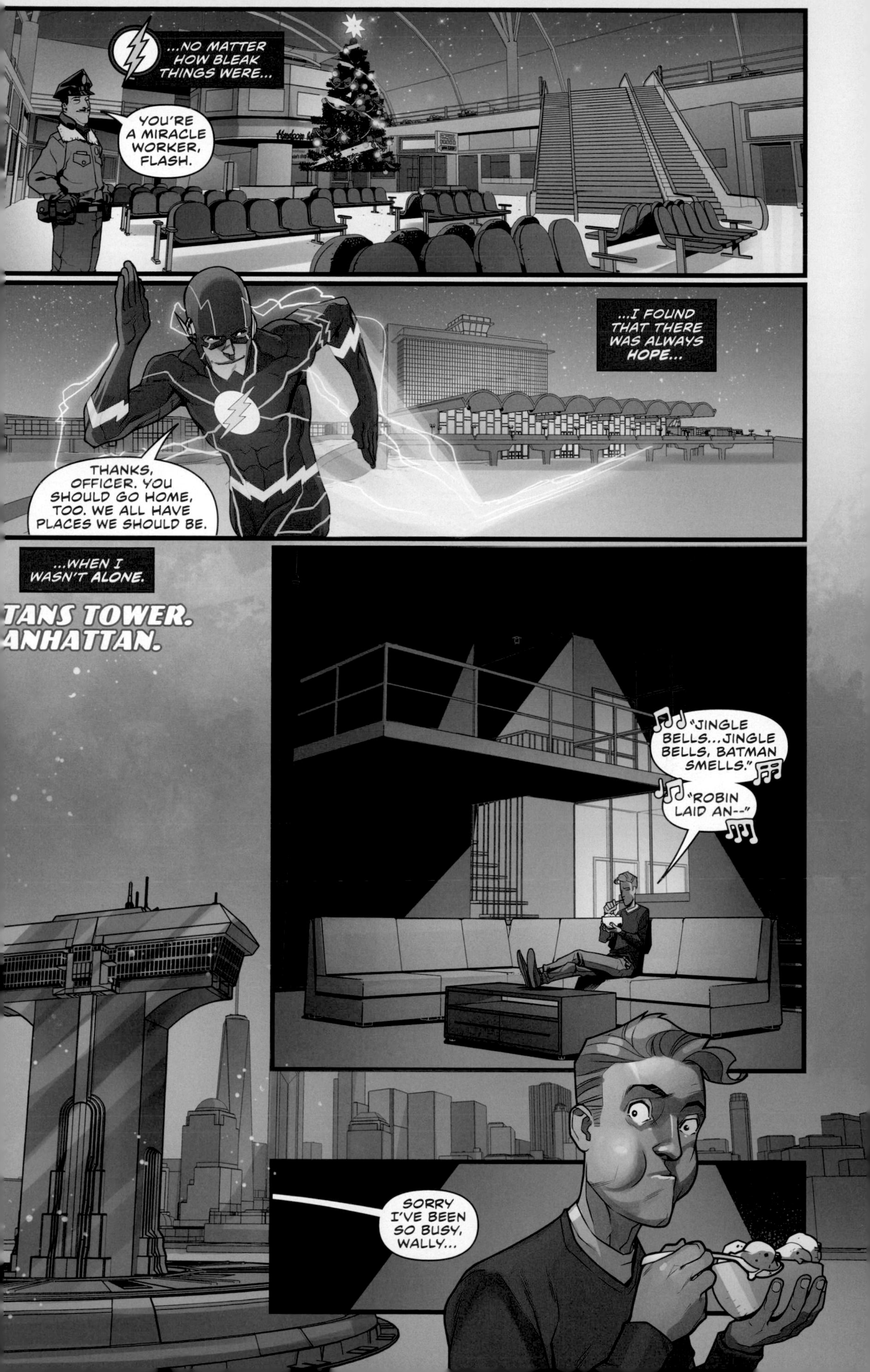

...NO MATTER HOW BLEAK THINGS WERE...
YOU'RE A MIRACLE WORKER, FLASH.
...I FOUND THAT THERE WAS ALWAYS HOPE...
THANKS, OFFICER. YOU SHOULD GO HOME, TOO. WE ALL HAVE PLACES WE SHOULD BE.
...WHEN I WASN'T ALONE.
TANS TOWER. ANHATTAN.
"JINGLE BELLS...JINGLE BELLS, BATMAN SMELLS."
"ROBIN LAID AN--"
SORRY I'VE BEEN SO BUSY, WALLY...

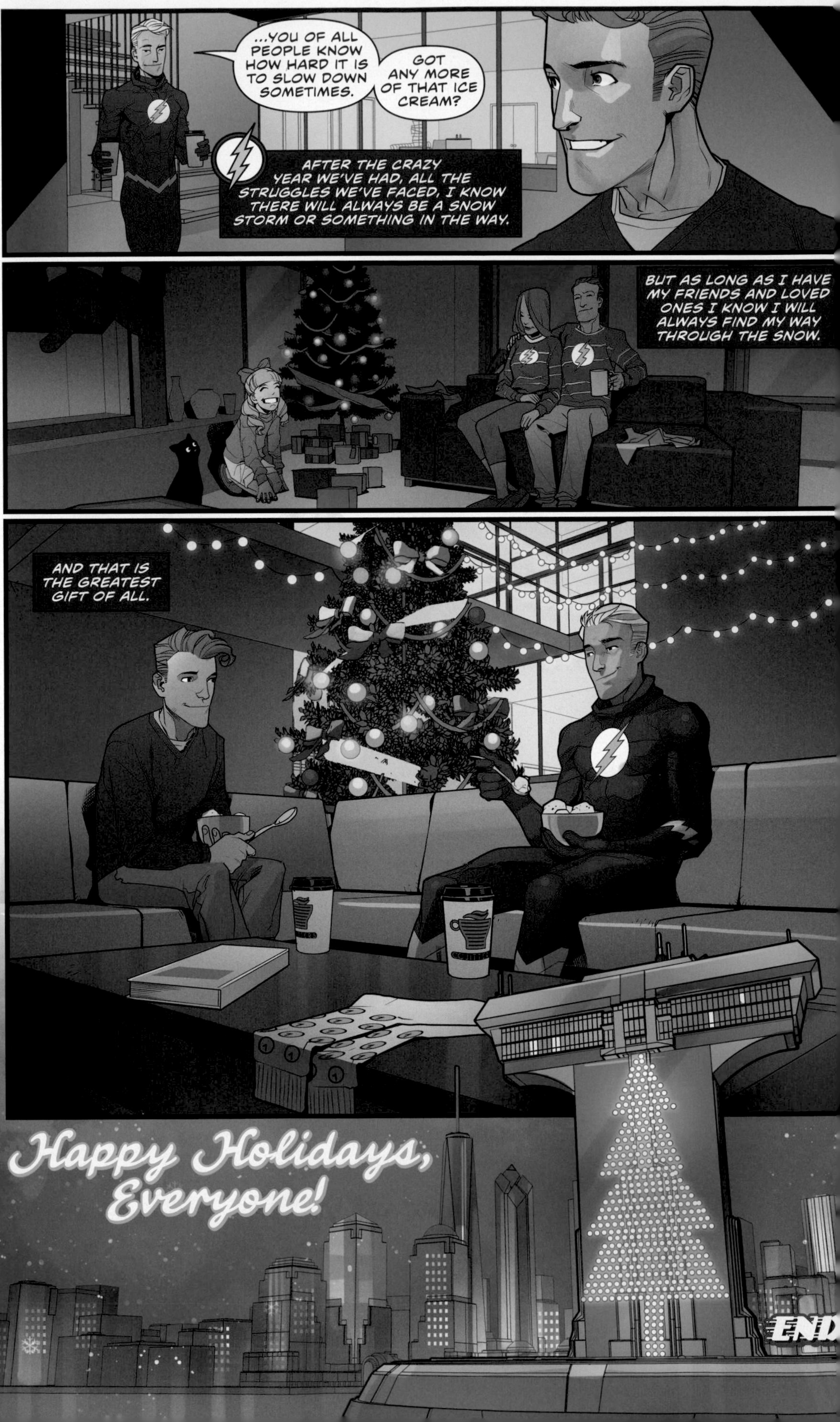
...YOU OF ALL PEOPLE KNOW HOW HARD IT IS TO SLOW DOWN SOMETIMES.
GOT ANY MORE OF THAT ICE CREAM?
AFTER THE CRAZY YEAR WE'VE HAD, ALL THE STRUGGLES WE'VE FACED, I KNOW THERE WILL ALWAYS BE A SNOW STORM OR SOMETHING IN THE WAY.
BUT AS LONG AS I HAVE MY FRIENDS AND LOVED ONES I KNOW I WILL ALWAYS FIND MY WAY THROUGH THE SNOW.
AND THAT IS THE GREATEST GIFT OF ALL.
Happy Holidays, Everyone!
END

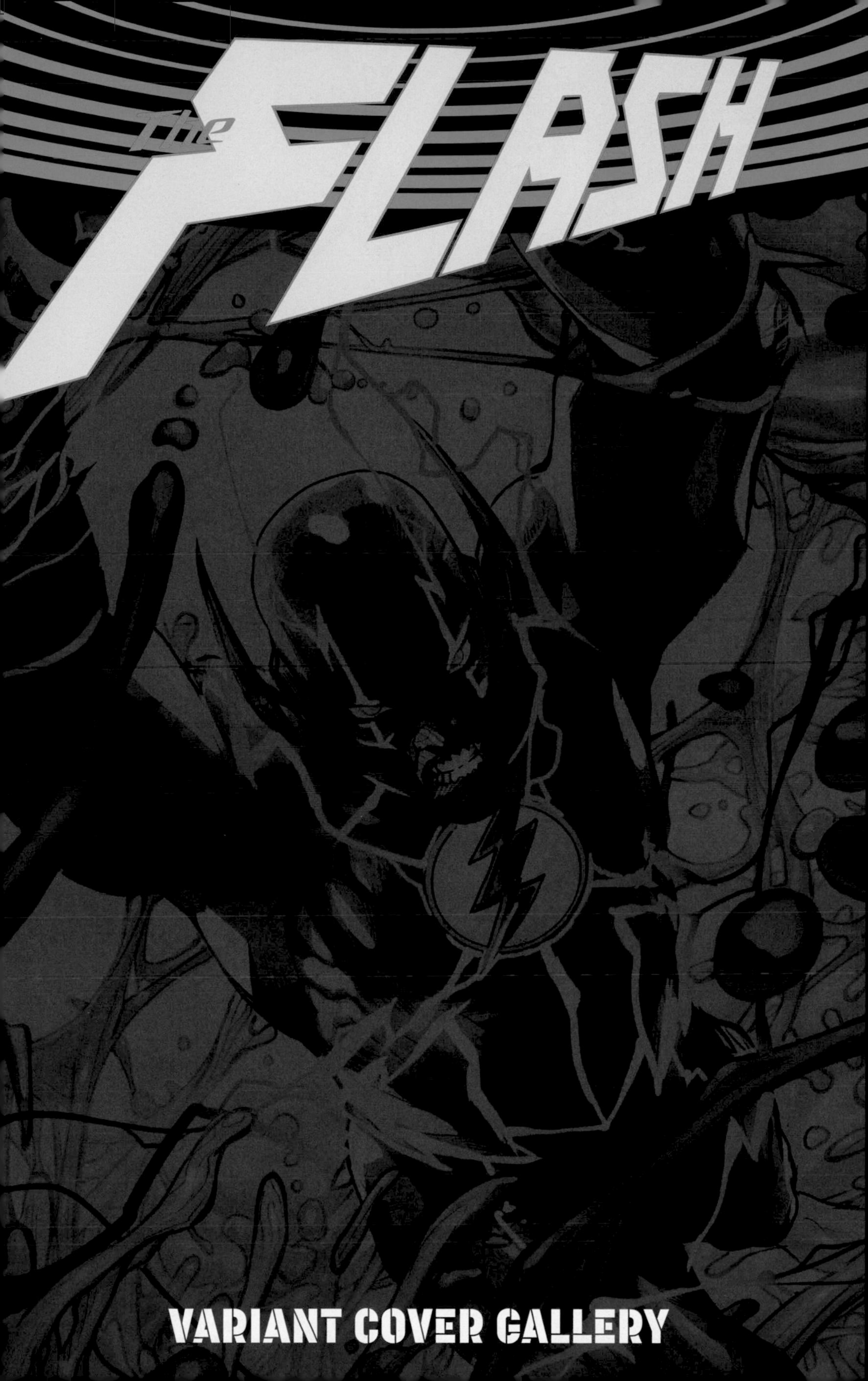
The FLASH
VARIANT COVER GALLERY

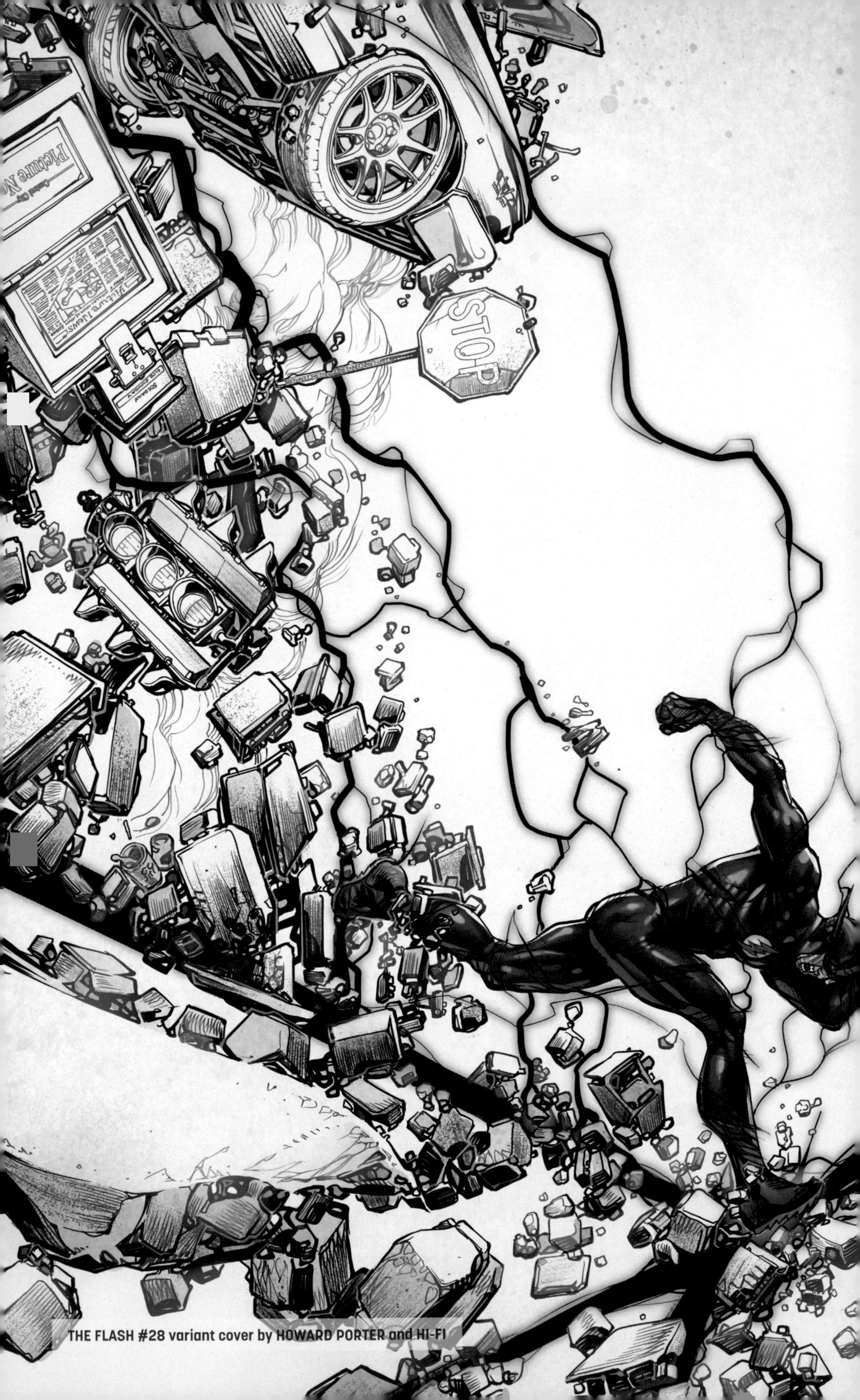
STOP
THE FLASH #28 variant cover by HOWARD PORTER and HI-FI

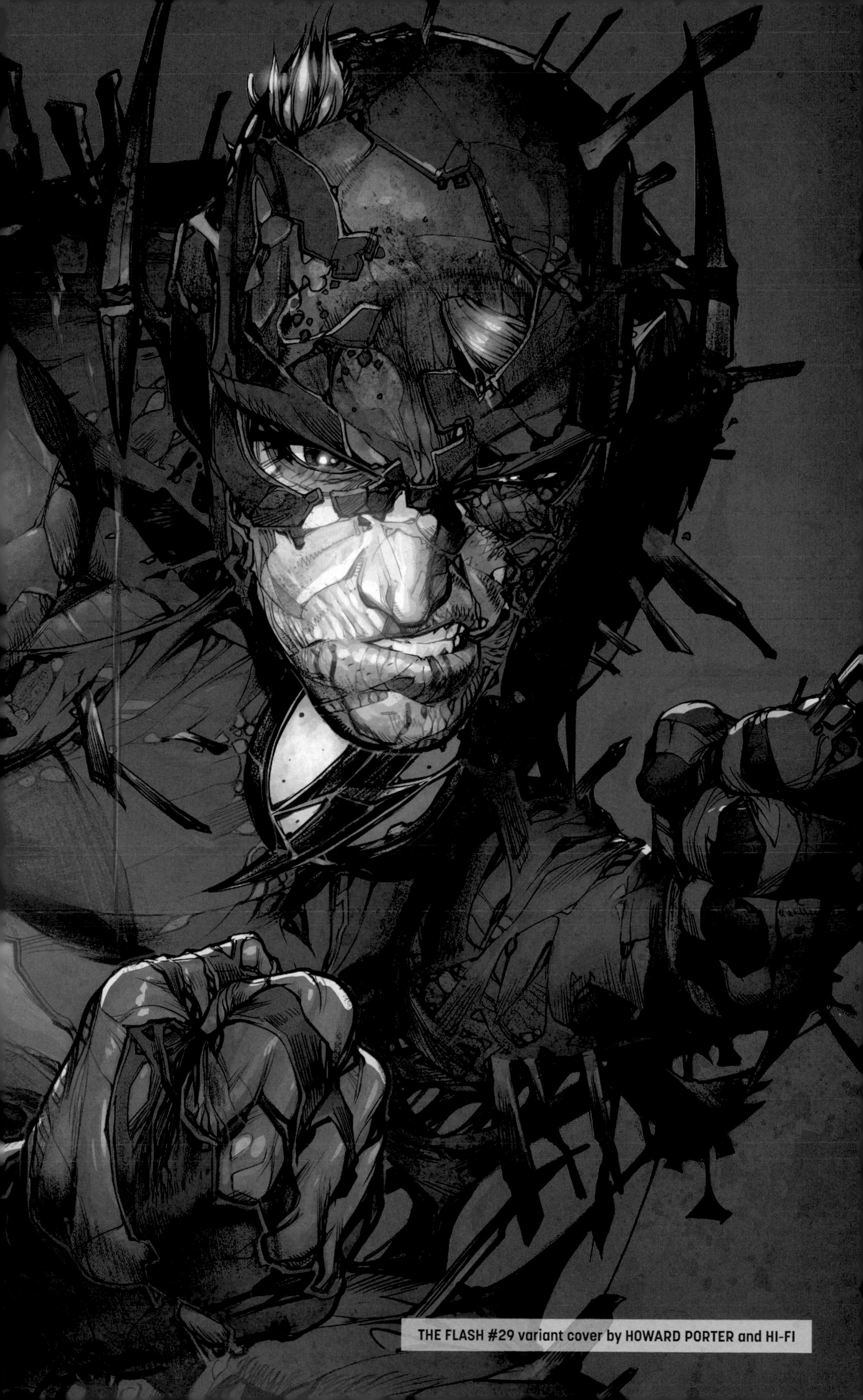

THE FLASH #29 variant cover by HOWARD PORTER and HI-FI

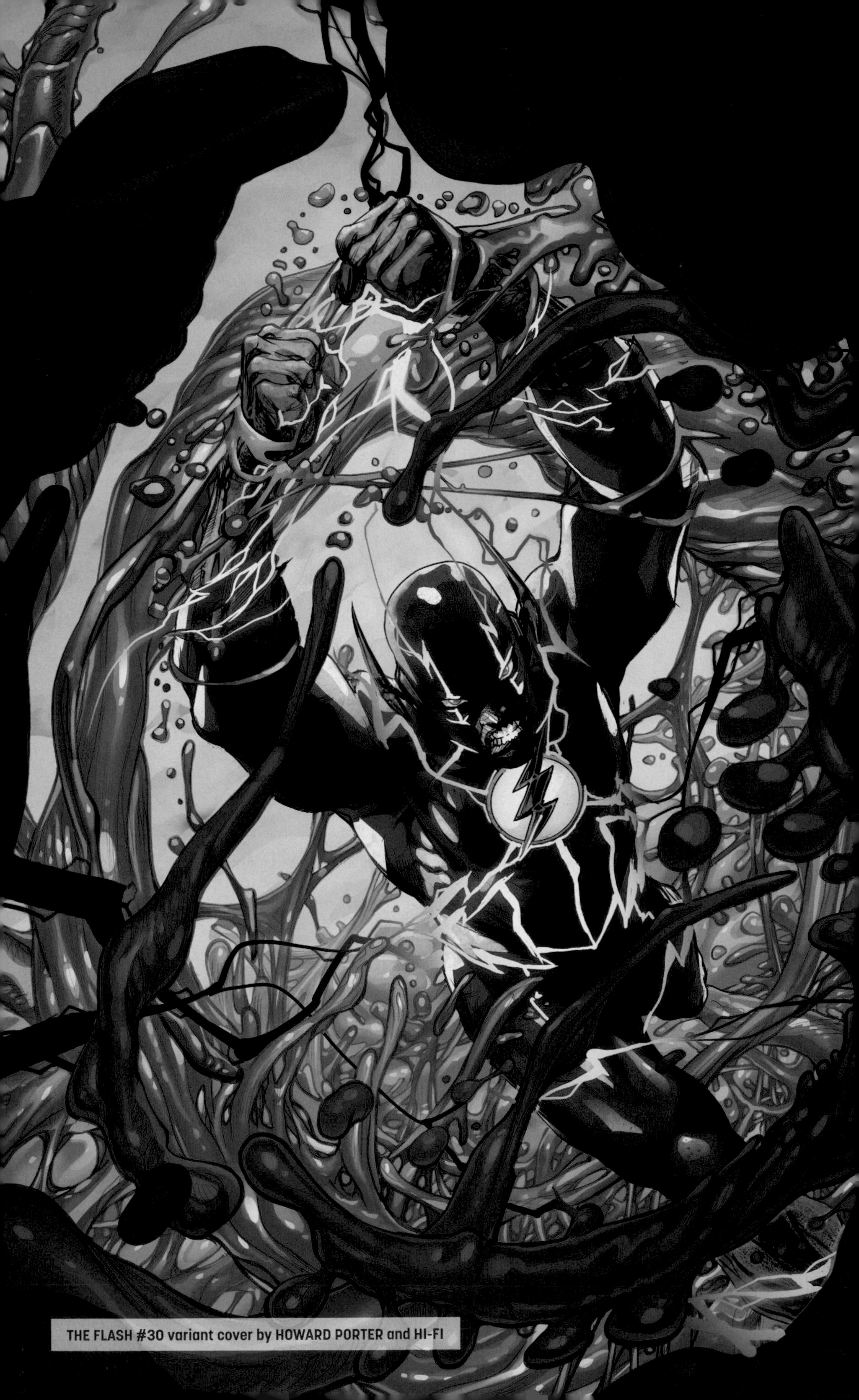

THE FLASH #30 variant cover by HOWARD PORTER and HI-FI

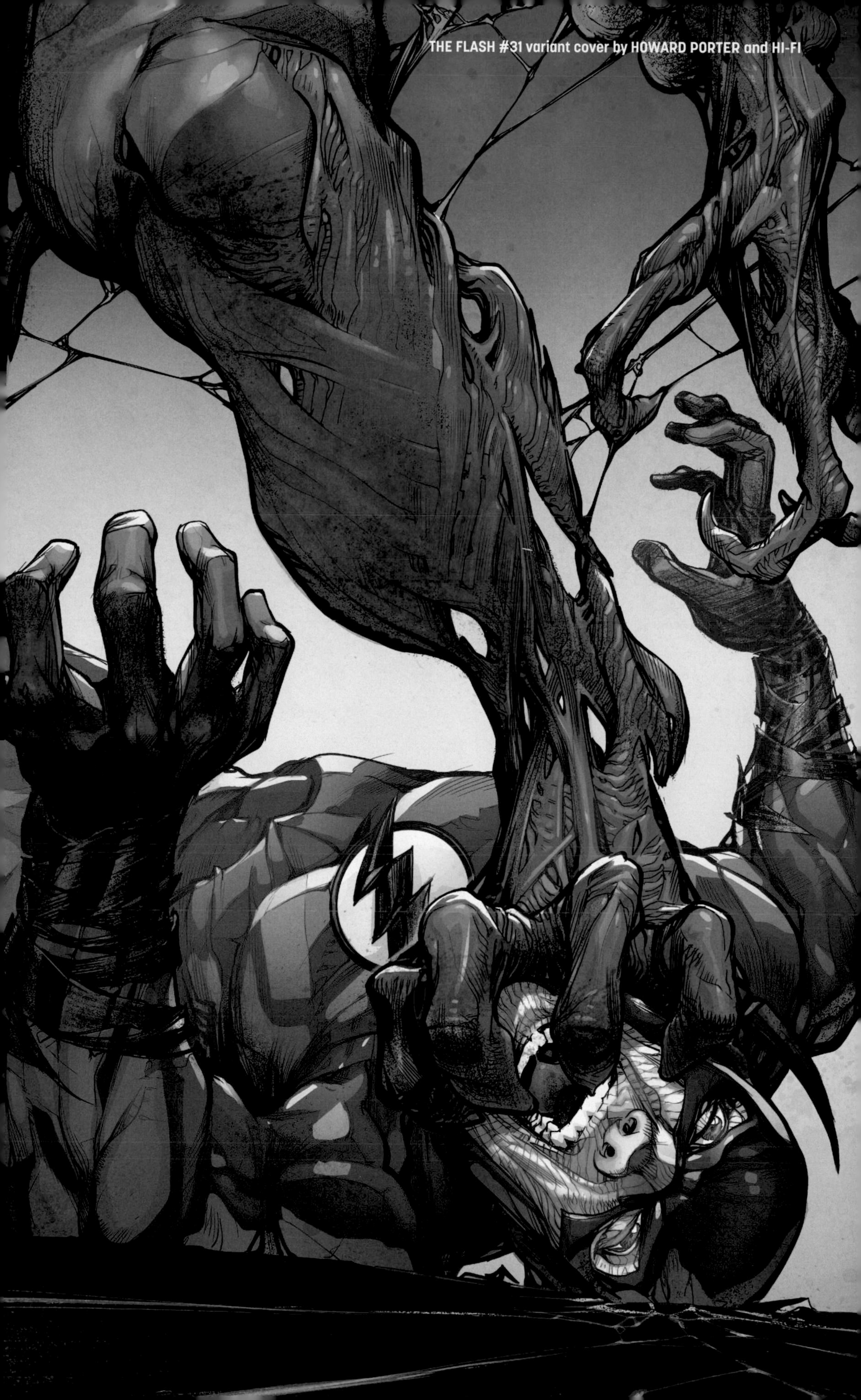

THE FLASH #31 variant cover by HOWARD PORTER and HI-FI

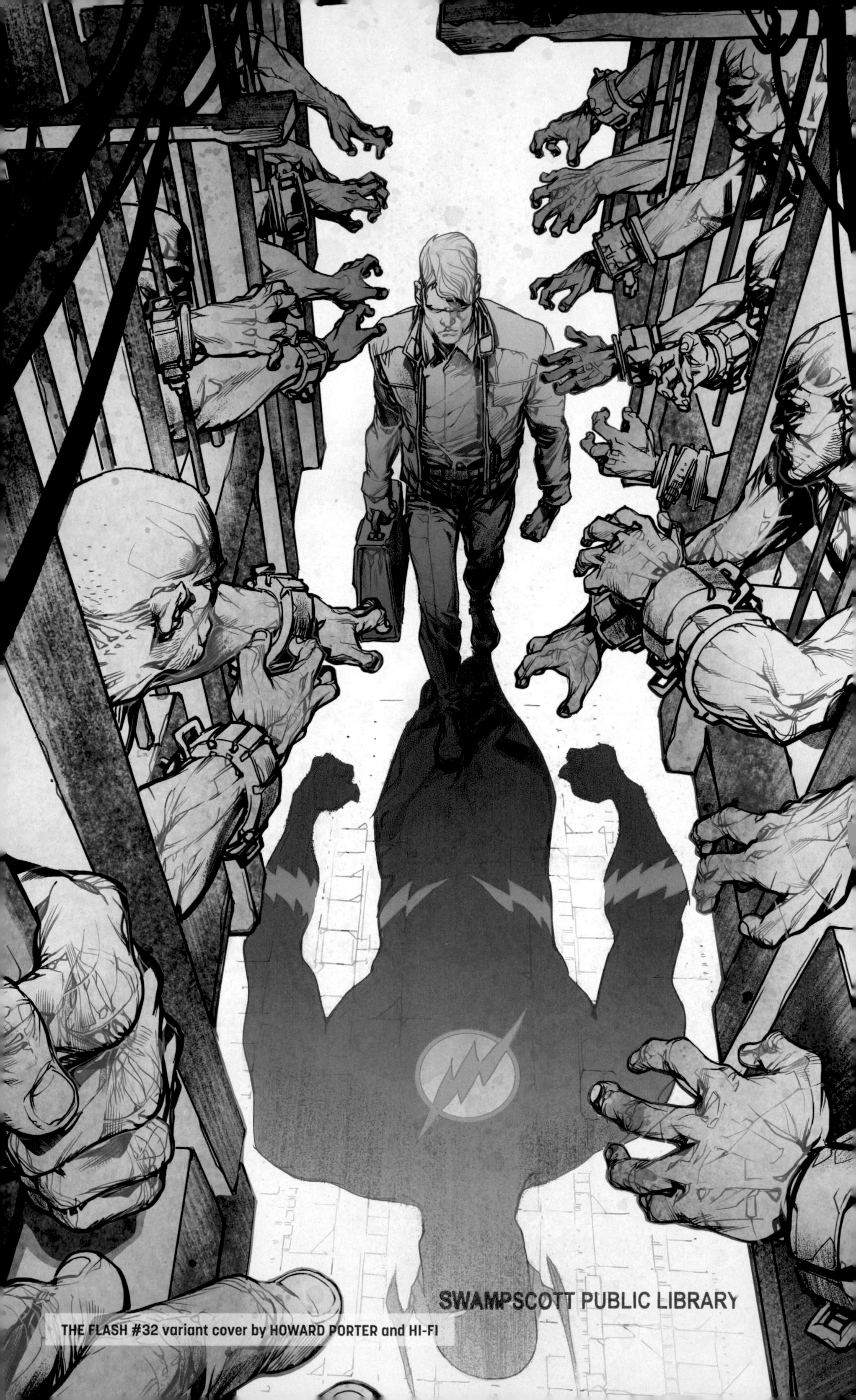

THE FLASH #32 variant cover by HOWARD PORTER and HI-FI